AF885000

Environmental Finance and Development

This book focuses on environmental financing in the process of alignment with the EU.

Based on a comparative analysis of national environmental strategies and financial needs and their links with strategic development documents in five selected countries (Bulgaria, Romania, Slovenia, Croatia, Turkey), the book identifies major achievements and remaining challenges in the main areas of environmental regulation: nature protection, water, waste, air and climate change.

For each area the same concept is applied: the current situation is presented, followed by an overview of institutional and legal frameworks. Division of competences between actors at the same or at different levels is addressed. Costs of implementation are estimated and possible sources of financing identified.

The analysis shows that a significant role in the decision making related to financing environmental protection has: (i) commercial value of environmental infrastructure necessary for services; (ii) issue of affordability; (iii) price setting mechanisms; (iv) risks for investors and creditors; and (v) policy stability and predictability.

Sanja Tišma is Director of the Institute for International Relations (IMO), Zagreb, Croatia

Ana-Maria Boromisa is Senior Research Fellow at the Institute for International Relations (IMO), Zagreb, Croatia

Ana Pavičić Kaselj is Assistant Minister at the Croatian Ministry of Construction and Physical Planning.

Routledge Studies in Ecological Economics

1 **Sustainability Networks**
Cognitive tools for expert collaboration in social-ecological eystems
Janne Hukkinen

2 **Drivers of Environmental Change in Uplands**
Aletta Bonn, Tim Allott, Klaus Hubacek and Jon Stewart

3 **Resilience, Reciprocity and Ecological Economics**
Northwest coast sustainability
Ronald L. Trosper

4 **Environment and Employment**
A reconciliation
Philip Lawn

5 **Philosophical Basics of Ecology and Economy**
Malte Faber and Reiner Manstetten

6 **Carbon Responsibility and Embodied Emissions**
Theory and measurement
João F. D. Rodrigues, Alexandra P.S. Marques and Tiago M.D. Domingos

7 **Environmental Social Accounting Matrices**
Theory and applications
Pablo Martínez de Anguita and John E. Wagner

8 **Greening the Economy**
Integrating economics and ecology to make effective change
Bob Williams

9 **Sustainable Development**
Capabilities, needs, and well-being
Edited by Felix Rauschmayer, Ines Omann and Johannes Frühmann

10 **The Planet in 2050**
The Lund Discourse of the future
Edited by Jill Jäger and Sarah Cornell

11 **Bioeconomics**
Edited by Mauro Bonaiuti

12 **Socioeconomic and Environmental Impacts on Agriculture in the New Europe**
Post-communist transition and accession to the European Union
By S. Serban Scrieciu

13 Waste and Recycling: Theory and Empirics
Takayoshi Shinkuma and Shunsuke Managi

14 Global Ecology and Unequal Exchange
Fetishism in a zero-sum world
Alf Hornborg

15 The Metabolic Pattern of Societies
Where economists fall short
Mario Giampietro, Kozo Mayumi and Alevgül H. Sorman

16 Energy Security for the EU in the 21st Century
Markets, geopolitics and corridors
Edited by José María Marín-Quemada, Javier García-Verdugo and Gonzalo Escribano

17 Hybrid Economic-Environmental Accounts
Edited by Valeria Costantini, Massimiliano Mazzanti and Anna Montini

18 Ecology and Power
Struggles over land and material resources in the past, present and future
Edited by Alf Hornborg, Brett Clark and Kenneth Hermele

19 Economic Theory and Sustainable Development
What can we preserve for future generations?
Vincent Martinet

20 Paving the Road to Sustainable Transport
Governance and innovation in low-carbon vehicles
Edited by Måns Nilsson, Karl Hillman, Annika Rickne and Thomas Magnusson

21 Creating a Sustainable Economy
An institutional and evolutionary approach to environmental policy
Edited by Gerardo Marletto

22 The Economics of Climate Change and the Change of Climate in Economics
Kevin Maréchal

23 Environmental Finance and Development
Sanja Tišma, Ana-Maria Boromisa and Ana Pavičić Kaselj

Environmental Finance and Development

Sanja Tišma, Ana-Maria Boromisa
and Ana Pavičić Kaselj

Routledge
Taylor & Francis Group
LONDON AND NEW YORK

First published 2012
by Routledge
2 Park Square, Milton Park, Abingdon, Oxon OX14 4RN

Simultaneously published in the USA and Canada
by Routledge
711 Third Avenue, New York, NY 10017

Routledge is an imprint of the Taylor & Francis Group, an informa business

© 2012 Sanja Tišma, Ana-Maria Boromisa and Ana Pavičić Kaselj

The rights of Sanja Tišma, Ana-Maria Boromisa and Ana Pavičić Kaselj to be identified as authors of this work have been asserted by them in accordance with the Copyright, Designs and Patent Act 1988.

All rights reserved. No part of this book may be reprinted or reproduced or utilised in any form or by any electronic, mechanical, or other means, now known or hereafter invented, including photocopying and recording, or in any information storage or retrieval system, without permission in writing from the publishers.

Trademark notice: Product or corporate names may be trademarks or registered trademarks, and are used only for identification and explanation without intent to infringe.

British Library Cataloguing in Publication Data
A catalogue record for this book is available from the British Library

Library of Congress Cataloging in Publication Data
A catalog record for this book has been requested

ISBN: 978-0-415-58609-2 (hbk)
ISBN: 978-0-203-11581-7 (ebk)

Typeset in Times New Roman
by Bookcraft Ltd, Stroud, Gloucestershire

Contents

List of figures and tables

Figures

Tables

Acknowledgements

The impetus for our research in the field of environmental financing was our involvement in the project 'Developing the capacity of environmental authorities through transfer of best practices and training to support effective use of financial resources' initiated by the European Commission, DG Environment in Brussels in 2008. The idea was to introduce strategic planning and financial management of environmental protection in the Republic of Croatia. We have learned a lot on the financial aspects of environmental protection from our excellent colleagues from Denmark – Daiva Semeniene and Michael Jacobsen to whom we are endlessly grateful, because they have opened up a whole new world of economics, environmental protection and development to us. We also thank our colleagues from the Institute for International Relations in Zagreb, and special thanks goes to our young colleagues Anastasya Raditya, Marija Martinko and Helena Čermak, who helped us in collecting and processing the data, analysis and studies, which presented a really comprehensive and challenging work, and to Andrea Ruk on her assistance in finalizing the text.

Most of all we thank our families, without whose understanding and support this book would never have been completed. Especially, big thanks to Jelena, Ivana, Juraj, Petra, Lovro and Tamara.

Authors

List of abbreviations

AAU	Assigned Amount Units
ACCOBAMS	Agreement on the Conservation of Cetaceans in the Black Sea, Mediterranean and Contiguous Atlantic Area
AURE	Agency for Efficient Use of Energy (Slovenia)
BAP	Biodiversity Action Plan
BGN	Bulgarian Lev
CBD	Convention on Biological Diversity
CCS	Carbon Capture and Storage
CDM	Clean Developing Mechanism
CEVKO	The Foundation for Environmental Protection and Reappraisal of Packaging Wastes (Turkey)
CITES	Convention on International Trade in Endangered Species
CLRTAP	Convention on Long-range Transboundary Air Pollution
CMS	Conservation of Migratory Species
CO_2	Carbon Dioxide
COP	Conference of Parties
DG	Directorate-General
DSI	State Hydraulic Works (*Devlet Su İşleri*)
EAFRD	European Agricultural Fund for Rural Development
EAP	Environmental Action Programme
EC	European Commission
ECU	European Currency Unit
EBRD	European Bank for Reconstruction and Development
EDF	European Development Fund
EEA	European Environment Agency
EEC	European Economic Community
EFF	European Fisheries Fund
EIONET	European Environment Information and Observation Network
EMEPA	Enterprise for Management of Environment Protection Activities
EPEEF	Environmental Protection and Energy Efficiency Fund
EPIs	Environmental Protection Inspectorates
ERDF	European Regional Development Fund
ESF	European Social Fund
ETS	Emissions Trading System

EU	European Union
GDP	Gross Domestic Product
GEF	Global Environment Facility
Gg	Giga Gram
GHG	Greenhouse Gas
GNI	Gross National Income
GNP	Gross National Product
GOCC	Government Office of Climate Change (Slovenia)
Ha	Hectare
HFCs	Hydrofluorocarbons
IFIs	International Financial Institutions
IISD	International Institute for Sustainable Development
IMF	International Monetary Fund
IPA	Instrument for Pre-accession Assistance
IPCC	Intergovernmental Panel on Climate Change
IPPC	Integrated Pollution Prevention and Control
IRSNC	Institute of the Republic of Slovenia for Nature Conservation
ISPA	Instrument for Structural Policies for Accession
JI	Joint Implementation
kg	Kilogram
km	Kilometre
kt	Kiloton
kWh	Kilowatt-hour
LCP	Large Combustion Plant
LMO	Living Modified Organism
LULUCF	Land Use, Land-Use Change and Forestry
m^3	Cubic Metre
MDGs	Millennium Development Goals
MEAs	Multilateral Environment Agreements
MEPPPC	Ministry of Environmental Protection, Physical Planning and Construction (Croatia)
MESP	Ministry of Environment and Spatial Planning (Slovenia)
MEWM	Ministry of Environment and Water Management
MHSW	Ministry of Health and Social Welfare (Croatia)
mm	Millimetre
MOEW	Ministry of Environment and Water (Bulgaria)
Mtoe	Million Tonnes of Oil Equivalent
MWFEP	Ministry of Waters, Forests and Environmental Protection
n.a.	not available
NDP	National Development Programme
NEPA	National Environmental Protection Agency
NH_3	Ammonia
NIR	National Inventory Report
NGO	Non-governmental Organization
NMVOC	Non-methane Volatile Organic Compounds
NO_x	Nitrogen Oxide

NRP	National Reform Programme
NSDS	National Sustainable Development Strategy
NSRF	National Strategic Reference Framework
NWMP	National Waste Management Programme/Plan (depending on country)
OECD	Organization for Economic Cooperation and Development
OP	Operational Programme
PAF	Protected Areas Fund
PCB	Polychlorinated Biphenyls
PCT	Polychlorinated Terphenyls
p.e.	Population Equivalent
PET	Polyethylene Terephthalate
PFCs	Per Fluorinated Compounds
PHARE	Poland and Hungary: Assistance for Restructuring their Economies
PM	Particulate Matter
PPP	Public-Private Partnership
R&D	Research and Development
RDP	Rural Development Plan
SAPARD	Special Accession Programme for Agriculture and Rural Development
SDS	Sustainable Development Strategy
SF_6	Sulphur Hexafluoride
SIT	Slovenian Tolar
SO_2	Sulphur Dioxide
SPAs	Special Protected Areas
TAP	Foundation of Transportable Battery Producers and Importers (Turkey)
Tg	Teragram
TRY	Turkish Lira
UNDP	United Nations Development Programme
UNECE	United Nations Economic Commission for Europe
UNEP	United Nations Environment Programme
UNFCCC	United Nations Framework Convention on Climate Change
USA	United States of America
USD	United States Dollars
VOCs	Volatile Organic Compounds
WB	World Bank
WEEE	Waste Electrical and Electronics Equipment
WFD	Water Framework Directive
WTO	World Trade Organization
WWF	World Wide Fund

Introduction

Environmental issues are becoming an increasingly important element of the economic and business environment. Mitigation and adaptation to climate change, conservation of biodiversity, increased energy security and efficiency, improved quality of living and working environment are challenges that have recently gained the status of the imperative and have direct implications on the economy. In the business context, this trend is manifested in two ways: as a threat and as an opportunity. On the one hand, the introduction of increasingly demanding environmental standards accelerates the contraction of polluting sectors and firms. On the other, a successfully restructured business becomes more resource and market efficient, as well as competitive, while a new kind of demand and rapidly growing 'green' markets create new business opportunities.

New challenges of green economics and environmental financing have gained particular importance on a global scale in the recent years of economic crisis. The financial and economic crises fostered a change of financial architecture and are now searching for additional challenges to 'standard' structural change. Integration of environmental topics into development strategies and green growth have become key development goals.

In 2011 the world economy is slowly recovering from the deepest recession since the Second World War. After the fall of GDP by 0.5 per cent in 2009, strong fiscal and monetary incentives in developed countries resulted with the growth at a rate of 5.1 per cent in 2010. However, the International Monetary Fund (IMF) forecasts growth slowing to 4.3 per cent in 2011 and 4.5 per cent in 2012 due to the necessity of fiscal consolidation. According to IMF forecasts, growth in developing countries will slow from 7.4 per cent in 2010 to 6.6 per cent in 2011, while in developed countries it will be reduced from 3.0 per cent to 2.2 per cent. There is an increased risk that these growth rates are going to be smaller because the recovery in most developed countries has been achieved with the tremendous growth of public debt and the extreme reduction in interest rates, while there are still significant structural problems and the financial sector is faced with a considerable burden of bad marketing. An exceptionally large increase in prices of raw materials (34.5 per cent for oil and 21.6 per cent for other raw materials) in 2011 will increase inflation in developed countries from 1.6 per cent in 2010 to 2.6 per cent in 2011.

Under these conditions, forecasts for 2012 and the next five years are very unreliable.[1] It is not a simple task for national economies to 'get stronger' by adapting to or even by taking advantage of a rapidly changing and rather unpredictable business environment. The main development challenge for economically powerful countries is inertia, which hinders structural change and requires adaptation to new market conditions. The main development challenge for countries with a weaker economy is the lack of information, expertise, financial and human resources and the achievement of a compromise between the need to accelerate rapid development and environmental protection.

The recent initiatives of international organizations demonstrate the significance of the problem. Since the United Nations (UN) Conference on Environment and Development in Rio de Janeiro in 1992, the United Nations Millennium Declaration, which was adopted in 2000 by the UN General Assembly, puts environmental protection and sustainable development as fundamental and global goals of humanity.

Most European states have set common standards of environmental protection and conservation and they have generally reached the agreed improvements in environmental management. An initial common reflection of environmental protection was initiated by the First Community Environmental Action Programme (1973–1977). Environmental financing appears only in the Fourth Programme (1987–1992), and the notions of polluter pays and user pays were set as two of the principles of the Sixth Community Environmental Action Programme.

Newer member states, such as Romania and Bulgaria, and those that will soon become members, like Croatia, as well as the ones that are in the process of preparation, such as Turkey and Serbia, have mostly aligned or are aligning their environmental legislation with the *acquis communautaire*, but have also agreed the transitional periods which should enable full implementation in practice. It is important to stress that the EU legislation in the field of environmental protection is one of the widest and most complex of about 300 legal documents sorted through several thematic groups: horizontal legislation, air quality and climate change, waste management, water management, industrial pollution control and risk management, chemical noise and nature conservation. The basic policy framework that should finance environmental protection is the polluter pays principle and the user pays principle but it requires prior infrastructural support for the implementation of environmental policies in order to meet environmental standards.

For the implementation of enacted laws, significant investments are needed, from private sector and public sources (either domestic of foreign). Rough estimates show that about 1.5 per cent of the GDP needs to be invested in the environmental sector alone. For example, it is estimated that about €10 billion need to be invested in environmental infrastructure (water, waste and air) in Croatia over the next 20 years. Thus, new financial tools have to be used. As a side effect at the global level, a fairly new discipline called 'environmental financing' is being developed, which is concerned mainly with the use of various financial instruments for the protection of the environment and biodiversity. As a scientific category, environmental financing can be viewed as part of environmental economics, which undertakes theoretical or empirical studies of the economic effects of environmental policies on local, regional and national development.

At a professional level, environmental financing is mentioned as an instrument used for promoting environmentally beneficial measures through financial institutions or independent funds. Multiple sources of funding for international environmental actions are now available, which in addition to classical forms of financing infrastructural investment through loans include specialized funding mechanisms (e.g. the Global Environment Facility (GEF), UN agencies, international environmental NGOs – WWF, etc.). A very preliminary and rough estimation of only the key global environmental governance institutions suggests that the basic funds being channelled by multilateral institutions, treaty mechanisms, the regional development banks and a few key environmental NGOs add up to nearly US$10 billion per annum (IISD, 2007). As they generally provide co-financing, at least the same amount is ensured from other sources, indicating that the occurrence of environmental financing is the notion that deserves double attention – conserved environment and incentives for economic development.

Various sectoral national strategies identify needs for heavy environmental infrastructure investments without clear intersections in the implementation of numerous strategies and plans. It is, therefore, a challenge to link sector-specific environmental strategies with financial and budgetary planning on one side and economic development strategies with green business potential on the other.

Through this book waste, air and nature/biodiversity[2] sectors are analysed in different countries in order to evaluate the level of interconnection within sectors. The analysis was prepared based on background documents and secondary sources trying to develop an overall picture and to support the creation of an enabling economic environment capable of providing long-term financing, and to establish a financing structure in a certain period with the necessary funding coming from different sources motivated by market principles and not just from national budgets or donor agencies.

Communication and future cooperation between the key actors in the establishment and operation of environmental financing will be a further challenge in the study of the role of environmental financing in the development of national economies, especially strengthening cooperation between environmental ministries and ministries responsible for the financial sector, financial institutions and funds in the case of grants.

In most of the analysed countries, legislation is generally harmonized with EU legislation and there is a clear identification of the environmental problem(s) to be solved. The policy approach of the environmental ministries are developed and elaborated with preferential financing measures, sources and methods for necessary financing (general budget, fees or donor funds) which are defined mainly in the environmental financing strategies of individual countries.

It is the responsibility of governments to do everything to implement environmental financing strategies in practice, according to clear environmental policy framework, to strictly enforce environmental standards; and it is the responsibility of financial institutions to include long-term financing of environmental projects and programmes in their development programmes.

Undoubtedly, the future success of environmental financing schemes will contribute to a safer and more stable development of society in the future.

1 Development strategies, environmental protection and financing

Sustainable development

Global policy framework

The 1992 Rio Summit[1] established sustainable development as the guiding principle for development. Sustainable is 'development that meets the needs of the present without compromising the ability of future generations to meet their own needs' (Brundtland, 1987). It integrates economic, social and environmental objectives and recognizes that economic growth is necessary, but not sufficient for economic development.

The principle of sustainable development was integrated in key documents produced at the Earth Summit:

- Agenda 21, the strategy for sustainable policies in 21st century.
- The Rio Declaration on Environment and Development, which states that the only way to long-term economic progress is to link it with environmental protection and health.
- Forest Principles, which deal with sustainable use of forests and balance the need to protect forests (for environmental and cultural reasons) and to use trees and other forest life for economic development.
- The Convention on Biological Diversity, aiming at sustainable use of biological diversity.
- The Framework Convention on Climate Change which sets the long-term objective to stabilize atmospheric greenhouse gas concentrations at a level that would prevent dangerous anthropogenic interference with the climate system, and an overall framework to tackle challenges posted by climate change.

The final declaration of the UN Millennium Summit, the Millennium Declaration, adopted in 2000 and signed by 189 countries, reaffirmed Agenda 21 and outlined the international agenda for development. The Millennium Declaration lists eight interdependent Millennium Development Goals (MDGs) to be achieved by 2015, including environmental sustainability. The interdependence of goals, activities and results at local, regional and global level makes it difficult to formulate, cost, finance and implement adequate policies. Despite these difficulties, MDGs articulated a long-term perspective and provided direction for the implementation of development strategies. They called specifically for integration of the principles of sustainable development into country policies and programmes. Based on the Agenda 21 and MDGs each country was expected to adopt its own national sustainable development strategy (NSDS) and begin implementing them by 2005.

EU approach

Sustainable development became a fundamental objective of the EU in 1997, when it was included in the Treaty of Amsterdam. It was reiterated in the Treaty of Lisbon.

The first EU Sustainable Development Strategy was launched by the European Council at the Gothenburg Summit in June 2001. The 2001 strategy was composed of two main parts: the first with objectives and policy measures, and the second which called for a new approach to policy making. Central to this new approach was impact assessment, which was expected to ensure that the EU's economic, social and environmental policies were mutually reinforcing. Persistence of unsustainable trends required revision of the Sustainable Development Strategy (SDS) in 2006. The renewed SDS set overall objectives and concrete actions for seven priority areas:

1 climate change and clean energy
2 sustainable transport
3 sustainable consumption and production
4 conservation and management of natural resources
5 public health
6 social inclusion, demography and migration, and
7 global poverty and sustainable development challenges.

However, the issue of Europe's economic competitiveness has dominated the political agenda. Thus, sustainable development has been regarded as a pillar of growth strategies (first the Lisbon Strategy, and since 2011 the EU 2020 Strategy) instead as an overreaching principle.

In accordance with the Agenda 21 and MDGs, the EU SDS also requires the EU member states to develop national sustainable development strategies and stipulates the importance of an external dimension of sustainable development, e.g. the need to tackle global poverty and strengthen cooperation with partners outside the EU. However, sustainable development is still regarded as one of the pillars of growth, and not the other way around.

Within the current EU's growth strategy, Europe 2020, a sustainable economy presents one of the three priorities – the other two being a smart economy and an inclusive economy. Based on these priorities, targets – on employment, innovation, education, social inclusion and climate/energy – were set to be reached by 2020. Inclusion of climate and energy targets (i.e. reducing greenhouse gas emissions by 20 per cent compared to 1990 levels, increasing the share of renewable in final energy consumption to 20 per cent and moving towards a 20 per cent increase in energy efficiency) among EU 2020 headline targets shows that the Europe 2020 Strategy recognizes that high standards of environmental quality and climate protection are necessary for long-term and sustainable development.

To achieve these targets, previously planned environmental measures have to be fully implemented and unsustainable trends (e.g. relating to loss of biodiversity and natural resources) reversed. Biodiversity conservation is recognized as one of the key environmental challenges of the EU 2020 Strategy (European Council, 2010: 6). The shift to 'a greener economy' (European Commission, 2010d), i.e. a safe and sustainable low-carbon and low input economy, will require more efficient and transparent governance structure and adequate investments in environmental protection (European Commission, 2011).

The implementation of the EU 2020 is guided by ten integrated guidelines and headline targets. Based on the guidelines, member states should develop their national reform programmes (NRPs), while the Stability and Growth Pact serves as the framework for the establishment of stability and convergence programmes.

According to the integrated guidelines the use of environmental taxation is seen as an instrument for achieving public finance stability. Shifting tax burden on environmentally harmful activities is considered as a measure that opens the space to lowering the tax burden on growth enhancing categories (e.g. labour) and boosts green growth, green technologies and green jobs, which is a long-term reform goal. The European Economy Recovery Plan tries to ensure consistency of the short-term anticrisis measures with the long-term goal: the transition of the EU towards an inclusive low-carbon and knowledge-based economy, as defined by EU SDS and EU 2020.

Based on the common principles (Agenda 21, MDGs, and for the EU member states EU SDS) each country was expected to prepare its sustainable development strategy.

Thus, NRPs should define short-term measures (for a three-year period) enabling economic recovery and reaching sustainable development goals, as defined by NSDS.

National policies

Slovenia

In 2005 Slovenia adopted the Development Strategy (Šušteršič *et al.*, 2005) for the period until 2013. The Development Strategy represents Slovenia's SDS and at the same time transposed the Lisbon Strategy goals into the national environment. The Development Strategy defines the vision and goals of the development of Slovenia and provides guidelines for institutional and development reforms after accession to the EU.

The Strategy serves as a long-term umbrella document for development planning and promotes principles of sustainable development and integration of development policies. It involves economic development, social, environmental, political, legal and cultural issues and defines five development priorities:

1 a competitive economy and faster economic growth
2 effective generation, two-way flow and application of the knowledge needed for economic development and quality jobs
3 an efficient and less costly state
4 a modern social state and higher employment, and
5 integration of measures to achieve sustainable development.

(Šušteršič *et al.*, 2005)

The integration of measures to achieve sustainable development covers development in the areas of the environment, sustained population growth, regional and spatial development and culture. In accordance with Slovenia's Development Strategy, the sectoral programmes were also adopted, for environment (the National Environmental Action Programme for the Period 2005–2012), for energy (The National Energy Plan) and waste (Waste Management Strategy).

The implementation of Slovenian Development Policy is guided by the National Strategic Reference Framework (NSRF), the National Development Programme 2007–2013 and operational programmes.

The NSRF is the basic document for the implementation of the EU cohesion policy. It defines the general strategy of an EU member state for achieving faster convergence, and also includes situation analysis, the definition of the strategy and determines basic mechanisms for achieving the goals set (i.e. operational programmes and basic financial arrangements). The NSRF 2007 served as a basis for the the National Development Programme (NDP) 2007–2013 and operational programmes.

The Development Strategy was updated in 2009 due to the financial and economic crisis and became the Exit Strategy. It sets the ground for a new development strategy, which is expected to lay out the key policy goals and guidelines up to 2020.

The Exit Strategy recognizes that the exit from the crisis should be accompanied by an active structural reform leading to an environmentally efficient, low-carbon society. It promotes reforms which are 'cost-free' (e.g. abolition and reduction of administrative barriers), investments into low-carbon technologies, and reform of the cohesion policy and provides for the implementation of 'green tax policies' and 'green public procurement' directing national and EU investment of funds into green technologies.

In 2010 the manner of development planning, policy making and designing of development priorities were revised and a closer link with the preparation of the programme budget was amended by a Decree on Development Planning Documents and Procedures for the Preparation of the Central and Local Government Budgets adopted by the government. A new framework for the coordination of development policies was set up: an umbrella group for development planning, a fiscal policy group and working groups for individual policies.

The new framework was applied for the preparation of the Slovenian NRP required for the implementation of the 'Europe 2020' strategy. The objective of the NRP is sustainable economic growth in the long term, which will be achieved by implementing economic policy measures, structural measures and institutional adjustments. The measures are chosen on the basis of their impact on eliminating 'bottlenecks to growth'. A gradual transition to an environmentally efficient, low-carbon society is horizontally integrated into all priority measures (NRP, 2011).

Bulgaria

Until its accession to the EU, Bulgaria treated development issues separately from environmental issues. A special inter-institutional council was established in 2006 with a view to elaborate an NSDS and set of indicators to be used to monitor its implementation. The draft prepared in 2007 corresponded to the renewed EU SDS, but it had not been adopted (European Sustainable Development Network, 2008).

In the absence of an SDS, development is primarily guided by national documents relevant for the implementation of the 'EU 2020' strategy, the EU structural policy and access to structural funds: the national reform programme, the national development plan, the strategic reference framework and operational programmes.

The NRP of the Republic of Bulgaria 2011–2015 is closely linked to the Convergence Programme of the Republic of Bulgaria 2011–2014 and focuses on fostering competitiveness in order to take full advantage of the economic recovery (NRP, 2011b). Structural policy related strategic documents include Bulgarian National Development Plan 2007–2013 containing the vision, strategic goals and national development priorities and identifying necessary financial resources and institutional framework required for their realization. The plan presents the governmental policies for accelerating the economic and social convergence and defines the long-term public investment programme of the country.

The NSRF 2007–2013 justifies financial support of the EU funds by setting the timetable and programme to implement pre-accession commitments, and the ways of reaching the overall long-term strategic objective to become a dynamic, competitive and accessible EU country with a high quality of life, income and social awareness by 2015. It identifies four priorities: infrastructure, employment, entrepreneurship and promotion of stable territorial development. There are seven national operational programmes dealing with:

1 transport
2 environment
3 regional development
4 competitiveness
5 technical assistance
6 human resources development, and
7 administrative capacity.

The NRP of the Republic of Bulgaria 2011–2015 is closely linked to the Convergence Programme of the Republic of Bulgaria 2011–2014 and focuses on fostering competitiveness in order to take full advantage of the economic recovery (NRP, 2011b).

Romania

Romania adopted a long-term NSDS in 1999 and subsequently prepared the National Action Plan for its implementation and introduced the Local Agenda 21. The current Romanian SDS was adopted in 2007, the same year that Romania entered the EU. It identifies objectives for 2013, 2020 and 2030 in seven key areas:

1 climate change and clean energy
2 sustainable transport
3 sustainable consumption and production
4 conservation and management of natural resources
5 public health
6 social inclusion, demography and migration, and
7 global poverty and the challenges of sustainable development.

(NSDS, 2008)

The short-term objective of the Romanian SDS (to be achieved by 2013) is to incorporate the principles and practices of sustainable development in all programmes and public policies. In the medium run (by 2020) Romania plans to reach the current average level of EU countries for the main indicators of sustainable development, while the long-term objective is to get significantly close to the average performance of EU member states in that year in term of sustainable development indicators (NSDS, 2008: 4).

Romanian SDS contains guidelines and action areas, as well as provides for the coordination of various policy areas. It sets a few quantified objectives (such as reducing final energy consumption by 13.5 per cent between 2008 and 2016 compared to the average consumption levels between 2001 and 2005; the rehabilitation of heating systems for at least 25 per cent of the multi-storied buildings; increase its share of renewable resources in the total consumption of primary energy from 11 per cent in 2010 to 11.2 per cent in 2015).

Based on the 'EU 2020' strategy, Romania has adopted its NRP 2011–2013 (NRP, 2011a). Its main measures are consistent with the provision of existing programmes and commitments (e.g. Convergence Programme 2011–2014 and Romania's commitments with the International Monetary Fund (IMF), European Commission (EC), the World Bank, and other international financial institutions). NRP 2011–2013 sets national targets for Europe 2020, including 20 percent target for reducing greenhouse gas (GHG) emissions, as compared to 1990 reference year, 24 percent share of energy from renewable sources in the gross final energy consumption, reduction of 19 per cent in the consumption of primary energy (about ten Mtoe) for 2020. A reduction of eight Mtoe in the consumption of primary energy is estimated for 2013.

In parallel to an SDS, Romania also adopted strategic development documents relevant for the implementation of the EU structural policy and access to structural funds, i.e. national development plan, strategic reference framework and operational programmes. A competitive, dynamic and prosperous Romania is the overall goal set by the Romanian National Development Plan 2007–2013 with a target to reach GDP per capita at 41 per cent of EU average by 2013 (NDP, 2005). The Strategic Reference Framework identifies four thematic priorities: development of basic infrastructure to European standards; increasing the long-term competitiveness of the Romanian economy; development and more efficient use of Romania's human capital; and building effective administrative capacity. Five national (technical assistance, environment, transport, regional operational programme and increase of economic competitiveness) and three cross-border operational programmes (Romania–Bulgaria, Hungary–Romania and South-East Europe) have been approved for the 2007–2013 programming period.

Croatia

Croatia's development strategy is contained in several documents: the SDS, the Strategy of Government Programmes, the Strategic Development Framework 2006–2013, the Strategic Reference Framework, the Pre-accession Economic Programme and a number of sector-specific strategies.

The NSDS was adopted in 2009. This document integrates key environmental challenges into the ultimate objective of achieving sustainable economic and social development, sets basic objectives and identifies key challenges in their realization. It focuses on eight key areas in which it is necessary to redirect the existing processes towards a more sustainable behaviour:

1 encouraging population growth in the Republic of Croatia
2 environment and natural resources
3 promoting sustainable production and consumption
4 ensuring social and territorial cohesion and justice
5 ensuring energy independence and increasing the efficiency of energy use
6 strengthening public health
7 interconnectedness of the Republic of Croatia, and
8 the protection of the Adriatic Sea, coastal area and islands.

The Strategy lists thematic indicators, but lacks headline objectives and measures to meet those objectives. As regards implementation, the Strategy refers to existing documents and institutions[2] or envisages adoption of action plans. The development of four action plans was launched in January 2011,[3] i.e. almost two years after the adoption of the Strategy. Delays in preparing action plans indicate that the SDS has not been the main strategic document guiding reforms.

The pre-accession instruments have received more attention: the Strategic Development Framework, the Strategic Cohesion Framework and the NSRF. The Strategic Development Framework identifies ten strategic areas requiring coordinated action in order to achieve the strategic goal: growth and employment in a competitive market economy operating in a European social state of the 21st century. These strategic areas include sustainable development and balanced regional development. The Strategic Development Framework 2006–2013 relies on existing sector-specific strategies in areas where they have been drafted.

The Strategic Coherence Framework 2007–2013 is the basic strategic document for the use of the Instrument for Pre-accession Assistance (IPA). It was adopted by the government and approved by the EC in 2007. Priorities are elaborated in detail at the level of sector-specific implementation documents, i.e. the Environmental Operational Programme, the Regional Competitiveness Operational Programme, the Transport Operational Programme, and the Human Resources Development Operational Programme. Individual state administration bodies were given responsibility for their preparation in accordance with their sector-specific competences. The priorities defined in this document are based on national strategies and the strategic guidelines of the European Union.

The NSRF is necessary for programming of EU structural funds and the cohesion fund upon the accession of Croatia to full membership in the European Union. It was prepared as a precondition for the closing of negotiations on Chapter 22 – 'Regional policy and coordination of structural instrument'. It analyses the socio-economic situation, thematic investment priorities, and priority axes for each investment area, the financial allocation plan and key aspects of implementation.

The Strategy of Government Programmes is a strategy document drafted annually on the basis of the strategic plans of the ministries and other state administration bodies. It encompasses the goals and priorities for the coming three-year period. The strategy plans provide an overview of all sector-specific goals, while the Strategy of Government Programmes secures the allocation of budget funds to the goals that will have the greatest effect in priority areas.

The process of linking strategy and budget planning started with the adoption of the strategy for the period 2010–2012.

Turkey

Turkey's main development document is the Ninth Development Action Plan 2007–2013. The Plan is the fundamental policy document outlining economic, social and cultural reforms necessary to transform Turkey into 'a country of information society, growing in stability, sharing more equitably, globally competitive and fully coherent with the European Union' as well as within the framework of the Long-term Strategy (2001–2023). The novelty of the Ninth Development Plan is the application of a strategic approach to development planning (instead of formulating each area in detail) and an effective monitoring and evaluation mechanism. The Ninth Development Plan is the basis for and ensures coherence among the necessary documents in the EU accession process like the Pre-accession Economic Programme, the Strategic Coherence Framework, and the Medium-term Programme, operational, sectoral and institutional strategy documents.

The Strategic Coherence Framework is a strategic document that provides a 'frame of reference' for the operational programmes under regional development and human resources development components of the IPA. The Strategic Coherence Framework 2007–2013 takes into account the priorities of Turkey and the EU and sets priorities for utilizing EU funds.

Environmental protection

International instruments

One of the key outputs of the 1992 Rio Summit was to highlight and focus attention on the environment. A number of conventions, conferences and other activities relating to different environmental issues have generated multilateral environment agreements (MEAs). MEAs regulate specific aspects of environmental sustainability, such as stopping the loss of biological diversity and developing national biodiversity strategies and action plans in line with the Convention on Biological Diversity (CBD).

MEAs may take the form of 'soft-law', setting out non-legally binding principles, which parties will respect when considering actions that affect a particular environmental issue, or 'hard-law' that specify legally binding actions to be taken to work toward an environmental objective.

Here we present selected multilateral environmental agreements that provide relevant policy framework for focus countries. They fall into six general environmental themes: governance, nature and biodiversity, water, waste, air and climate change (see Table 1.1).

Table 1.1 Main international environmental agreements relevant for focus countries

Theme	*Agreement*
Governance	Aarhus Convention (1998) Espoo Convention (1991)
Nature and biodiversity	Convention on Biological Diversity (1992) and its protocols: Cartagena Biosafety Protocol (2000); Nagoya Protocol (2010) Bonn Convention on the Conservation of Migratory Species (1979) Bern Convention on European Wildlife and Habitats (1979) The Ramsar Convention (1971) CITES (1973)
Water	Helsinki Convention on Watercourses and International Lakes (1992) Barcelona Convention (1976) as amended and its protocol
Waste	Basel Convention on hazardous wastes (1989)
Air	Geneva Convention on Long-range Transboundary Air Pollution (1979) and its protocols (including Gothenburg Protocol)
Climate Change and Ozone Depletion	UNFCCC Framework Convention on Climate Change (1992) and Kyoto protocol (1997) Vienna Convention for the Protection of the Ozone Layer (1985) and Montreal protocol (1987) as amended

Source: Authors' compilation

Governance

The Convention on Access to Information, Public Participation in Decision making and Access to Justice in Environmental Matters (the so-called 'Aarhus Convention') and the Convention on Environmental Impact Assessment in a Transboundary Context (the so-called 'Espoo Convention') require considering environmental issues in decision making processes. The Aarhus Convention regulates public participation in the decision making process at national level, while the Espoo defines minimum information necessary to be presented to decision makers for projects that might have a significant adverse transboundary impact. By improving the quality of information presented to decision makers, the Espoo Convention aims to prevent, reduce and control significant adverse transboundary environmental impacts on proposed activities. By enabling the right of access to information, public participation in decision making and access to justice in environmental matters, the Aarhus Convention contributes to the quality and implementation of decisions and the strengthening of the democracy. Both conventions provide for consideration of environmental factors at an early stage in the decision making process.

Nature and biodiversity

Here we present selected multilateral agreements which include the Convention on Biological Diversity (1992) and its Cartagena Biosafety Protocol (2000) and Nagoya Protocol (2010), the Bonn Convention on the Conservation of Migratory Species (1979), the Bern Convention on European Wildlife and Habitats (1979), the Ramsar Convention (1971) and the Convention on International Trade in Endangered Species of Wild Fauna and Flora (CITES) (1973) (see Table 1.1).

The conservation of biological diversity, the sustainable use of its components and the fair and equitable sharing of benefits arising from the use of genetic resources are the aims of the CBD.

Its target to significantly reduce the rate of biodiversity loss at the global, regional and national levels by 2010 as a contribution to poverty alleviation and for the benefit of all life on Earth was subsequently endorsed by the World Summit on Sustainable Development and the United Nations General Assembly. The target itself stipulates the link between biodiversity and poverty alleviation and is incorporated in the MDGs (Target 7.B: Reduce biodiversity loss, achieving, by 2010, a significant reduction in the rate of loss). The progress towards goals has not been sufficient, thus a new strategic plan was adopted in 2010 which identifies five strategic goals (to be achieved by 2050) and 20 Aichi Biodiversity Targets (to be met by 2020, at the latest).

The Cartagena Biosafety Protocol to the CBD deals with the protection of biological diversity from any adverse effects of living modified organisms (LMOs). Its aim is to minimize adverse effects that LMOs could have on biological diversity as well as risks to human health by regulating safe handling, transport and the use of LMOs resulting from modern biotechnology.

The Nagoya Protocol on Access to Genetic Resources and the Fair and Equitable Sharing of Benefits Arising from their Utilization to the Convention on Biological Diversity adopted in 2010, supports the implementation of the main goals of the CBD, fair and equitable sharing of the benefits arising from the use of genetic resources, which includes appropriate access to genetic resources and the transfer of relevant technologies.

The Convention on the Conservation of Migratory Species of Wild Animals (also known as CMS or the Bonn Convention) deals with conservation of migratory species. The CMS aims to conserve terrestrial, marine and avian migratory species on a global scale, by protecting their habitats (conserving or restoring the places where they live) and migration routes (mitigating obstacles to migration). The CMS encourages states whose territories include areas that a migratory specie inhabits, stays in temporarily, crosses or overflies at any time on its normal migration route to conclude specific agreement in order to facilitate cooperation and contribute to protection of specific animals, such as bats (Agreement on the Conservation of Populations of European Bats), migratory water birds (Agreement on the Conservation of African–Eurasian Migratory Water Birds) or cetaceans (Agreement on the Conservation of Cetaceans of the Black Sea, Mediterranean and Contiguous Atlantic Area –ACCOBAMS).

The Convention on European Wildlife and Habitats (Convention on the Conservation of European Wildlife and Natural Habitats, 1979), also deals with the protection of migratory endangered and vulnerable species. Its aims are threefold:

- to conserve wild flora and fauna and natural habitats, especially those species and habitats whose conservation requires the cooperation of several states;
- to promote cooperation between states;
- to give particular attention to endangered and vulnerable species, including (but not focused to as Bonn Convention) to endangered and vulnerable migratory species.

The Bern Convention provides for the monitoring and control of endangered species and the provision of assistance concerning legal and scientific issues. The Convention led to the creation of the Emerald Network of Areas of Special Conservation Interest in 1998 throughout the territory of the parties to the Convention. The Emerald Network operates alongside the European Union's Natura 2000 programme.[4]

The Ramsar Convention (the Convention on Wetlands of International Importance) provides the framework for national action and international cooperation for the conservation and wise use of wetlands and their resources. It is the only global environmental treaty that deals with a particular ecosystem (wetlands), and the Convention's member countries cover all geographic regions of the planet including EU member states, as well as Croatia and Turkey. The Ramsar contracting parties committed themselves to:

- designate at least one site that meets the Ramsar criteria for inclusion in the List of Wetlands of International Importance
- protect the ecological character of listed sites

- include wetland conservation within their national land-use planning
- establish nature reserves on wetlands and promote wetland training
- consult with other contracting parties about the implementation of the Convention.

CITES aims to ensure that international trade in specimens of wild animals and plants does not threaten their survival.

Water

Essentially, the transboundary nature of water resources and associated sovereignty issues require tackling the major water related problems at international level, as by the UN Economic Commission for Europe (UNECE) Convention on the Protection and Use of Transboundary Watercourses and International Lakes (Helsinki Convention). The Helsinki Convention deals with water quality (contaminated water resulting in water related diseases) and water quantity (increasing droughts and floods). It replaces an earlier focus on localized sources of pollution and management of separate components of the ecosystem with a holistic approach based on integrated water resources management. Its main goals are threefold:

1 prevention of transboundary impacts
2 control of transboundary impact, and
3 reduction of transboundary impacts on the environment, human health and socio-economic conditions.

It provides for the implementation of the ecosystem approach guided by two main principles: precautionary principle and polluter pays principle.

Waste

The trend observed in the 1980s, when toxic traders were shipping hazardous waste to developing and Eastern European countries, led to the creation of the Basel Convention on the Control of Transboundary Movements of Hazardous Wastes and their Disposal. It sets up a framework to control transboundary movements of hazardous wastes, and defines criteria for waste management and a control system based on prior written notification. This should lead to environmentally sound management which is the central goal of the convention drafted by the United Nations Environment Programme (UNEP). Obligations of the parties are:

- to inform other parties if a country decides to prohibit the import of hazardous waste or other waste and to prohibit export of wastes to parties that prohibit import.
- to ensure that production of hazardous waste is kept to a minimum; that adequate disposal facilities are available; that pollution is prevented; that

transboundary movement of hazardous wastes are kept to a minimum; that information and documents for transboundary movement are provided; and that cooperation with other parties are conducted.
- to take legal measure in case of violation of the Convention, and illegal transboundary movements are considered crimes.
- to review periodically the possibility to reduce the amount of waste exported.

Air

The 1979 Geneva Convention on Long-range Transboundary Air Pollution (CLRTAP) was the first international legally binding instrument to deal with the problems of air pollution on a broad regional basis. The Convention was the result of cooperation, which aimed at fighting acidification initiated after scientific evidence (provided in the 1960s) of a correlation between sulphur air emissions in continental Europe and the fact that Scandinavian lakes became acidic. Later (between 1972 and 1977) several studies confirmed the hypothesis that air pollutants could travel several thousand kilometres before being deposited and damage occurred. Thus, CLRTAP laid down the general principles of international cooperation for air pollution abatement (such as requirements for information exchange). Its aim is to reduce and prevent air pollution including long-range transboundary air pollution. It, therefore, requires each party to gradually limit and reduce air pollution and long-range transboundary air pollution. To this end, CLRTAP and its eight legally binding protocols[5] set out emission limit values for many air-polluting substances, including sulphur dioxide, nitrogen oxide, persistent organic pollutants, volatile organic compounds, lead and mercury.

One of the most successful examples of legal instruments for environmental management is set by the Vienna Convention for the Protection of the Ozone Layer and its Montreal Protocol on Substances that Deplete the Ozone Layer. In 2009, the Vienna Convention and its Montreal Protocol became the first treaties of any kind to achieve universal ratification (196 countries).

The Vienna Convention for the Protection of the Ozone Layer is often called a framework convention, because it served as a framework for efforts to protect the globe's ozone layer. It was adopted in 1985 and entered into force in 1988. The objectives of the Convention are to promote cooperation by means of systematic observations, research and information exchange on the effects of human activities on the ozone layer and to adopt legislative or administrative measures against activities likely to have adverse effects on the ozone layer.

The Vienna Convention does not require concrete actions to control ozone depleting substances. It is the Montreal Protocol which requires phasing out ozone depleting substances, chloro-fluorocarbons and halons.

Climate change

The United Nations Framework Convention on Climate Change (UNFCCC) sets the overall framework for intergovernmental efforts to tackle the challenge posted by climate change. Its long-term objective is 'to stabilize atmospheric greenhouse gas concentrations at a level that would prevent dangerous anthropogenic interference with the climate system'. Under the Convention, governments gather and share information on GHG emissions, national policies and best practices, launch national strategies for addressing GHG emissions and adapting to expected impacts, including the provision of financial and technological support to developing countries, and cooperate in preparing for adaptation to the impacts of climate change.

MEAs provide a general policy framework, but the adoption and effective implementation of proper environmental policies and regulations require strong regulatory and enforcement institutions. MEAs often lack the capacity for effective implementation, thus international organizations with established structures and budgets support their functioning. These organizations include multinational economic institutions (the World Bank, IMF, WTO), the UN entities with environmental responsibilities (UNEP, Commission for Sustainable Development, UNDP, UNCTAD, etc.), as well as non-governmental organizations committed to drawing into the international policymaking process the best data, thinking, analysis and policy experience. Multinational economic institutions have gradually included environmental mainstreaming into its policies and country strategies. Since the adoption of its first environmental strategy in 2001, the World Bank has undertaken two main types of environmental related activities: assessments (of environmental conditions, and institutional and governance structures) and lending operations geared towards technical capacity development. Support for addressing environment and natural resources themes has increased from about 5 per cent in 2002 to 11 per cent in 2009. The new environmental strategy, which is currently being drafted, is expected to enable a differentiated approach to clients, based on the detailed assessments of local conditions. These will be evaluated on the basis of a country environmental assessment (which enables integration of environmental considerations into country assistance strategies and can guide institutional reform and capacity development efforts) and strategic environmental assessment (which integrates environmental and social considerations at the policy, plan or programme level).

While focusing on monetary cooperation, financial stability and facilitating international trade, the IMF also promotes high employment, sustainable economic growth and poverty reduction. Environmental degradation is regarded as a potential threat to economic performance, and the IMF's concept of 'high quality growth' defined as sustainable growth with domestic and external financial stability embraces environmental considerations. It is considered that sustainable development, protection and preservation of the environment complement the WTO's objective to reduce trade barriers and eliminate discriminatory treatment in international trade relations.

Among the UN entities with environmental responsibilities the UNEP has played a significant role in developing international environmental conventions, promoting environmental science and information. UNEP regularly convenes meetings of representatives of the MEA secretariats, including secretariats or interim secretariats for:

- the Convention on Biological Diversity
- the UNFCCC and the Kyoto Protocol
- the Convention on the Conservation of Migratory Species of Wild Animals
- the Basel Convention on the Control of Transboundary Movements of Hazardous Wastes and their Disposal
- the Vienna Convention for the Protection of the Ozone Layer and for the Montreal Protocol on Substances that Deplete the Ozone Layer
- the Convention on International Trade in Endangered Species of Wild Fauna and Flora
- the Convention on Wetlands of International Importance Especially as Water Flow Habitat (Ramsar Convention).

UNEP is the implementing agency for the Global Environmental Facility (GEF) and the Multilateral Fund for the Implementation of the Montreal Protocol. It is also a member of the United Nations Development Group which was created to improve the effectiveness of UN development activities at the country level.

EU policy framework

Under the Lisbon Treaty the objectives of the EU policy on environment are to preserve, protect and improve the quality of environment, protecting human health, prudent and rational utilization of natural resources and to promote measures at international level to deal with regional or worldwide environmental problems, and in particular combating climate change.

The EU environmental policy is created in accordance with the ordinary legislative procedure by the European Parliament and the Council, after consulting the Economic and Social Committee and the Committee of the regions. The European Environment Agency (EEA) provides information necessary for EU and national policymaking.

Environmental policy is based on preventive action: the polluter pays principle, fighting environmental damage at source, shared responsibility and the integration of environmental protection into other EU policies. Thus, a number of strategic documents determine the policy context and influence the setting of priorities: environmental action plans (currently the Sixth Environmental Action Programme – 6th EAP), development strategies (the EU SDS), growth strategies (the EU 2020 Strategy, Economy Recovery Plan), and sector-specific policies (agriculture, research, external action, cohesion).

Environmental action programmes guide the implementation of environmental policy. The 6th EAP launched in 2002 provides a strategic framework for environmental policy up to 2012. It promotes the application of impact assessments and increased use of market-based instruments and highlights the importance of solid scientific foundations as instrumental for better policy making. The thematic strategies (on air, pesticides, waste prevention and recycling, natural resources, soil, marine environment, urban environment)[6] developed within the 6th EAP focused on environmental policy integration and led to the adoption of new, or the revision of existing, legislative instruments (comprised over 200 major legal acts) to improve coherence and to address specific gaps.

New policies have been prepared for the period up to 2020: a new strategy to halt the loss of biodiversity and ecosystem services in the EU by 2020 (European Commission, 2011d) a Roadmap for moving to a low-carbon economy in 2050 (European Commission, 2011b), a White Paper on Transport (European Commission, 2011f), Communications on energy 2020 – an Energy Efficiency Plan 2011 (European Commission, 2010c) and a Roadmap to a resource-efficient Europe (European Commission, 2011g). Preparations for the Rio+20 Conference are under way (European Commission, 2011e). The agenda for 2012 includes a blueprint for water policy and a review of the Sustainable Consumption and Production and Sustainable Industrial Policy Action Plan (European Commission, 2008a). Air quality policy is to be reviewed in 2013. The proposals to reform the Common Agricultural Policy, the Common Fisheries Policy and the Cohesion Policy are also being prepared (European Commission, 2011i).

The new policies emphasize the importance of the green growth and a resource-efficient, low-carbon economy and should enable economic transformation in the long term. If successful, the EU model could serve as policy guidance for global economic transformation.

National policies

Slovenia

The Constitution of the Republic of Slovenia (which defines that the state is responsible for protecting nature and maintaining a healthy environment) membership in multilateral environmental agreements (see Table 1.2), and in the EU accession process (launched with the adoption of the Environmental Accession Strategy of Slovenia, as an Appendix to the National Programme for Adoption of the *Acquis Communautaire* in 1998) have provided a framework for environmental policy development.

Slovenia was the first among Eastern European countries which set up the environment fund, where polluters were made responsible for the damage they caused and where an environmental tax was introduced. The environment fund was replaced by an environmental development fund set up in 1994 as a financial instrument for investment. Currently the Eco Fund (*Eko Sklad*) promotes environmental investment in Slovenia. This public financial institution finances various investment schemes in the form of loans, such as loans for environmental protection at national and local level and for technology aimed at environmental protection. The rates of interest for these loans are lower than others.

Key acts regulating the protection of environment, nature conservation and the protection of the natural heritage of Slovenia are the Environmental Protection Act and the Nature Conservation Act. Environmental provisions have also been incorporated in civil and criminal law.

The objectives, principles and instruments for the protection of the environment are established by the Environmental Protection Act which covers the

Table 1.2 Participation in MEAs and focal points

Convention name	*Bulgaria*	*Croatia*	*Romania*	*Slovenia*	*Turkey*	
Aarhus	2003	2007	2000	2004	–	Ratification year
	MEW	MEPPPC	MEF	MESP	–	National focal point
Espoo	1995	1996	2001	1998	–	Ratification year
	MEW	MEPPPC	MEF	MESP	–	National focal point
Basel Convention	1996	1994	1991	1993	1994	Ratification year
	MEW	MEPPPC	MEFNEPA	MESP	MOEF	National focal point
Cartagena Protocol	2003	2003	2003	2003	2004	Ratification year
	MEW	MOC	MEF	MESP	MARA	National focal point
CBD	1996	1996	1994	1996	1997	Ratification year
	MEW	MOC	MEF	MESP	MOEF	National focal point
Nagoya Protocol	–	–	–	–	–	Ratification year
	–	–	–	–	–	National focal point
CITES	1991	2000	1994	2000	1996	Ratification year
	MEW	MOC	MEF	MESP	MOEF	National focal point
CMS	1999	2000	1998	1999	–	Ratification year
	MEW	MOC	MEF	MESP	–	National focal point
Kyoto Protocol	2005	2007	2005	2005	2009	Ratification year
	MEW	MEPPPC	MEF	MESP	MOEF	National focal point
Montreal Protocol	1990	1992	1993	1992	1991	Ratification year
	–	–	–	–	–	National focal point
Ramsar Convention	1976	1991	1991	1991	1994	Ratification year
	MEW	MOC	MEF	MESP	MOEF	National focal point
Rotterdam	2000	2007	2003	1999	–	Ratification year
	MEW	MHSW	MEF	MOH	MOEFMARA	National focal point
Stockholm	2005	2007	2004	2004	2009	Ratification year
	MEW	MEPPPC	MEF	MOH	MOEF	National focal point
UNCCD	2001	2001	1998	2001	1998	Ratification year
	MEW	MEPPPC	MEF	MESP	MOEF	National focal point
UNFCCC	1995	1996	1994	1996	2004	Ratification year
	MEW	MEPPPC	MEF	GOCC	MOEF	National focal point
Vienna Convention	1990	1992	1993	1882	1991	Ratification year
						National focal point

Source: Authors' compilation

protection of land, water and air, flora and fauna and the use of natural resources. It embraces the polluter pays and pollution prevention principles and stipulates that incentives should be provided for environment friendly conduct and the use of environment friendly technologies (Kraus, 1998).

The Nature Conservation Act regulates the environmental permits, the environmental impact assessment, the environmental taxes and tradable emission permits.

The National Development Plan and the National Environmental Protection Plan and Action Programme are the main strategic documents defining national environmental policy and the major objectives. The EU support is guided by the national operational programme for development of environmental protection, transport infrastructure and sustainable use of energy in the period 2007–2013.

The Slovenian Ministry of the Environment and Spatial Planning is the key governmental organization for environmental protection. It has been reorganized several times and its authority extended from the protection of water resources to the inclusion of all areas of environmental protection and nature protection.

The Environmental Agency of the Republic of Slovenia, a body of the Ministry of the Environment and Spatial Planning, performs monitoring activities. Subordinate agencies to the Ministry include the Nature Protection Agency, the Geophysical Monitoring Authority, and the Nuclear Inspectorate, the Agency for Efficient Use of Energy and the Department of Efficient Energy Use and Use of Renewable Energy Sources, which is in charge of implementing national programmes in different sectors.

Line ministries deal with specific issues, e.g. the Ministry of Health for drinking water quality and for the implementation of Rotterdam and Stockholm Conventions (see Table 1.2), and the Ministry of Agriculture for forest management.

Local authorities are responsible for implementing government decisions on environmental policy but also have jurisdiction in matters of local significance. The Inspectorate of the Republic of Slovenia supervises the execution of regulations and general acts that regulate environmental protection and nature conservation.

The Health Inspection Service controls the protection of public health and the implementation of sector-specific acts and regulations.

Bulgaria

Participation in MEAs (see Table 1.2) and integration into the European Union influenced the policy and domestic environmental legislation.

The Constitution of the Republic of Bulgaria provides that the state ensures the protection of the environment, the maintenance and diversity of wildlife and the appropriate utilization of Bulgaria's natural resources.

The main piece of environmental legislation in Bulgaria is the Environment Protection Act which sets up the basic principles of the environmental law, such as: health protection, prevention of pollution and conservation of biological diversity and regulates access to environmental information.[7] It also defines rights and obligations of the state, municipalities and persons in respect of environmental protection and provides for development of environmental strategies, programmes and plans.

The main framework of the environmental protection is defined by the Development Plan and Environmental Strategy. The environmental component of the Development Plan focuses on strengthening institutional capacity of central and local authorities involved in environmental issues and finding ways and instruments to encourage companies to comply with environmental legislation.

The Ministry of the Environment and Water, the Regional Inspectorates of the Environment and Water, the Basin Directorates, the National Parks Directorate and local government authorities are responsible for implementing environmental legislation. The Environmental Executive Agency (which is subordinated to the Ministry) monitors the environment.

Ex ante (environmental impact assessment for planned investments, licences), *ex post* (control results of implementation of measures required by environmental impact assessments, licences, permits) and ongoing control (monitoring the compliance with the terms and conditions of the licences) are the main instruments for the enforcement of the environmental legislation.

The Enterprise for Management of Environmental Protection Activities is the institution that facilitates implementation of environmental rules and encourages companies to comply with environmental legislation by financing ecoprojects and awareness raising activities.

The current National Environmental Strategy 2009–2018 and the Strategy Action Plan emphasize the importance of environmental quality for economic development and regional convergence.[8]

National strategies and action plans have also been adopted for other sectors (e.g. development of ecotourism and sustainable development of tourism, development of the forestry sector, waste management, water supply and sewage, regional development, fishery and aquaculture, biodiversity). Relevant line ministries are responsible for implementation, namely the Ministry of Economy, Energy and Tourism, the Ministry of Transport and the Ministry of Health (see Table 1.2). The EU support is guided by the National Operational Programme: Environment 2007–2013.

Romania

The building of new structures for environmental protection started in 1990 when the Ministry of Environment was established. The implementation of ratified multilateral environmental agreements (see Table 1.2) and the alignment with the EU rules have influenced policy formulation and measures in sectors and activities that have environmental impact.

Economic activities that have a significant impact on the environment must be authorized by the National Agency for Environmental Protection, specialized authority of the public central administration, also responsible for environmental monitoring (drawing up a report on the state of the environment; reporting to the EEA) and subordinated to the Ministry of Environment and Forests.

The Ministry of Environment and Forests is the key central authority for the administration, compliance checking and enforcement of legislation relating to environmental protection. It is responsible for environmental strategies, drafting laws, issuing administrative regulations, environmental impact assessment, environmental monitoring and management of protected areas, environmental inspection and international and public relations. The Ministry of Environment is also the management authority for the Operational Programme Environment, one of the most important programming documents enabling the implementation of sectoral and national environmental strategies, such as the NDP 2007–2013, the NSRF, the National Environmental Action Plan, the NSDS 2013–2020–2030 and guides EU support. National financing is provided by the Environmental Fund, a financial instrument for supporting environmental protection priority projects.

While the local governments have some environmental authority, they have less powers than local branch authorities of the ministries acting in the field of environment (e.g. the Ministry of Environment and Forests, the Ministry of Health, see Table 1.2) and limited financial resources for implementation.

Croatia

Croatian integration to the European Union and the process of adjustment of Croatian legislation with *acquis communitaire* has influenced the Croatian environment legislation. The EU conditionality approach has influenced also Croatian accession to the MEAs (see Table 1.2).[9]

According to the Constitution, conservation of nature and the environment is among the highest values. Everyone shall have the right to a healthy life. The state shall ensure conditions for a healthy environment. Everyone shall be bound, within their powers and activities, to pay special attention to the protection of public health, nature and environment.

These principles and environmental protection requirements have been gradually integrated into all relevant sectoral policy areas (transport, energy, agriculture, tourism, etc.) and legislation (primarily the Environmental Protection Act). The strategy documents that determine the national environmental policy framework in Croatia include the Strategic Development Framework 2006–2013 as a general framework, the National Environmental Strategy and the National Environmental Action Plan, which guide enforcement of environmental law. Support provided by the EU and programmed in the Operational Programme Environment facilitates implementation.

The National Environmental Strategy attempts to reconcile two basic strategic directions of action: incentives and sanctions. It includes principles of integration of the environmental protection policy into other sectoral policies, the principles of partnership and shared responsibility, the principle of subsidiary, the change of behaviour in production and the use of a large number of instruments, mainly economic ones.

Environmental protection is thus gradually included in policies and regulation related to energy, transport, agriculture, tourism and other sectors.

The Ministry of Environmental Protection, Physical Planning and Construction performs administrative and other activities relating to general policy on environmental protection. The Spatial Planning and Environmental Protection

Committee of the Croatian Parliament establishes and monitors the implementation of policy, and is a competent working body in procedures to enact legislation and other regulations related to environment protection. The Agency for Environmental Protection, established in 2002, collects and processes environmental data, monitors and reports on the state of the environment. The Fund for Environment Protection and Energy Efficiency, established in 2004, finances, among others, the preparation, realization and development of programmes, projects and similar activities in the area of preservation, sustainable use, protection and enhancement of the environment.

Turkey

According to the Turkish Constitution, the development and protection of the environment and the prevention of environmental pollution are the duty of all public institutions and organizations, as well as of the citizens.

The EU accession process has fostered a series of fundamental reforms, as approximation requires transposition and enforcement of legislation and also the reorganization of institutional structure. The approximation process in the environment field has been carried out by the Ministry of Environment and Forestry, which is mainly responsible for environmental legislation and policy development in Turkey. The Ministry of Environment was established in 1991 and merged with the Ministry of Forests in 2003. The Ministry, together with its local staff in the provinces, guarantees legal arrangements on environmental protection.

Apart from the Ministry of Environment, other ministries (the Ministry of Foreign Affairs, the Ministry of Energy and Natural Resources, the Ministry of Culture and Tourism, the Ministry of Industry and Trade, the Ministry of Labour and Social Security, the Ministry of Interior, the Ministry of Public Works and Settlement, the Ministry of Agriculture and Rural Affairs, the Ministry of Health), government agencies (the State Planning Organization, the General Secretariat of European Union, the State Hydraulic Works, Undersecretariat of Maritime Affairs, Undersecretariat of Treasury, Undersecretariat of Foreign Trade) are in charge of integrating environmental policy targets as well. Local authorities and municipalities have also established their own administrative structures, such as water and sewerage administrations in the cities of Istanbul, Izmir and Ankara. Apart from the authorities, the Bank of Provinces is mainly responsible for municipality investment in water and sewerage systems and provides funds and technical supports to the municipalities for their investment in the framework of the national development programmes.

The steps taken by Turkey on the path to EU membership and the harmonization process of environmental legislation will directly increase environmental standards and ensure sustainable development. Since the adoption of the Turkish National Programme for Adoption of the EU *Acquis* in 2003, which established a priority list for enforcement of environmental regulations, a substantial body of legislation has been transposed. The National Environment Law is a milestone in environmental protection in Turkey and has many sector-specific regulations.

Implementation is facilitated by the Operational Programme Environment which is one of the basic planning and action documents.

Financing

It is formally recognized, since the Rio Summit, that sustainable development should be the guiding principle for design and implementation of reform policies. However, the issue of economic competitiveness has dominated the political agenda and sustainable development has been regarded as the pillar of growth.

Having growth as the top priority, public investment is mainly geared towards growth related policies.[10] As a result there is limited public financing for environmental protection, especially in the already strained public budgets in the time of crisis, and environmental investment depends on private initiatives. This means that projects must be sufficiently profitable. The commercial value of environmental services being offered on the market plays a decisive role on investment in environmental infrastructure. The commercial value of environmental infrastructure depends on the price of service and demand, as well as the price of substitute, which is pollution, i.e. the higher the pollution costs, the higher the demand for environmental services. On the other hand, an increased price reduces affordability and demand. The rising price thus has ambiguous impact on the commercial value of environmental infrastructure. Determining the price of pollution (i.e. full application of polluter pays principle) and setting the right price for environmental services are thus crucial for investment decisions.

Besides investors, the key role in project preparation lies with creditors. The availability of capital depends on risk assessment and profit related to each project. Projects must be technically, commercially and financially viable over the project duration (typically 20 years or more), and the risks must be predictable and acceptable.

In times of financial and economic crisis the access to capital is more difficult. Reduced economic activity decreases environmental pressures and demand for environmental services. The commercial value of infrastructure drops, which is an additional difficulty for new investments.

Conversely, if environmental protection is the top priority, investment decisions are based on environmental goals (e.g. those set by multilateral environmental agreements) and might receive public financing. As public budgets are limited, access to finance depends on the risk evaluation by creditors. Thus, investments that are not necessarily profitable might be financed provided that they are feasible, financially sustainable and provide economic benefits.[11]

In brief, investment decisions related to environmental infrastructure depend on:

1 commercial value of environmental infrastructure necessary for services
2 issue of affordability
3 price setting mechanism
4 risks for investors and creditors; and
5 policy stability and predictability.

Bearing this in mind, it is not surprising that indicative cost estimates show that implementation of Agenda 21 and reaching the MDGs have to be financed mainly from a country's own public and private sources.[12] However, growth alone is not sufficient. There is a need for external financing, including a grant component which exceeds official development assistance and requires new and additional financial tools.

Developed countries have agreed to provide 0.7 per cent of GNI for official development assistance by 2015 and committed to mobilizing US$100 billion a year by 2020 to address the needs of developing countries in the context of international climate negotiations. The EU member states that joined EU after 2002 are supposed to provide a minimum of 0.33 per cent of GNI to official development assistance in 2015, while the EU as a whole has to achieve 0.7 per cent target, i.e. new member states (including Slovenia, Bulgaria and Romania) are expected to gradually change their role, from donor recipients to donors. They should be able to finance their own development and to provide development aid. This also requires the change of financial tools used for investment in environmental protection and sustainable development.

Financial tools necessary to further sustainable development include information resources for financial decision making, cost saving mechanisms, partnership ideas, and financing options such as grants and loans.

Increased use of market-based instruments, including loans from international financial institutions, the World Bank (through support to environmentally sound projects and policies) and the IMF (by integrating growth, social and environmental goals into development objectives) and full application of polluter pays principle, as opposed to technical assistance from the EU and the partnership through the GEF, might be considered as essential conditions for long-term economic growth.

Long-term growth requires transformation to the green economy. A green economy is the one that results in 'improved human well-being and social equity, while significantly reducing environmental risks and ecological scarcities' (UNEP, 2011). In line with the MDGs, reducing environmental risks and ecological scarcities means ensuring environmental sustainability,[13] which requires the integration of the principles of sustainable development into policies and programmes, reversing loss of environmental resources, as well as reducing biodiversity loss. Funding needs for global biodiversity and ecosystems are estimated at €4–40 billion a year (European Commission 2011a: 117). For comparison:

- Multilateral Environmental Fund of the Montreal protocol, which is one of the most successful examples of legal instrument for environmental management, since 1991 has provided about US$2.6 billion for assistance (industrial conversion, technical assistance, training and capacity building).
- The GEF has, since it was established in 1991 to 2009, allocated US$10.4 billion (supplemented by more than US$44 billion in co-financing) to various projects addressing global environmental issues.
- The rescue package for Greece agreed by heads of states or governments of the Eurozone in July 2011 amounted to €109 billion, while net voluntary support of the private sector is estimated at €37 billion.

At the EU level, environmental and climate action related investments are ensured through a combination of mainstreaming of environmental and climate concerns into other policies' areas and their respective funds (cohesion, agriculture, research, external action), and a dedicated instrument (LIFE+).

Under current multiannual financial framework (2007–2012) environment related actions represent some 9 per cent of the EU budget (some €12–13 billion a year) and climate related actions 5 per cent (approximately €7 billion a year).[14] EU funds allocated directly to the environment and climate are €450 million a year, which is less than estimated cost of implementing thematic strategies within the 6th EAP.[15]

Financing environment related actions results from an integration of environmental financing into other major funding programmes. These include:

- some €6.5 billion per year for environmental infrastructure from the structural/cohesion funds, focusing on waste water, water supply and waste,
- some €5 billion per year for environmental measures in agriculture and forestry from the European Agricultural Fund for Rural Development,
- some €0.4 billion per year for innovation and research, from Seventh Research Programme and the Competitiveness and Innovation Programme.

Most substantial sources of financing for climate related actions come from cohesion policy (€4.1 billion per year), the Seventh Research Framework Programme (€0.9 billion per year) and Common Agricultural Policy (€1.5 billion per year). In addition, some €1 billion per year is spent on external environment and climate actions as a result of a mix of mainstreaming in the IPA, the European Neighbourhood and Partnership Instrument, the geographical programme in the Development Cooperation Instrument, and the Tenth European Development Fund (10th EDF), as well as from the thematic programme for Environment and Sustainable Management of Natural Resources including energy.

The budget proposal for the next multiannual financial framework 2014–2020 recognizes that the EU environmental policy contributes to the EU 2020 objectives of smart, sustainable and inclusive growth. Environmental policy priorities will be mainstreamed into all the major EU funding instruments, including cohesion, agriculture, maritime and fisheries, research and innovation and external aid. In external action, the IPA will finance environmental infrastructure and capacity building in candidate countries. Support for the environment will also be mainstreamed under the European Neighbourhood and Partnership Instrument. Biodiversity and ecosystems will be part of the thematic programme for global public goods and challenges. In addition to mainstreaming, LIFE+ programme is proposed to continue and align with Europe 2020 objectives. The environment subprogramme will be organized according to three priorities: biodiversity, environment (i.e. implementation of environmental legislation relevant to the EU 2020 resource efficiency objectives) and governance. It will focus on two types of projects: new integrated projects (the number and financial share of which will gradually increase) and traditional projects. LIFE+

integrated projects will support a series of specific activities and measures for the implementation of environmental actions plans (e.g. a prioritized action framework under the Habitats Directive for an air pollution abatement plan to meet air quality requirements).

For the period 2014–2020, the proposed budget allocation is €2.4 billion, excluding funds for mainstreaming which are included within budgetary allocations for sectoral funding instruments.

The total environmental and climate change costs in the EU, based on an assessment of non-action, would be in the order of €650 billion per year, about 5–6 per cent of EU's GDP (GHK, *et al.*, 2011). There are significant financial needs for achieving the environmental and climate objectives for the environmental protection requirements and climate actions identified throughout the EU. For example, the costs of managing and restoring the Natura 2000 network are estimated by member states at €5.6 billion per year; the implementation of the Water Framework Directive around €30 billion per year; soil action needs €4.5 billion, and waste water treatment €6.5 billion a year (EC, 2011a: 116). Over the next 40 years additional annual private and public investment equivalent of 1.5 per cent of EU's GDP or around €270 billion (EC, 2011a: 112) would be needed on top of current annual investment to make EU economies energy efficient and climate friendly.

Costs and financing sources at national level considerably depend on a number of factors, such as structure of the economy, prevailing environmental impact, effectiveness and timeliness of action etc. Thus, we present financial needs and sources for selected EU member states and candidates.

Slovenia

The financial requirements for investment in the five environmental fields (water, waste, waste water, renewable energy sources and risk prevention) for the period 2000–2013 are estimated at €1.5 billion (Gobec and De Sutter, 2006: 78). In the period 2000–2006, €156 million were invested, and the financial need for the period 2007–2013 is estimated at €1.3 billion, out of which €383 million is expected to be financed from EU funds.

Slovene environmental expenditures are financed mainly through the state budget, local governments and municipalities, the National Environmental Protection Fund as well as from the private sector and external sources. External sources include the European Bank for Reconstruction and Development (EBRD) and the World Bank and bilateral donors (the governments of Austria, the Netherlands, the United Kingdom and France). Co-funding of environmental investments is also a common scheme in Slovenia, which enables financing for up to 30 per cent of total investment from an eco fund, whose sources of funding include earmarked revenue (form environmental taxes), grants (from EU funds) and loans (International Bank for Reconstruction and Development, European Investment Bank).

Since 2001, general government expenditure for environmental protection has been between 0.7– 1.09 per cent of GPD (€180–246 million), and according to the

National Environment Action Plan (for the period until accession) 1.5 per cent GDP is necessary for implementing foreseen measures.

Significant parts of the general government expenditure for environment are subsidies. General subsidies increased from €349.9 to €660.3 million in the period 2000–2009. Their share in GDP, after remaining unchanged for several years (1.6 per cent of GDP) increased to 1.9 per cent in 2009. The increased share of subsidies in GDP is the result of the GDP decline and increase of subsidies by 12.4 per cent in nominal terms, mainly due to the stimulus measures taken to offset the economic crisis (see Table 1.3).

The share of subsidies for environmental protection does not follow this trend. Environmental subsidies declined in 2009 in nominal terms and their share in subsidies also declined, indicating that environmental integration is not the highest priority for recovery.

As regards revenues, it is planned that the gap between needed and available funds will be gradually bridged with a progressive setting up of the polluter pays system. The progress can be illustrated by the fact that revenues from environmental taxes in 2008 represented 3.0 per cent of GDP, and 3.8 per cent in 2009.

Bulgaria

The necessary expenditures for investment and institutional reform resulting from the harmonization of the Bulgarian with the environmental *acquis* in the period 2001–2004 were estimated between €5.4 and €8.0 billion, or between €1.222 and €1.691 billion a year (see Table 1.4). For the period 2005–2013 necessary public investments are estimated at €5.3 billion (Tonchevski and Lust, 2006).

Necessary investments in all areas relating to the environment significantly exceed Bulgarian capacity to finance. PHARE (around €60 million), ISPA (€430 million) and SAPARD[16] (€211 million) in the 2001–2006 periods provide external support and facilitate alignment with the EU *acquis*. However, Bulgaria was not able to fully implement the environmental *acquis* by the date of accession. Thus transitional periods were negotiated based on the implementation plans of

Table 1.3 General government subsidies and environmental subsidies in Slovenia, 2000–2009

	2000	*2005*	*2006*	*2007*	*2008*	*2009*
Total subsidies (million euros)	349.9	452.1	503.1	549.7	587.2	660.3
Subsidies as per cent of GDP (%)	1.9	1.6	1.6	1.6	1.6	1.9
Environmental subsidies (million euros)	29.4	51.6	44.1	46.8	49.1	36.9
Share of environmental subsidies in total subsidies (%)	8.4	11.4	8.8	8.5	8.4	5.6

Source: Authors' calculation based on Šušteršič, *et al.*, 2005

Table 1.4 Environmental investment costs, in million euros

Sector	*Total investment costs*		*Annual investment costs**		*Annual operation and maintenance costs*		*Total annual costs*	
	Min	*Max*	*Min*	*Max*	*Min*	*Max*	*Min*	*Max*
Air pollution	3,051	3,260	359	383	391	428	750	811
Drinking water	246	1,463	29	172	16	53	45	225
Sewage	734	1,114	86	131	16	22	102	153
Wastewater treatment	476	850	56	100	49	102	105	202
Waste management	850	1,150	100	135	93	132	193	267
Nitrates	103	155	12	18			12	18
Other**	30	30	3	3	12	12	15	15
Total	5,490	8,022	645	942	577	749	1,222	1,691

Source: OP Environment 2007–2013, 2007

Notes

* All costs related to maintenance and capacity building of the public administration, as well as the subsidies for nature protection.

** These do not include the costs for nuclear safety, commerce and elimination of past pollution. The costs for the transport and industrial sector are partially included.

so-called 'heavy' directives. Implementation plans identify necessary investments and sources of financing, including the support from the EU Cohesion and Structural Funds form 2007–2013 (see Table 1.5).

The total amount of EU funds under the cohesion fund for 2008 was €6,674 million. Environment and risk activities were supported with €1,461 million in 2008. These activities were financed mainly under the priorities of the Environmental Operational Programme. Some €636 million were allocated for R&D in general, of which €23 million were related to environmental processes. The Operational Programme 'Regional Development' 2007–2013 provides support for decreasing fuel consumption in public transport, energy efficiency in public buildings (hospitals, schools, social centres for disabled, etc.), as well as rehabilitation (including energy efficiency) in about 2000 apartment buildings.

The National Innovation Fund for promoting new technologies had a budget of BGN3 million (€1.5 million) in 2008. The sum of BGN500,000 (€257,500) will be allocated to support scientific and research projects; likewise, the amount of BGN15 million (€7,724 million) will be set aside for technical, economical and pre-project research.

An increased focus on the environment is illustrated by the Ministry of Environment and Water budget growth between 2007 and 2009. In 2007 the Ministry of Environment budget was €136 million, in 2009 €289 million, while in 2009 it reached €570 million.[17]

Table 1.5 Total investment costs for implementation of heavy directives, the public sector, in million euros

Sector	*Total investment costs*	*Investment costs up to 2005*	*Investment costs for the period 2005–2009 (annual and cumulative)*						*Investment costs after 2009*
			2005	*2006*	*2007*	*2008*	*2009*	*2005–2009*	
Water*	2,218	144	120	151	175	211	239	896	1,177
Waste	445	53	51	52	54	29	31	216	176
IPPC	47	16	8	7	7	6	4	31	0
LCP	657	137	164	195	161	0	0	520	0
Total	3,367	350	343	405	396	245	274	1,663	1,353

Source: OP Environment 2007–2013, 2007: 36

Note
* The Implementation Programme for the requirements of Directive 91/271/EC only includes investments for sewage systems, including waste water treatment plants.

Romania

Under the current financial programming period, estimated investment requirement for the implementation of the National Development Plan 2007–2013, amounts to €58.67 billion. The structural instruments and the EU agriculture and fisheries funds might provide about €32 billion, if the highest possible national absorption capacity is ensured.

The balance is covered from the state budget, external borrowing and other sources. There will be some additional financing needed for the objectives of the NSDS. The SDS does not identify how much additional financing is needed, but recognizes the opportunity to submit projects on a competitive basis to EU funds that are not part of the structural or cohesion funds,[18] funds allocated through the Financial Mechanism of the European Economic Area[19] and from bilateral schemes operated by EU member states or other European countries (Norway, Switzerland). The revisions of strategy are planned for the period after 2011, and it is expected that the objectives and targets of the SDS will be used as the reference points for the drafting of national and local budgets (annual and multi-annual) and for the formulation and promotion of Romania's proposals toward the preparation and approval of allocations under the next EU financial programming periods (2014–2020 and 2021–2027).

Potential financial sources include:

- EU contribution (European Regional development Fund, European Social Fund, European Cohesion Fund, European Agriculture Fund for Rural Development, European Fisheries Fund)
- Funds from the state and the local budgets (primarily for co-financing investments of EU structural instruments)

- External borrowing (from international financial institutions: European Investment Bank, EBRD, World Bank, etc. and other sources: sovereign funds, private investment funds, etc.)
- Other financial sources (foreign direct investment, active utilization of capital markets, especially by launching initial public offers, enlarging the lending base of the banking sector by encouraging domestic savings, developing long-term saving and investment instruments, concession of infrastructure and public utilities projects, promoting public-private partnerships, etc.)

Croatia

Alignment with the EU environmental *acquis* has imposed a heavy financial burden on the already strained Croatian public budget. Historically, spending from the public sector on the environment in Croatia is 0.65 per cent of the GDP, which means that the financial needs for environmental purposes cannot be met solely from the public sector. To ease this financial burden, the EU has provided financial and technical assistance. In covering the financial gap, Croatia has also been strongly supported by the international financial institutions, mainly the World Bank and EBRD. For example, the EC assistance to Croatia over the period 2001–2008 reached €489.64 million, out of which €90.59 million for environment. Nevertheless, environmental investment in Croatia has so far been unsatisfactory to meet all the EU requirements. Therefore, the expenses of Croatian environmental harmonization are estimated to rise to €10 billion in the upcoming 15–20 years (Tišma and Maleković, 2009: 29).

The special Energy Efficiency and Nature Protection Fund was established in 2004 to facilitate investments. Its revenues come from environmental fees, fees paid for the use of environment for economic activity, penalties paid for the violation of the Environmental Protection Act, utilization and concession fees collected under the Geological and Mining Law, fees determined under the Water Management Act and also the act on recycling of decommissioned vehicles, local budgets and external sources. Since co-financing mostly takes the form of loans, the National Fund constitutes a 'renewable source of financing' for environmental protection projects.

Turkey

The cost of environmental infrastructure necessary to align Turkey with the EU *acquis* is estimated at about €59 billion. It is planned that 80 per cent of this cost will be financed by the public and 20 per cent by private sector (EU Integrated Environmental Approximation Strategy 2007–2023, 2006). For the period 2007–2023 local administrations are expected to ensure 33 per cent of the total investment needed in the environmental sector, 12 per cent Iller Bank, and the international financial institutions (World Bank, European Investment Bank, German Investment and Development Bank, Japan Bank for International Cooperation and the credits of Spanish Government) are expected to finance 2 per cent of environmental investments, with 26 per cent coming from the private sector. The rest is expected to be financed from the general budget, grants and other instruments (see Table 1.6).

Table 1.6 Turkish investment in environmental protection in TRY

	Toplam	*2007*	*2008*	*2009*	*2010*	*2011*	*2012*	*2013*	*2014*
1 Central administration	7,738	299	314	330	347	364	382	401	421
2 Local Administration	21,814	1,078	1,233	1,423	1,553	1,189	1,221	1,227	1,296
Municipal resources	13,023	643	783	966	1,117	741	772	767	827
Bank of Provinces	6,980	296	312	313	323	344	350	366	377
External credits	994	139	116	115	83	71	61	53	47
PPP (YID)	817	0	23	30	30	34	38	41	45
3 Private sector	15,138	111	210	581	612	648	690	723	771
4 Public Economic Enterprises	1,187	32	34	38	46	57	62	66	69
5 Funds (EU + Other + Fund)	12,708	71	75	80	102	508	558	614	674
General total	58,585	1,591	1,866	2,452	2,660	2,766	2,913	3,031	3,231

	2015	*2016*	*2017*	*2018*	*2019*	*2020*	*2021*	*2022*	*2023*
1 Central administration	442	465	488	512	538	565	593	623	654
2 Local administration	1,431	1,465	1,462	1,411	1,407	1,328	1,083	1,078	927
Municipal resources	946	960	938	864	836	729	459	426	248
Bank of Provinces	395	413	433	453	474	497	520	545	570
External credits	42	38	35	34	32	32	32	32	32
PPP (YID)	49	53	57	60	64	71	72	75	76
3 Private sector	821	763	1,143	1,193	1,252	1,309	1,371	1,436	1,504
4 Public economic enterprises	72	74	78	82	86	91	95	100	105
5 Funds (EU + Other + Fund)	740	814	895	984	1,082	1,188	1,306	1,438	1,581
General total	3,507	3,580	4,066	4,183	4,365	4,481	4,448	4,674	4,771

Source: EU Integrated Environmental Approximation Strategy 2007–2023, 2006: 62

Note
* €1/TRY1.86
TRY726 million of TÜPRAS fuel quality investment is not included

Users' fees are earmarked revenue of the public budget and should be used for both renewals and new investment expenditures. The revenues of local administration include: consumer fees which are collected from water and wastewater services; municipal taxes (environment tax, environmental cleaning tax, which is the only financial resource of solid waste management services, electricity–gas consumption tax, etc.); fee income (natural spring water fee, registration and renewal fee and similar fees); and service revenues (water, waste water and similar services). Iller Bank disburses 6 per cent of general budget tax revenues to municipalities based on their population, provides credits for the municipalities and acts as an agent in the usage of external credits by the municipalities.

Conclusions

Since the Rio Summit, sustainable development is recognized as the principle that should guide the design and implementation of reform policies. Thus, poverty reduction, growth or development strategy, as well as environmental protection strategy should be regarded as components of an SDS. In reality, however, the issue of economic competitiveness has dominated the political agenda and sustainable development, and is regarded as a pillar of the growth strategy.

As growth strategies provide general policy framework, financial institutions (World Bank, IMF) act as regulatory and enforcement institutions. They have gradually included environmental mainstreaming into their policies and country strategies as it is recognized that environmental degradation, if neglected, might impede economic performance. Thus, environmental considerations are included in IMF's concept of 'high quality growth' defined as sustainable growth with domestic and external financial stability. The World Bank's new environmental strategy is expected to enable a differentiated approach to clients, based on country environmental assessment and strategic environmental assessment.

Having growth as the top priority, public investment is mainly oriented to growth related policies. There is limited public financing for environmental protection, especially in the strained public budgets at times of crisis. Environmental investment depends on private initiatives, which mean that projects must be sufficiently profitable. Profits depend on the price of environmental services and demand, which is closely related to the price of substitute (i.e. pollution) and the issues of affordability. Full implementation of polluter pays principle is not affordable, thus there is a need for external financing.

Multilateral environmental agreements often lack institutional and financial capacities for effective implementation of identified environmental protection goals.

The EU also lacks an effective governance structure. Thus, national policies are essential for achieving globally recognized goals.

In selected EU members states (Slovenia, Bulgaria, Romania) and candidates (Croatia, Turkey) national sustainable development strategies that have been developed as a basis for identifying reform priorities, and for the justification of needs for financial support from EU funds, can be regarded as the framework for the development of sector-specific, operational plans with a clear division of authorities and financial plans. On the other hand, sustainable development strategies that have been adopted after the planning documents necessary for the justification of needs for financial support from EU funds are less likely to be implemented, as they generally lack financial and institutional implementing instruments.

Mere existence of the sustainable development strategies shows a progressive shift from addressing specific environmental concerns at the project level towards integrating the dimension of environmental sustainability into the expected results of the mainstream development activities.

New EU member states are expected to gradually change their role from donor recipients to donors. They should be able to finance their own development and provide aid to developing countries.

As affordability issues prevent increased use of market-based instruments, including loans from international financial institutions and full application of polluter pays principle. The use of market-based instruments, as opposed to technical assistance from the EU and the partnership through the GEF, might be considered as development indicators and pre-conditions for greening the economy.

Significant roles in the decision making related to financing environmental protection have:

1 commercial value of environmental infrastructure necessary for services
2 issue of affordability
3 a price setting mechanism
4 risks for investors and creditors, and
5 policy stability and predictability.

2 Nature protection

EU requirements

The EU nature protection policy and legislation have developed according to the most significant international biodiversity conventions: United Nations Convention on Biological Diversity (CBD), the Ramsar Convention on Wetlands, the Convention on Trade of Endangered Species (CITES), the Convention on the Conservation of Migratory Species of Wild Animals (the Bonn Convention) and the Bern Convention on European Wildlife and Habitats.[1] The main goal of the EU nature protection policy is halting the loss of biological diversity, which is considered key for achieving long-term sustainable development, as stipulated in the EU Sustainable Development Strategy. Protection of the biodiversity is also one of four priorities of the EU's Sixth Environmental Action Programme.

Key rules are defined by the Habitats and Birds Directives. The Birds Directive adopted in 1979[2] created the first European nature protection policy. It led to the establishment of special protected areas for birds. This Directive, together with the 1979 Bern Convention on the Conservation of European Wildlife and Natural Habitats, laid the foundation for the Habitats Directive in 1992. It identifies the most at-risk and valuable natural resources – roughly 200 habitats and 1,000 species of animals and plants. The goal of the Directive is to ensure their long-term sustainability – known as 'favourable conservation status'. The two main means to achieve this goal are:

1 designation of special areas of conservation, known as the Natura 2000 network of conservation sites, and
2 a strict system of species protection.

The European ecological network of special areas of conservation, Natura 2000, consists of core areas, corridor zones, buffer zones and, if needed, nature rehabilitation areas for the re-establishment of nature. It works on a principle of conservation and sustainable use, aiming for harmonious co-existence between human activities and nature. Economic activities such as farming, tourism, fishing and forestry are encouraged, provided that they integrate nature protection requirements (i.e. that they are nature-friendly).

Natura 2000 is the largest network of protected areas in the world. Between €5.6 and €6.1 billion per year are necessary for the effective management of the network (Gantioler, *et al.*, 2010; Final Report on Financing Natura, 2000). These costs are co-financed between the EU and the countries hosting Natura 2000 sites. Allocations for Natura 2000 from the EU budget are roughly estimated between €550 and €1,150 million per year (Kettunen, *et al.*, 2011) which is 9–19 per cent of the estimated financing needs. Co-financing from the EU budget includes allocations from the Financial Instrument for the Environment (LIFE+) and horizontal instruments: structural funds – European Social Fund (ESF) and European Regional Development Fund (ERDF); the Cohesion Fund; the European Agricultural Fund for Rural Development (EAFRD); the European Fisheries Fund, and the Seventh Research Framework Programme (European Commission, 2004).

Sustaining the financial requirements of the Natura 2000 network thus ultimately depends on national governments (to make resources directly available to Natura 2000 sites) and the capacities of Natura 2000 managers (to access these funds through competitive process and/or lobbying). Such approach makes it difficult for protected areas to make independent choices and adopt long-term strategies. Therefore, Natura 2000 sites should be encouraged to engage into market-based mechanisms to contribute autonomously to their funding needs and create a solid management base. Nevertheless there does not seem to be a coherent policy (or sets of policies) able to facilitate or promote the use of market-based mechanisms for Natura 2000 funding.

National plans and financing

Slovenia

The present state

Slovenia is a small territory characterized by extremely diverse and relatively well-preserved nature. One of the most important and oldest mechanisms for the preservation of plant and animal species and their habitats has been the designation of protected areas. The most threatened types of habitat are: wetlands, coastal and marine, standing and running waters, subterranean, and dry and humid grasslands. At least nine breeds of indigenous domestic animals have been classified endangered (Countdown 2010, 2007).

Protected nature areas account for around 11 per cent of the territory. These include 47 national, regional and landscape parks as well as nature reserves and natural monuments. Slovenia also has four marine protected areas, one World Heritage Site (Skocjanske jame), two 'Man and Biosphere'[3] areas (Karst, the Julian Alps) and three Ramsar sites (Secoveljske soline, Skocjanske jame, Cerknisko jezero z okolico). Forests in Slovenia cover approximately 60 per cent of the country's surface area.

Around 48 per cent of Slovenia is covered by areas defined as being of ecological importance. Two-thirds of these areas (covering 36 per cent of the territory of Slovenia) are included in the European Natura 2000 network. There are 286 Natura 2000 sites: 260 according to the Habitats Directive and 26 according to the Wild Birds Directive.

Policy and regulation

Relevant UN conventions and the EU legislation provide the general framework for Slovenian nature protection policy.

A nature conservation act is the main legislative document that defines nature protection in Slovenia. Its purpose is to protect and conserve plant and animal species, their habitats and valuable natural features. It provides for the establishment of a system of permits in the area of nature conservation, an indemnity system for proceedings related to damage caused by wildlife and for controlling the import and export of endangered species of wildlife flora and fauna in accordance with the CITES Convention. According to the Slovenian Environmental Agency, these systems are effective (Slovenian Environmental Agency, 2009a).

Based on the Nature Conservation Act, the National Environmental Action Programme was developed, and includes the National Nature Conservation Programme. This Programme links goals with measures: preservation of biodiversity with measures for the protection of plant and animal species, their habitats and ecosystems; protection of natural values with a programme for the establishment of protected areas and the restoration of valuable natural features; the route to fulfilment of international obligations; education in the area of nature conservation; raising public awareness of the importance of nature conservation; and securing financial resources for implementing nature protection.

The Biodiversity Conservation Strategy was adopted in line with the CBD. However, it lacks action plans, which were, according to the Strategy, to be adopted for a four-year period as operational programmes (OP) (species, ecosystems or habitat types, and genetic resources) for the main sectors (agriculture, forestry, hunting and fishing, water management, industry and energy, transport and tourism, significantly affecting the sustainable use of biodiversity components) relevant for the protection of biodiversity.

However, conservation and sustainable use requirements have gradually been integrated in development planning (National Development Strategy, Regional Development Programmes), forestry policy, hunting and fishing policies, agriculture (the Rural Development Programme, Programme on the Agro-environmental Measures), water management and spatial planning (National Strategy of Spatial Development) in the pre-accession period and, at a slower pace in transport, energy and tourism. Integration of nature protection policies in other sectoral policies was further strengthened in 2007, when the government adopted the Natura 2000 Site Management OP 2007–2013. The Programme defines conservation objectives and measures for each specie and/or habitat type at each Natura 2000 site[4] and identifies the competent sectors (protected area management plans, forestry, fishery and hunting).

According to the OP, conservation measures have to be incorporated in relevant sector management plans, once they are updated. Such provisions are already implemented in the spatial (land use) planning policy (Spatial Development Strategy) and the Rural Development Programme. The Spatial Development Strategy includes nature conservation (biodiversity and protected areas) goals and references to landscape integrity and environmental measures. At the local level, the municipal spatial development strategies should also include specific measures for the protection of biodiversity and contribute to the decreased degradation of natural habitats.

The Rural Development Programme (2007) for the period 2007–2013 provides for a gradual increase of area included in the implementation of agro-environmental measures, from 328,364ha in 2007 to 365,000ha of utilized agricultural area by 2013. The measures provide for improving soil and water quality, the preservation of cultural landscape and biodiversity and expansion of organic farming. The area under organic farming increased from 2,400ha in 1999 to 29,332ha in 2007, from 0.5 to 5.9 per cent of utilized agricultural area (Slovenian Environmental Agency, 2009).

Institutions

There are three main state institutions in Slovenia that are responsible for nature protection: the Ministry for the Environment and Spatial Planning (i.e. Department for Nature Protection within the Environment Directorate), the Environmental Agency of the Republic of Slovenia (Department for Nature Protection), and the Institute of the Republic of Slovenia for Nature Conservation. The Ministry directs the nature protection policy, the Agency takes care of the consistent and effective implementation through administrative and regulatory issues, and the Institute is responsible for the nature protection professional issues. Nature conservation inspectors, at the Inspectorate for the Environment and Spatial Planning, supervise the implementation of regulations and general acts.

Financing

The long-term objective of the National Environmental Action Plan is to finance biodiversity projects mostly relying on existing environmental taxes. In the period 2005–2008 CO_2 tax – introduced in Slovenian environmental policy in 1998 – and the national budget were identified as domestic sources for financing biodiversity preservation (see Table 2.1).

While the contribution of a national budget for the financing of the biodiversity sector in Slovenia was planned to remain constant in the 2005–2008 period, contributions of CO_2 tax were expected to triple (from €1.5 to €4.6 million).[5] Contributions from the ERDF and the European Agricultural Guidance and Guarantee Fund were expected to increase significantly following Slovenia's accession to the EU in 2004. The EU support for Slovenia in the period from accession to the end of the EU Multiannual Financial Framework 2004–2006 was programmed according to the two Slovenian development documents: Single Programming Document and Rural Development Plan (RDP). In the

Table 2.1 Financial sources for conservation of biodiversity and valuable natural features (including Natura 2000 areas) 2005–2008, in million euros

Financial source	*2005*	*2006*	*2007*	*2008*	*Total*
CO_2 tax	1.54	2.80	3.63	4.59	12.56
National budget	5.17	5.17	5.17	5.17	20.68
Agricultural forestry policy measures*	2.09	12.52	25.04	34.09	73.74
Total	8.80	20.49	33.84	43.85	106.98

Source: Resolution on the National Environmental Action Programme 2005–2012, 2005: 118

Note

* Financial scheme of the Rural Development Programme and the European Agricultural Guidance and Guarantee Fund

period 2004–2006 more than €700 million was provided from domestic and EU financial resources, mainly for introducing principles of good farming practice and agro-environment activities which led to the improvement of the nature sector in Slovenia (see Table 2.2). It is estimated that roughly 10 per cent of the budget was allocated to nature and biodiversity spending (European Commission, 2006a: 10).

In the 2007–2013 programming period, financial resources for nature protection are allocated in the OP 'Strengthening the Regional Development Potentials'. The OP includes five priority axes including 'Integration of Natural and Cultural Potentials'. This priority axis includes, but is not limited to, nature protection. This priority axis alone amounts to over €300 million for the period 2007–2013, with ERDF contributing around €263 million, which is more than 80 per cent of the budget, the rest being the national contribution. The share for nature at €57.3 million (Slovenian Ministry of Environment and Spatial Planning, 2007: 41) is expressed as set no. 51 'promoting biodiversity and nature protection' and set no. 56, the 'protection and development of natural heritage'. Set no. 51 also funds the programme Natura 2000, which provided around €7.6 million for the year 2007 and €6.5 million for the year 2008.

Besides the funding provided by the ERDF, the financial framework for nature protection is also available from EAFRD and stated in the country's RDP in Axes 3 and 4 (see Table 2.3). Axis 3 of the RDP aims to increase the quality of life in rural areas and diversification of the rural economy, while Axis 4 aims to

Table 2.2 Overview of financial support for rural development in Slovenia 2004–2006, in million euros

Programme	*Public expenditure*	*EU contribution*
RDP	353.1	281.6
SPD	47.1	23.6
Total	400.2	305.2

Source: European Commission DG Agriculture (n.d.)

encourage local decision making on the development of individual rural areas. The total amount of the budget for both Axes for the entire period of 2007–2013 is over €165 million, of which EAFRD contributes around €126 million.

However, information about the share aimed at nature protection is not available. Until 2006, Slovenia has gained very limited experience in using the LIFE programme for financing nature protection projects (European Commission DG Environment, 2009: 9). There was no project conducted in Slovenia during the LIFE II period, and there were only three projects during the LIFE III and III extension for the period 2000–2006. These three projects were budgeted at no more than €1.8 million, and from that amount the co-financing from LIFE was only €0.7 million (see Table 2.4). However, during 2007–2013, according to Natura 2000 Site Management OP 2007–2013, Slovenia expects €2–2.5 million annually from the LIFE+ programme.

Apart from the EU, the main financial assistance in the nature conservation sector in Slovenia has come from international financial institutions such as the Global Environment Facility (GEF) and from bilateral cooperation from the governments of Netherlands, Norway and Great Britain. These grants exceed the

Table 2.3 Financial plan of Axis 3 and Axis 4, entire period, in euros

Axis	*Total*	*EAFRD contribution*	*Percentage of EAFRD co-financing*
3	132,039,136	99,029,352	75
4	33,760,006	27,008,005	80

Source: Slovenian Ministry of Agriculture, Forestry and Food, 2007

Table 2.4 Summary tables on LIFE environment projects in Slovenia

Generation	*Year*	*Number of projects*	*Total budget (€million)*	*Total LIFE co-financing (€million)*
LIFE II	1996	0	0	0
	1997	0	0	0
	1998	0	0	0
	1999	0	0	0
LIFE III	2000	1	0.6	0.2
	2001	0	0	0
	2002	0	0	0
	2003	2	1.2	0.4
	2004	0	0	0
LIFE III	2005	0	0	0
extension	2006	0	0	0
Total		3	1.8	0.6

Source European Commission DG Environment 2009: 9

amounts financed by EU, e.g. the grants provided by European Environmental Agency (EEA) and the Norway grants scheme will finance the programmes aimed at halting the loss of biodiversity until 2014 with €3.75 million (EEA Grants–Norway Grants, 2011).

Bulgaria

The present state

According to the Bulgarian National Biodiversity Conservation Strategy, Bulgaria ranks among the countries with the greatest biological diversity in Europe (Bulgarian Council of Ministers, 2009). A variety of landscapes, geology and microclimates have resulted in a rich diversity of species, communities and natural habitats. Bulgaria contains three biogeographic areas (alpine, Black Sea and continental), a variety of communities and ecosystems and almost all major European habitat types. There are 11 Ramsar sites in Bulgaria (Srebarna, Ropotamo Complex, Atanasovsko Lake, Durankulak Lake, Dragoman Marsh Karst Complex, Lake Shabla, Belene Islands Complex, Ibisha Island, Poda, Pomorie Wetland Complex, and Vaya Lake) and two UNESCO heritage sites (Pirin National Park and Srebarna Maintained Reserve). There are six protected area management categories defined by the Protected Areas Law of Bulgaria, incorporating (with some differences) classification of the International Union for the Conservation of Nature.[6] At the end of 2008 there were 950 protected areas with a total area of 581,736ha (5.2 per cent of the state territory). The area covered by the protected areas is set to increase in stages to reach about 7 per cent in 2018.

Bulgaria has some of the largest Natura 2000 areas in Europe covering 34 per cent of its territory: 114 Natura 2000 sites for wild birds (20 per cent of territory) and 228 Natura 2000 sites for habitats (30 per cent of territory). There are ten sites designated under the both directives.

Policy and regulation

Bulgaria is party to almost all global and European conventions dealing with environment and nature conservation. Participation in the international processes has contributed to policy development and application of good international ecological practices.

The Environmental Protection Act, adopted in 1992, provided for the elaboration of specialized laws, such as the Protected Areas Act or the Biological Diversity Act. The Protected Areas Act, adopted in 1998, is the first specialized nature conservation act which introduces a system of protected areas categories and defines the interactions between the institutions, responsible for their management. The Biological Diversity Act, adopted in 2002, regulates the protection of habitats, of species of plants and animals and their biotopes, the elaboration of action plans, as well as hunting, gathering and their trade. It transposes the requirements of the Habitats and the Birds Directives into national legislation, focusing on preservation of habitats types and biotopes of plant and animal species. The Biological Diversity Act envisages the establishment of a national ecological network, consisting of three elements – protected zones, protected areas and buffer zones, based on already identified relevant sites (e.g. Ramsar sites).

During the pre-accession period, a number of strategies and action plans were elaborated: the National Development Plan until the year 2006 – Environment Sector Programme; the National Environment Strategy and Action Plan 2000–2006; the National Biodiversity Conservation Strategy (first for the period 1999–2004 and the second for 2005–2010); the Action Plan for the Protection and Restoration of Floodplain Forest on the Bulgarian Danube Islands 2003–2007, the action plans for the conservation of threatened species, Bulgarian Forest Development Project.

Some of these strategies have been updated, but since the integration with the EU, main efforts aimed at nature protection have been gradually incorporated into policies dealing with agriculture, forestry, fishery, climate change, tourism, technology and alien species. The basis for such approach was adopted in 2007, when the 'Regulation on condition and order for compatibility assessment of plans, projects and development proposal with the purpose and objective of Natura 2000 sites' came into force. Objectives related to nature protection integrated in sectoral expertise include:

- mitigating forestation, (Strategic Development Forestry Plan for 2007–2011)
- protection of the natural resources and conservation of environment in the rural areas, (National Strategic Plan for Agricultural and Rural Development 2007–2013)
- introduction of ecological methods in agricultural production in order to conserve or improve the environment and contribute to sustainable land management and conservation of Bulgaria's natural resources (National Agro Ecological Programme 2007–2013).

Institutions

The Ministry of Environment and Water is the key body responsible for implementation of the set biodiversity protection measures at the national level. Some of the tasks related to nature protection at the national level are also assigned to the Ministry of Agriculture and Forestry (sustainable use of agricultural surfaces and exploitation of forests), the Ministry of Regional Development and Public Works (sustainable regional development and urbanization with the respect of natural limitations), the Ministry of Economy, Energy and Tourism (sound and sustainable tourism development in line with the limitations of sensitive biodiversity resources). In order to achieve greater coordination among responsible bodies as well as to avoid any overlapping of their obligations, the Biodiversity Act (2002) regulates the relations among the state, environmental funds and the municipalities, as well as calling for greater integration of biodiversity conservation issues in sectored policies, especially spatial planning. For example, the National Nature

Protection Service was founded as the specialized directorate of the Ministry of Environment and Water which conducts the national policy relating to biodiversity and protected areas, while the regional inspectorates of environment and local levels of governance have the task of organizing and implementing the biodiversity conservation of the landscape and the natural heritage of the territory within their authority. Furthermore, the task of the Executive Environment Agency is to design and manage the National Management Biodiversity System and to conduct activities foreseen in the National Biodiversity Conservation Plan, as well as the assessment of the Plan's effectiveness.

Financing

The National Biodiversity Conservation Plan 1999–2003 included the estimate of necessary funds (from €3–5 million a year) and sources for its implementation (see Table 2.5).

Table 2.5 Bulgaria's financial needs for the national plan and sources of financing for nature protection 1999–2003, in thousand euros

	Amount	*1999*	*2000*	*2001*	*2002*	*2003*
A NEPF	6,010	1,095	1,387	1,293	1,188	1,047
B Bulgarian Forest National Fund	1,028	176	175	215	223	238
D State Budget	2,584	89	438	629	681	747
E Foreign sources – total	2,179	1,333	613	88	68	68
E.1 GEF Project	701	701	0	0	0	0
E.2 Bulgarian–Swiss Programme	378	149	230	0	0	0
E.3 Le Balkan Foundation	115	38	38	13	13	13
E.4 PHARE	231	116	116	0	0	0
E.5 UNEP	55	55	0	0	0	0
E.6 Bird Life International	69	14	14	14	14	14
E.7 Ramsar Bureau	18	18	0	0	0	0
E.8 UNESCO	12	12	0	0	0	0
E.9 Monaco Project	5	5	0	0	0	0
E.10 Avalon Fund	31	10	10	10	0	0
E.11 Bulgarian–Swiss Programme: Forest	538	192	192	51	51	51
E.12 WWF	26	13	13	0	0	0
Non-secured funds	10,877	468	1,761	2,665	2,901	3,082
Necessary funds	22,678	3,152	4,374	4,891	5,069	5,192
Financial gap, %	52	14	60	45	42	41

Source: Bulgarian Council of Ministers, 1999: 37

The Plan identified a financial gap of roughly 50 per cent for the whole period and relied mostly on the state budget, the National Environmental Protection Fund and the Bulgarian Forest Fund. Identified potential external donors included the GEF, bilateral donors, private foundations, and corporations. While there is no report on the implementation, available data show that actual sources of financing were different from those planned: until 2001, the USAID has been the lead donor in the area of biodiversity in Bulgaria, investing approximately €0.7 million per year (up to 2001) in protected areas management and related institutional and policy strengthening at the national level. With USAID support, Bulgaria became the first country to develop a National Biodiversity Conservation Strategy after the country signed the Biodiversity Convention at the Rio Convention in 1992 (Grimes *et al.*, 2002).

In order to find additional funds for further financing of protected areas, in 2003 the Bulgarian government issued the Protection Areas Fund Strategy with the idea of making a fund that would serve to raise additional financial resources meant to be invested in biodiversity protection and eventually lead to ensuring the long-term protection of biodiversity in Bulgaria.

In 2004 the Protected Areas Fund was set up as a specialized internal fund of the private, non-profit National Trust Eco Fund, which had been established in the mid-1990s through a 'debt for nature swap' with the government of Switzerland. Over the years, it has demonstrated satisfactory management of more than €17 million in addition to other donations from the Danish Development Agency and the World Bank. The fund has financed numerous biodiversity and environmental activities throughout Bulgaria.

According to the Strategy, prepared as a basis for establishment of the Protected Areas Fund, the Bulgarian government was expected to match international grants of up to €7 million to the fund, and to continue to support the annual budget of the protected areas system at a cost of €0.7 million in 2003, increasing by 20 per cent per year until 2007 (Bulgarian Protected Areas Fund Strategy, 2003: 3). However, there is no comprehensive implementation report.

In addition to the Protected Areas Fund, a non-profit institution under direct supervision of the Ministry of Environment and Waters, the Enterprise for Management of Environmental Protection Activities (successor or the National Environment Protection Fund), finances some of the nature protection activities, such as operational costs of national parks and nature reserves. In 2004 up to €2 million were allocated for such costs for three national parks. The enterprise also finances a national monitoring system including laboratories and protected area activities, with 5–9 per cent of its revenue, which come from nature and visitor fees, compensation, concession agreements, penalties, sanctions and donations (€25 million in 2004).

With regard to the implementation of Bulgarian commitments to preserve and restore biological diversity in the process of negotiations with the EU, no transitional periods have been negotiated.

The pre-accession instruments PHARE, ISPA and SAPARD played a significant role in improving the state of the environment in the country. PHARE has been supporting an approximation of the Bulgarian nature protection and biodiversity legislation to that of the EU: improvement of state officials for ecological management of natural resources; cross-border cooperation in nature protection; and facilitated integration of Bulgarian protected areas in the Natura 2000 network (see Table 2.6).

From 2004–2009 the Norwegian government and EEA provided €16 million grants for energy, biodiversity and environment protection (EEA Grants–Norway Grants, 2012). Out of that €1 million was used specifically for biodiversity

Table 2.6 List of international projects in Bulgaria in the nature sector from 2001 – ongoing, in euros

LIFE	10,200,000
• LIFE+ (2009–2010)	
SAPARD (2000–2007)[a]	364,868
Investment in sustainable agro-environmental measures	
GEF/WB/UNDP	27,953,000
• Small Grants Programme – GEF (2006–2010)[b]	2,200,000
• Wetland Restoration and Pollution Reduction Project – WB/GEF Strategic Partnership for Nutrient Reduction in the Danube River and Black Sea (2002–2008)	9,500,000
• Conservation of Globally Significant Biodiversity in the Landscape of Bulgaria's Rhodope Mountains (2004–2009)	13,000,000
• Support for the Implementation of the National Biosafety Framework for Bulgaria (2002–2006)	353,000
• Lake Pomorie Conservation, Restoration and Sustainable Management Project (2005–2010)	1,400,000
• Conservation of Globally Important Biodiversity in High Nature Value Semi-natural Grasslands through Support for the Traditional Local Economy (2007–2012)	1,500,000
Bilateral	3,309,500
• Swiss government (2004–2007)	3,000,000
• Danish government[c]	309,500
PHARE	8,200,000
• Wild flora and fauna (2000)	800,000
• Wetland areas (2002)	1,800,000
• CBC Nature protection (2004)	3,500,000
• CBC Erma river (2004)	800,000
• CBC Mesta river (2004)	1,300,000
Total 2001–2011	50,027,368

Source: Authors' calculations

Notes

a The SAPARD Regulation identifies a list of priorities that can be included in the plan, most of them not directly related to nature conservation. However, from an integration point of view, SAPARD offers a wide variety of measures of interest for nature conservation (e.g. promotion of sustainable land exploitation, valorisation of protected areas through sustainable tourism development, improvement of forests, erosion prevention etc.). These measures can be used to generate income in protected areas from tourism or the sale of quality products from sustainable farming systems that help maintain certain habitats.

b http://sgp.undp.org/index.cfm?module=Projects&page=SearchResults&CountryID=BUL

c Conservation of Species and Habitats in Bulgaria: EU–Approximation, 2002–2005 http://www.natura2000bg.org/natura/eng/index1.php

support: preservation of *Castanea sativa* on Belasitsa mountain; protection of plant glacial relicts; and for implementation of the Biodiversity Monitoring System (Pitija, 2010).

The indicative forecast for the period 2007–2013 shows that the necessary financial resources for the fulfilment of the Republic of Bulgaria commitments in the biodiversity sector amount to approximately €203 million (OP Environment 2007–2013). Around €103 million are programmed under Priority 3 'Preservation and restoration of biological diversity' of the OP 'Environment 2007–2013'. The indicative forecast shows that €15 million can be provided from the state budget and within the framework of the LIFE+ programme. According to the LIFE nature and biodiversity component, the latest available data indicate that investments are likely to exceed expectations; projects worth €10.2 million have been contracted, out of which the European Union will contribute €6.8 million. From 2011–2014 projects funded by the current LIFE+ programme (2007–2013) in the biodiversity sector in Bulgaria are planned to amount to €5 million per year, out of which nearly €3 million will be an EU contribution (European Community, 2009), i.e. instead of €15 million, €25 million is expected to be invested through LIFE + projects. However, there is still a significant financial gap.

The identified sources for financing the investment costs necessary for the implementation of the requirements of the Birds and Habitats Directives for the period 2007–2013 can provide approximately 60.7 per cent coverage of financial needs, i.e. there is a financial gap of approximately €80 million (€70 million, if LIFE+ projects are implemented as planned).

Therefore the needs from additional investments in all areas relevant to nature and biodiversity protection in Bulgaria are evident. The World Bank study on the necessary resources for implementation of EU requirements for conservation and management of the environment shows that they significantly exceed the potentiality of the existing national financial resources and proves the need for additional external financial sources.

In the coming years, Bulgaria will significantly rely on EU Cohesion and Structural Funds as well as on the opportunities that could be provided through the international financial institutions and the public-private partnerships. Also, the Norwegian government and EEA have allocated bigger green funding (€43 million) for protecting the environment, boosting energy efficiency and promoting green innovation for the period 2009–2014.

Romania

The present state

Romania possesses five of the ten biogeographic regions officially recognized by the European Union (alpine, continental, pannonian, pontian, and steppe), and the only EU country possessing steppe and pontian regions. It is, therefore, the most biogeographically diverse country of the EU. Native steppe and steppe-associated wet meadows have been systematically converted to cropland and pastures, thus it is estimated that less than 10 per cent remains of some types of grassland and shallow marsh ecosystems that were once common in Romania. There is also a trend for desertification on 20 per cent of the total arable land (CBD, 2011).

The total biodiversity protected areas have reached around 20 per cent of Romanian territory. Natura 2000 sites include 273 special areas of conservation and 108 special protected areas; there are six Ramsar sites and 22 biosphere reserves, including Romania's Danube Delta Biosphere Reserve, which is home to Europe's second largest wetland, is the 22nd largest protected area in the world and the third largest in Europe. It contains the greatest expanse of reed beds worldwide and one of the worlds' largest wet habitat zones (CBD, 2011a).

Policy and regulation

Romania has played an active role in many international environmental issues and is a contracting party to most international and regional environmental agreements and conventions. Based on international obligations, Romania integrated biodiversity protection into the Romanian regulatory framework, which has been further strengthened with the process of integration into the EU.

There are various national laws and regulations that address biological diversity and attempt to support nature protection and conservation. Despite these strong efforts to incorporate environmental principles into the regulatory framework, these laws and regulations are often unclear, overlap and are conflicting. Furthermore, they are inconsistently enforced by the responsible authorities.

The main objectives of the preservation of the biological diversity are integrated in Romania's National Development Plan 2007–2013 (NDP, 2005) which focuses on the sustainable use of natural habitats, of wild flora and fauna species, as well as the ecological reconstruction of damaged systems.

The Romanian National Sustainable Development Strategy (NSDS) sets key development objectives for the short, medium and long term in the Horizon 2013–2020–2030. The concrete targets proposed for 2015 include the augmentation of those protected areas and Natura 2000 sites that operate in accordance with approved management plans, from three in 2006 to 240 in 2015, as well as the expansion of such units to 60 per cent of all protected areas. There are proposed measures for the conservation, rehabilitation and development of forests in accordance with the EU Forest Action Plan.

Institutions

A variety of Romanian governmental organizations have responsibility for some aspects relating to biodiversity, and it can be safely said that the institutional arrangements for biodiversity conservation and the management of protected areas are not clearly defined. Efforts to protect biodiversity are, therefore, hindered given that no single governmental organization acts as a central coordinator for biodiversity/nature conservation/sustainable development issues and can coordinate the involvement of other national institutions, set policy and implement programmes, and direct and manage organizations active at the field level.

The largest part of the responsibility for nature protection and management belongs to the Ministry of Waters, Forests and Environmental Protection (MWFEP) and the branches or agencies affiliated with the MWFEP. The Danube Delta Biosphere Reserve, however, has its own management structure (assisted with international support). The Commission for the Protection of Nature Monuments of the Romanian Academy is the legal scientific authority for nature conservation and protected areas. For the protected areas located on forest land, the management is ensured by the autonomous Agency ROMSILVA. Local authorities are responsible for land-use planning but with no capacity and qualified staff for incorporating biodiversity/nature conservation into their policies. The 41 Environmental Protection Agencies (County MWFEP offices) have legal responsibility for environmental monitoring and nature conservation. It is important that the new laws stipulate the separation of the regulatory responsibilities from the functions and management responsibilities for natural resources.

The Fund for the Environment collects taxes for pollution and exploitation of biological resources from economic agents, and co-finances (in some cases with the Ministry of Environment and Water Management) projects on biodiversity conservation and management of biological resources.

In 2008, the National Agency for Protected Natural Areas was legally established as a public institution. Its key task is to administer protected areas at national level and to ensure smooth implementation of the management plans for each of the areas designated for protection.

Financing

Estimated costs of halting the biodiversity loss amount to approximately €172 million, of which 80 per cent will be covered by EU co-financing from the ERDF (NSDS Romania, 2008: 61). Implementation is programmed through the Sectoral OP Environment 2007–2013. The envisaged funds for nature protection through both management of nature protected areas and implementing the Natura 2000 network are €215 million: 172 from the EU (i.e. 80 per cent), and €43 million from national public financing (Romanian Ministry of Environment and Sustainable Development, 2007: 100). However, the estimate included in the same document indicates that around €150 million can be provided from EU funds (Romanian Ministry of Environment and Sustainable Development, 2007: 39).

Funded projects aim to ensure the appropriate management of protected natural areas and, by default, halt biodiversity loss and degradation of natural resources. The establishment of the specialized National Agency for Protected Natural Areas and Biodiversity Conservation (which was realized in 2008) was also programmed within the OP Environment. The Agency should help to build management capacity and face pressure from illegal exploitation and hunting, uncontrolled tourism and construction, which lead to irreversible losses of biodiversity in Romania.

Domestic financing comes from the state budget and Fund for the Environment. The Ministry of Environment and Water Management supports biodiversity related projects and facilities the co-financing of applications to the Fund for the Environment.

In the pre-accession period, Romania was the first EU candidate country from Central and Eastern Europe to receive direct financial support from the LIFE nature programme in 1999. Between 1992 and 2006 (i.e. during the LIFE I, II and III programmes), the LIFE nature component (now called nature and biodiversity) co-financed 27 projects in Romania. These projects represented a total investment of €13.3 million, of which €8.4 million were contributed by the European Union. Seven projects have been co-financed under the LIFE+ programme. These represent a total investment of €5.5 million, of which the European Union will contribute €4.10 million (European Commission DG Environment, n.d.) (see Table 2.7).

Nature protection projects became eligible for financing under the PHARE programme in the period 2005–2006, when grant schemes were launched in that environmental domain, too.

Some of the nature protection components, related to sustainable community development inside and around protected areas comprise: development of eco and agrotourism; sustainable use of natural resources; waste management pilot initiatives; raising awareness on climate change and other environmental issues; promotion of renewable energy sources; wetland protection; promotion of ecological, organic and sustainable farming; the management of persistent organic pollutants in medical waste. These components are financed through

Table 2.7 List of international projects in Romania in the nature sector from 1994 – ongoing, in euros

LIFE	18,000,000
• LIFE II and LIFE III, 1996–2006	12,500,000
• LIFE +, 2009–2010	5,500,000
GEF/WB/UNDP	**21,120,000**
• GEF Small Grants Programme	3,300,000
• Danube Delta Biodiversity, 1994–2000	3,500,000
Biodiversity Conservation Management Project, 1999–2006	6,300,000
• Strengthening Romania's Protected Area System by Demonstrating Best Practices for Management of Small Protected Areas in Macin Mountains National Park, 2005–ongoing	2,100,000
• Strengthening Romania's Protected Area System by Demonstrating Government–NGO Partnership in Romania's	1,600,000
Maramures Nature Park, 2005–2009	4,000,000
• Improving the Financial Sustainability of the Carpathian System of	
Protected Areas , 2009 – ongoing	320,000
• Support to Alignment of NBSAP with CBD Obligations and Development of CHM, 2008 – ongoing	
PHARE	**11,100,000**
• CBC Danube River, 2000	2,800,000
• Danube wetlands, 2001	2,000,000
• Mures River, 2001	2,000,000
• CBC Biodiversity, 2003	4,300,000
2001–2011 TOTAL	**50,220,000**

Source: Authors' calculation

different instruments, such as GEF Small Grants Programme, EARDF, as well as measures under the SAPARD programme.

Until 2011 GEF Small Grants Programme funded 78 projects amounting to almost €1.7 million, with additional €1.6 million leveraged as co-financing. The Romanian Rural Development Programme for the period 2007–2013 includes biodiversity related activities under Axis 2, which will have a total public cost of €2,293 million, of which the EAFRD finances €1,880 million or 82 per cent of the total cost. Nature protection related activities include Natura payments (€32 million), forestation (€283 million) and agro-environmental payments (€672 million). The special measure of the SAPARD programme has been developed to contribute to green agriculture and agricultural biodiversity conservation. Financial support is strictly limited to the projects of institutions subordinated to the Ministry of Environment and Water Management and the Ministry of Agriculture, Forests and Rural Development and for international co-financing. Bilateral external funding plays a significant role, coming from the Netherlands, Germany, Denmark, USA and other countries, multilateral funding from the EU and in the past from the GEF.

Croatia

The present state

The biological, landscape and geological diversity is considered an essential Croatian asset and the major resource for future development. The protected areas – including those under preventive protection – cover 9 per cent of its total territory (11.37 per cent of Croatia's land and 3.40 per cent of its territorial sea). The Nature Protection Act of Croatia defines nine different categories of protected areas. There are four Ramsar sites in Croatia. The ecological network in Croatia covers 47 per cent of its land and 38 per cent of its sea. Most of the national ecological network will be designated as Natura 2000 sites. A large share of potential Natura 2000 sites are located in agricultural areas (33 per cent or 739,000 ha). Conservation of habitats and species in accordance with the Birds and Habitats Directives requires maintaining a favourable conservation status. This implies low input of small-scale farming and needs conservation measures that can easily be implemented by farmers who live and work in the region.

Policy and regulation

Croatia has developed and greatly improved the overall system of protection and conservation of natural values and resources and the sustainable use of natural (biological) stocks since the early 1990s. Progress was made both in the area of inventory and evaluation of biological and landscape diversity, as well as in the development of legislative and institutional framework and the improvement of a system for the protection of natural values and the management of natural resources.

The policy has developed on the basis of National Strategy and Action Plan for the Protection of Biological and Landscape Diversity. The fundamental act for regulating nature protection is the Nature Protection Act, adopted in 2005 (and amended in 2008 and 2011).

The Nature Protection Act incorporated main provisions of international agreements and the relevant EU rules. It was based on the first National Strategy and Action Plan for the Protection of Biological and Landscape Diversity of Croatia, which was adopted in 1999. This Strategy determined the long-term goals and guidelines for preserving biological and landscape diversity and protected natural values, and ways of its implementation, in line with the overall economic, social and cultural development of Croatia.

Consolidated data on the status of biological and landscape diversity and their protection, included in the report on the status of nature and nature protection in Croatia for the period 2000–2007, served as the premise for revision of the National Strategy and Action Plan for the Protection of Biological and Landscape Diversity. The revised Strategy adopted in 2008 included protection of geodiversity in addition to biological and landscape diversity.

The Strategy defines general objectives and provides for more than 100 action plans, many of them calling for an integration of nature protection requirements into sector-specific policies.

Nature protection requirements have been included into sector-specific documents dealing with forestry, hunting, spatial planning and especially by establishing the national ecological network. However, there are still sectors that have not incorporated natural ecological network requirements (e.g. acceptability assessments) into their legislation (fishery, mineral exploitation etc.) or incorporated the requirements specifically (e.g. not in the basic regulation – agriculture). Croatia has yet to formulate an agro-environmental policy.

While most of the necessary legislation is in place, more efforts should be directed to the implementation of action plans, and it is necessary to work further on strengthening the institutional framework and the allocation of significantly more resources for the nature protection from the state and regional/local budgets.

Institutions

The Ministry of Culture (Nature Protection Directorate) is the governmental body responsible for administrative and expert affairs in the nature protection field. The Ministry of Culture manages the Register of Protected Natural Assets (including areas under preventive protection), approves management plans for protected areas, including national ecological network, and implements a uniform Protected Area Management System covering all institutions at national and regional levels responsible for the management of protected areas and/or other protected values.

The State Institute for Nature Protection is centrally responsible for specialized nature protection expertise in Croatia. These tasks include, among others, responsibility for organizing and implementing biodiversity inventorying, monitoring and operating a nature protection information system. The State Institute is also responsible for the evaluation of management plans for protected areas, technical tasks in connection with drawing up the evaluation of nature impact assessment, preparation and implementation of project and programmes in the field of nature protection, and organization and implementation of educational and promotional activities. It is financed from the state budget through the Ministry of Culture.

Depending on the category of protection, protected areas are managed by the public institutions established by central (national), regional (county) or local (town or municipality) authorities. Currently, there are 19 public institutes at the national level, which are financed from the state budget through the Ministry of Culture, 20 public institutes at the county level (financed through county budget) and seven public institutions at the local level.

As regards integration of nature protection requirements in other policy areas, the Ministry of Culture is responsible for preliminary assessments for the areas of ecological network, while the Ministry of Environment is in charge of environmental impact assessments.

Financing

The highest protected area categories are funded by a mix of national government budget, their own self-generated income, and various other sources such as international aid and donations. Self-generated income is predominantly derived from visitor fees,[7] as well as concessions for recreational activities, and at some sites from hotels, restaurants and camping areas owned by the park public institutions. The vast majority of national parks and other conservation areas in Croatia require some financial assistance from the Ministry of Culture through the annual budgeting process. The latest allocation (for 2011) was €1 million (see Table 2.8).

The share of spending for protected areas in the state budget ranges between 0.05 and 0.075 per cent (Spurgeon *et al.*, 2009.) In addition to the state budget, nature protection activities are financed from a domestic extra-budgetary fund (the Environmental Protection and Energy Efficiency Fund) and external sources.

The Ministry of Culture, in cooperation with the Environmental Protection and Energy Efficiency Fund allocated around €300,000 for research and biological diversity monitoring in 2008. Until then, the role of the Environmental

Table 2.8 Summary of Ministry of Culture's expenditure for protected areas in 2010 and 2011, in thousand euros

	Public institutions managing PAs	*SINP*	*Total*
2010	1,697.8	82.41	1,780.21
2011	932.2	67.66	999.86
Total	2,630	150.07	2,780.07

Source: Croatian Ministry of Culture, 2010, 2011

Protection and Energy Efficiency Fund in the area of biological and landscape diversity was rather limited. Between 2004 and 2009, €1.9 million out of €663 million (i.e. 0.3 per cent) of the approved funds were allocated to biological and landscape diversity.

In 2006, GEF estimated that the total baseline funding on investments aiming to mainstream biodiversity into tourism, agriculture or fisheries sector in Croatia was approximately €40 million (UNDP and GEF, n.d.).

The EAFRD is one of the main funding mechanisms for the implementation of Natura 2000, especially its Axis 2: Improving the environment and the countryside. EAFRD focuses on land managers as beneficiaries and its potential lies in supporting specific land management practices. Several measures under the Axis 2 are contributing either directly or indirectly to nature protection, the three most important being agro-environment programmes, support to less favoured areas and payments for Natura 2000 areas.

Over the past years, the Croatian government has received considerable financial support from a variety of international sources for the management of protected areas. This funding from 2001– 2011 amounted to more than €45 million (see Table 2.9).

In the period 2011–2016 Croatia plans to invest €44 million to:

1 support park and county public institutions to implement Natura 2000 objectives in investment programmes
2 strengthen capacity for EU-compliant reporting and biodiversity monitoring, and
3 introduce programmes that involve a wider group of stakeholders in Natura 2000 network management.

The International Bank for Reconstruction and Development provided a loan of €20.8 million, the Government of the Republic of Croatia participates with €2.88 million, and co-financing through Parallel EU Structural Funds of up to €20 million is expected.

Turkey

The present state

There are several distinct biogeographic regions in Turkey: the Caucasian Mountain forests, with the temperate deciduous forest and alpine meadows; Central and Eastern Anatolian steppe grasslands; and the Mediterranean region, which includes the world's largest remaining cypress forests and Lebanon cedar forests.

Turkey hosts 75 per cent of the total number of plant species found in Europe and its wetlands are of crucial importance for many breeding species of birds, including the globally threatened species Dalmatian pelican and white-headed duck.

Table 2.9 List of international projects in Croatia in the nature protection sector from 2001 – ongoing, in euros

LIFE	3,690,686
• Towards wise use in Lonjsko Polje Nature Park, Croatia, 2001–2004	535,467
• Corine Land Cover Database for Croatia, 2002–2005	749,320
• Conservation and Management of Wolves in Croatia , 2002–2005	664,810
• Croatian National Ecological Network , 2002–2005	539,700
• Establishing Institutional Capacities for Protection of Mura River landscape, 2004–2006	349,487
• Central Posavina-Wading toward Integrated Basin Management,2005–2008	791,902
• The Protection of Biodiversity of the Sava River Basin Floodplains, 2007–2009	60,000
USAID	**200,000**
• Croatia National Park Programme, 2001–2003	
Ramsar	**50,000**
• Development of the Croatian Wetland Inventory, 2003–2004	
CARDS 2002	**497,000**
• Institutional Strengthening of the SINP, 2005–2006	
EF/WB/UNDP	**29,659,400**
• Kopački Rit Wetlands Management Project, 1998–2003	1,300,000
• Karst Ecosystem Conservation Project, 2003–2007	6,000,000
• Sustainable Financing Review for Croatia Protected Areas, 2009	169,400
• Conservation and Sustainable Use of Biodiversity in the Dalmatian Coast through Greening Coastal Development, 2007–2011	22,190,000
Bilateral	**3,200,000**
• Norwegian government – Protected Areas Management System, 2006–2009	
PHARE 2005	**3,919,250**
• Implementation of Natura 2000 in Croatia, 2006–2007	2,600,000
• Institutional Building and Implementation of Natura 2000 in Croatia, 2008–2010	1,319,250
WWF	**4,200,000**
• The Dinaric Arc Ecoregion project, 2007–2011	200,000
• MedPAN South Project, 2009–2012	4,000,000
2001–2011 Total	**45,416,336**
IPA 2009	**1,700,000**
• Capacity building for preparation of management plans and strengthening of nature protection inspection for proposed Natura 2000 sites (2010–2012)	
WB	**20,800,000**
• Nature Protection Investment Project, 2011–2016	
2011 – ongoing Total	**22,500,000**
European Union Natura 2000 Integration Project	43,680,000
EU Structural Funds	20,000,000
Future EU assistance Total	63,680,000

Source: Authors' calculation

Deterioration of the habitats causes a decrease in population of existing species, which are in situ and protected in areas covering around 6 per cent of the territory. Protected areas include national parks, nature reserves, nature conservation areas, natural sites, wildlife development areas, special environment conservation areas and internationally significant wetlands. The Ramsar list consists of 13 sites.

Policy and regulation

With rising human pressures on the environment, nature conservation policies started developing in the 1970s. The Fifth Five-Year Development Plan (1985–1989) included, for the first time, an environmental sector in national programmes as part of development plans. The subsequent Development Plans and Annual Programmes have included issues of biological diversity in the environmental and agricultural sectors. Policies, as well as implementing measures, gradually evolved for the conservation and sustainable development of biological diversity and for the augmentation of its economic value. The National Environmental Strategy adopted in 2006 strengthened the nature conservation system that was based on a number of national environmental strategies, plans and programmes: National Environmental Action Plan (1998), National Plan for in situ Conservation of Plant Genetic Diversity (1998), National Biological Diversity Strategy and Action Plan (2001), National Agenda 21 Programme (2001), National Wetland Strategy (2003), Turkish National Forestry Programme (2004), National Science and Technology Policies 2003–2023 Strategy Document (2004) and Turkish National Action Programme Against Desertification (2005). The aim of the Strategy includes protecting biological diversity, ensuring its sustainable use and preventing the loss of biological diversity. The current Ninth Development Plan (2007–2013) determines as a priority conservation of the biological diversity and its economic evaluation. In 2007, Turkey adopted the National Biodiversity Strategy and Action Plan, in line with the CBD.

The legal status of biological diversity in Turkey is reflected in the legal documents, including the Constitution, laws, international conventions, protocols and related regulations. The Environmental Law states the importance of protecting biological diversity and introduces penal sanctions against damage to the environment, including the destruction of biological diversity, when detected through inspection and audits.

Specific laws and regulations deal with species and site protection, such as the Law on National Parks, the Law for the Protection of Cultural and Natural Assets, the Terrestrial Hunting Law, the Regulation for the Protection of Wetlands, the Regulation for Implementing the Convention on International Trade in Endangered Species of Wild Fauna and Flora.[8]

It is expected that the identification of Natura 2000 areas and the related corridors will be accomplished by 2016 and that the share of the Turkish protected area will increase in parallel to implementing the EU environmental requirements. In the context of biodiversity conservation in Turkey, it is initially required to finalize the preparation of the Draft Law on Biodiversity and Nature Protection, to prepare an inventory regarding species and habitats of areas, to begin the preliminary studies for establishing the scientific authority and to employ and educate the personnel anticipated in the transition period.

Institutions

Various institutions, ministries and organizations have undertaken duties and responsibilities for conserving biological diversity. There is no overall coordinating system for conservation activities in Turkey. Due to various overlaps of mandates there are also no dedicated agencies for conservation of biodiversity in specific ecosystems (Turkish Ministry of Environment and Forestry, 2007: 36)

The Ministry of Environment creates policies and coordinates the activities concerning conservation/protection of wild flora, fauna and their habitats and implementation of international conventions and agreements regarding the conservation of nature. The Ministry of Environment has duplicated responsibilities with the Ministry of Forestry, the Ministry of Agriculture and Rural Affairs, and the Ministry of Culture and Tourism. The Ministry of Agriculture and Rural Affairs is responsible for coordination and utilization of all resources related to agriculture and has the authority over the use of pesticides and chemicals. The Ministry of Forestry is responsible for the management of protected areas declared under the National Parks Law, for the conservation of wildlife and for the regulation and supervision of terrestrial hunting. In addition, the State Planning Organization develops environmental policies under the five-year national development plans.

The Agency for Specially Protected Areas, under the Ministry of Environment, is responsible for special protected areas; and the Conservation Council of the Cultural and Natural Heritage is responsible for determining countrywide sites to be preserved and giving decisions about interventions to these sites. These councils are supported by the General Directorate for the Preservation of the Cultural and Natural Heritage within the Ministry of Culture and Supreme Council of the Cultural and Natural Heritage Conservation.

Financing

Funding for environmental conservation activities, ranging from planning and programming to implementation, carries low priority in relevant institutions' budgets. Large administrative and staffing budgets leave proportionally smaller allocations for operational activities. According to the National Environmental Strategy, €134.52 million is required within the framework of Habitats and Birds Directives for personnel expenses (i.e. 53 per cent of expenses) and €120.4 million for investment (47 per cent of expense) in the period 2007–2023 (see Table 2.10). An additional €3 million is necessary for institutional capacity building for Habitats and Birds Directives, €120,000 for scientific purposes and €1.7 million to keep a regular inventory of habitat and species (EU Integrated Environmental Approximation Strategy, 2006: 51).

The CITES Directive will require €8 million for implementation, and zoos €2 million. A total of €263.31 million is required for the implementation of Habitats

Table 2.10 The investment needs for protection of the Turkish nature sector 2007–2023, in million euros

	Total	*2007*	*2008*	*2009*	*2010*	*2011*	*2012*	*2013*	*2014*
Habitats and Birds Directives	254	3	5	8	10	11	13	14	15
CITES Directives	8	1	1	1	1	1	1	1	1
Zoos	2	n.a.	1	1	n.a.	n.a.	n.a.	n.a.	n.a.
Total	264	4	7	10	11	12	14	15	16
	2015	*2016*	*2017*	*2018*	*2019*	*2020*	*2021*	*2022*	*2023*
Habitats and Birds Directives	16	17	18	20	21	18	19	22	24
CITES Directives	n.a.	n.a.	n.a.	n.a.	n.a.	n.a.	n.a.	n.a.	n.a.
Zoos	n.a.	n.a.	n.a.	n.a.	n.a.	n.a.	n.a.	n.a.	n.a.
Total	16	17	18	20	21	18	19	22	24

Source: Turkish Ministry of Environment and Forestry, 2006: 52

and Birds Directives and directives concerning CITES and zoos in Turkey for the period 2007–2023. Information about actual funding is limited. According to available data, external funding to tackle globally significant biodiversity threats in all types of ecosystems, provided by GEF small grant programme since 1993 reached around €1.5 million (UNDP Turkey, 2011) (see Table 2.11).

As regards domestic sources, there was no nature protection sector in overall environmental spending from the state budget until 2009, when, according to

Table 2.11 List of international projects in Turkey in the nature protection sector from 1993 –ongoing, in euros

GEF/WB/UNDP/UNEP	
• GEF Small Grant Programme, since 1993	1,500,000
• In Situ Conservation of Genetic Biodiversity, 1993–1998	4,000,000
• Enhancing Coverage and Management Effectiveness of the Subsystem of Forest Protected Areas in Turkey's National System of Protected Areas (2008 – ongoing)	1,700,000
• Consultation for National Reporting, Participation in the National Clearing House Mechanism and Further Development of the National Biodiversity Strategy and Action Plan, 2005–2007	320,000
• Strengthening Protected Area Network of Turkey – Catalysing Sustainability of Marine and Coastal Protected Areas, 2008 – ongoing	4,400,000
• BS Support for the Implementation of the National Biosafety Framework (2010 – ongoing)	900,000
• Biodiversity and Natural Resources Management Project (2000–2008)	8,300,000
2001–2011 Total	21,120,000

Source: Authors' calculations

the TurkStat, the Turkish government spent €69 million on the nature protection sector (TurkStat, 2011).

Conclusions

All the focus countries are parties to the CBD and have developed biodiversity strategies. Slovenia alone does not have an action plan. However, implementation is partial.

Generally, two phases of the development of the nature protection policy can be identified: in the first, specific nature protection strategies were elaborated, while in the second nature protection has gradually been integrated into other policies.

The responsibilities for nature protection are not clearly allocated among various competent institutions and capacities need strengthening.

Spending targeted on nature protection is rather limited. Integration of nature protection into other policies makes it difficult to allocate the required level of funds to nature protection. Roughly, analysed EU member countries (Slovenia, Bulgaria and Romania) spend up to 2.5 per cent of cohesion and structural expenditure to promote nature conservation and biodiversity (see Table 2.12).

The cost estimates exceed investment plans. Funding for (reduced) investment plans are missing. Thus, the level of investment is underperforming at this stage.

The protection of biodiversity in agriculture is usually associated with low input small-scale farming. Agro-environmental measures are thus relevant for achieving nature protection goals. Allocations of the EAFRD resources for the 2007–2013 period indicate that this was identified (see Table 2.13).

The share of planned investments into agro-environmental schemes is rather limited (10–27 per cent, see Table 2.13), especially considering the size of protected areas and the relevance of agriculture in those areas (e.g. Natura 2000 sites for habitats cover 30 per cent of the terrestrial area of Bulgaria).

Table 2.12 Cohesion and structural expenditure promoting nature conservation and biodiversity, 2007–2013, in million euros

	Slovenia	Bulgaria	Romania	Total
Total CSF amount	4,101.05	6,673.63	19,213.04	29,987.72
Biodiversity Protection in Cohesion and Structural Policy	97.25	159.11	351.40	607.76
Biodiversity Protection in Cohesion and Structural Funds (%)	2.4%	2.4%	1.8%	
Actual allocation to selected operations (% of progress 2007– Sept 2009 for nature conservation and biodiversity)	58.1%	43.1%	1.3%	

Sources: Authors' calculations based on the European Commission, 2010a

Overall, level of investment in biodiversity in focus countries has been rather low. Its effectiveness cannot be estimated, as the methodology for measuring biodiversity is missing.

There are considerable investment needs for Natura 2000 sites alone (see Table 2.14). Lack of available public resources for investment can be regarded as a challenge, and also as an opportunity for innovation and development of new market-based instruments.

Table 2.13 Planned allocation, as of January 2010, of EAFRD resources for the period 2007–2013, in million euros

	Romania	*Slovenia*	*Bulgaria*
EAFRD	8,124	916	2,642
Total public expenditure (EAFRD + national contribution)	10,097	1,176	3,241
EAFRD Axis 2 – Improving the environment and the countryside	1,908	474	637
EAFRD Axis 2 – Payments for supporting agro-environment schemes	817	248	357
Agro-environment schemes (% of total EAFRD)	10.06%	27.12%	13.51%

Source: Authors' calculation based on MS country assessment report on implementing the EU Biodiversity Action Plan 2010

Table 2.14 Future estimated investments in Natura 2000, potential sources of financing, in million euros

	Bulgaria	*Romania*	*Slovenia*	*Croatia*	*Turkey*
Estimations of future investment in Natura 2000	203.1	n.a.	146.9	n.a.	263.3
Type of financing					
Structural funds n.a. EAFRD	103.3	215	57.3	63.7	n.a.
LIFE +	15	15	16.1	n.a.	n.a.
Rural development	n.a.	n.a.	21	n.a.	n.a.
National budget	n.a.	n.a.	52.5	n.a.	n.a.
GAP	84.8	n.a.	0	n.a.	n.a.
GAP (%)	41.75%	n.a.	0%	n.a.	n.a.

Source: Authors' calculations

3 Water sector

EU requirements

European water policy is based on a number of water related EU directives (see Table 3.1), as well as measures based on international obligations (e.g. Barcelona Convention for the Protection of the Mediterranean; Helsinki Convention on the protection of the Baltic Sea; Helsinki Convention on transboundary watercourse and international lakes; Convention for the Protection of the Rhine, OSPAR Convention).[1]

The Water Framework Directive (WFD), adopted in 2000 is the leading EU operational tool for water protection, i.e. inland surface water, groundwater, transitional waters and coastal waters. It is based on the idea that water management needs to take account of ecological, economic and social functions throughout the entire river basin. Objectives of the WFD include preventing and reducing pollution, promoting sustainable water usage, environmental protection, improving aquatic ecosystems and mitigating the effects of floods and droughts. The WFD sets a number of requirements and deadlines in order to achieve 'good ecological and chemical status' for all EU waters by 2015 (see Table 3.2).

According to the Directive, member states had to identify (by 2003) all the river basins lying within their national territory, assign them to individual river basin districts (or international river basin districts if they cover the territory of more than one member state) and designate a competent authority for application of the rules. Analysis of water, including:

1. the characteristics of each river basin district
2. review of the impact of human activity on water
3. an economic analysis of water use
4. a register of areas requiring special protection, and
5. a survey of all bodies of water used for abstracting water for human consumption and producing more than 10m^3 per day or serving more than 50 persons was expected to be prepared by 2004, revised in 2013 and every six years thereafter.

Management plans for each river basin district for the period 2009–2015 were to be prepared by 2009. The implementation of management plans should

Table 3.1 Selected EU water and related legislation

Framework legislation	*Purpose*
Directive 2000/60/EC, as amended	Water Framework Directive (WFD); the cornerstone of the EU water policies
Water quality objective oriented	
Drinking Water Directive (98/83/EC)	Sets quality standards for drinking water. Obliges member states to regular monitoring of drinking water.
Bathing Water Directive (76/160/EEC, to be repealed and replaced by the new Bathing Directive 2006/7/EC at latest by 2014)	Ensures good bathing water quality by setting limits to certain physical, chemical and microbiological parameters.
Shellfish Waters Directive (79/923/EEC), integrated into the WFD, to be repealed under the WFD as from 22.12.2003	Aims to protect shellfish populations by maintaining the quality of water areas where shellfish grow and reproduce
Fish Water Directive (78/658/EEC), integrated into WFD, to be repealed under the WFD as from 22.12.2003.	Relates to the quality of fresh waters in order to support fish life
Emission-control oriented	
Urban Wastewater Treatment Directive (91/217/EEC) and related Decision 93/481/EC	Aims to protect the environment from the adverse effects of urban waste water discharges as well from discharges from certain industrial sectors
Nitrates Directive (91/676/EEC)	Protects water quality by preventing pollution from nitrates used in agriculture and by promoting good farming practice
Groundwater Directive (80/68/EEC), 'Daughter Directive', integrated into WFD, to be repealed under the WFD as from 22.12.2003; after 2013 protection regime should be continued through the WFD and the new Groundwater Daughter Directive (2006/118/EC)	Requires preventing and monitoring of the groundwater pollution in order to achieve and maintain good groundwater chemical status
Dangerous Substances Directive (76/464/EEC), to be repealed under the WFD as from 22.12.2013; proposal for a new Directive setting limits for 41 substances was adopted on 17/07/2006	Sets measures to prevent pollution of inland surface waters, territorial waters, inland coastal waters and ground waters
Integrated Pollution Prevention and Control Directive (IPPC, 96/61/EEC)	Demands that industrial and agricultural activities with a high pollution potential get a permit after meeting certain environmental requirements
Flood Risk Management	
Directive on Flood Risk Management	Aims to reduce and manage risks that floods pose to human health, environment and overall economic activity

Source: Kampa et al., 2008:11

Table 3.2 Key milestones and set deadlines of the WFD requirements

Deadline	*Issue*
2003	Streamlining legislation: i.e. transposition of the WFD in national legislation, identification of river basin districts and authorities, expanding the scope of water protection to all waters, surface water and groundwater
2004	Characterization of river basin: pressures, impacts and economic analysis
2006	Establishment of monitoring programmes for the assessment of water status. Start public consultation (at the latest); getting citizens involved more closely
2008	Present draft river basin management plan
2009	Finalize river basin management plans including programme of measures
2010	Introduce pricing policies (introduce polluter pays principle)
2012	Programmes of measures operational at the latest
2015	Achievement 'good status' for all waters, updated the first river management plan, first flood risk management plan adopted
2021	Second management cycle ends
2027	Third management cycle ends, final deadline for meeting objectives

Source: European Commission, 2009a

start in 2012. It should lead to an achievement of good chemical and ecological status of surface water by 2015; protection of the groundwater and preservation of protected areas. According to need, the management plans for river basin districts can be complemented by more detailed management programmes and plans for a sub-basin, a sector or a particular type of water.

WFD requires public information, specifically regarding management plans for river basin districts. Projects from the management plans must be submitted to public consultation for at least six months. Responsibility for certain water management activities has to be fully decentralized to local governance. Consultations between the European Commission (EC) and the member states are also foreseen.

Economic instruments, primarily pricing policy, are promoted as tools to reduce negative impact on the environment and improve resource efficiency. By 2010 member states had to ensure that the proportion of the cost of water services (pumping, weirs, dams, channels, supply system – with a negative impact on the environment) is paid by the users (agriculture, hydropower, households). Costs should be split according to the 'polluter pays principle' and must take account of the principle of recovery of the costs of water services, including environmental and resource costs, as well as issues of affordability. The WFD requires an affordable price to guarantee a basic level of domestic water supply. To this end, well before introducing new pricing policies (deadline by 2010), an economic analysis had to be prepared (by 2004), including infrastructure for other than drinking water supply and wastewater treatment. If this is not the case, there is a major risk that such infrastructure already identified as creating major environmental problems will be exempt from adequate pricing policies. Consequently, the economic burden of water bodies reaching 'good status' by 2015 will remain with citizens, who already pay high prices for water services.

Significant financial resources are necessary for implementation of the requirements, such as improving their drinking water supply, constructing water purification stations and upgrading water management. Thus, potential investors in the water sector were identified to facilitate implementation (see Table 3.3.)

However, the achievement of EU water policy goals appears to be challenging, according to the European Environment Agency's 2010 State of the Environment Report. The EU is, therefore, preparing the Blueprint to Safeguard Europe's Water which will provide policy recommendation for the period until 2020. Focus will be given to land management, in particular to water related

Table 3.3 Potential investors in the EU water sector

	Potential investor	*Heavy investment*	*Other investment*
Drinking Water Directive	Municipalities, water utilities/companies	Water collection/ abstraction; Water treatment plants; Water delivery/supply system	Surface water monitoring; DW quality monitoring (at treatment plan and as tap)
Urban Wastewater Treatment Directive	Municipalities, water utilities/companies; industrial companies	Wastewater collection systems; wastewater treatment plants	Effluent monitoring
Sewage Sludge Directive	Industrial companies; Public or privatized water companies	Sludge dewatering systems; Sewage sludge incinerators; composting/treatment plants; Pre-treatment of industrial discharges to sewers	Sludge transport system; land spreading systems; Monitoring systems
Urban Wastewater Treatment Directive	Industrial companies	Wastewater treatment systems; New processes (cleaner technology)	Water quality monitoring; Modelling systems
Nitrates Directive	Agricultural enterprises	Animal waste storage facilities; Wastewater treatment systems	Water quality monitoring; Modelling systems;
Water Framework Directive	Regional governments (river basin authorities); Industrial companies; Agricultural enterprises	Wastewater treatment plants (municipal/ industrial); Animal waste storage facilities, etc.	Water quality monitoring
Bathing Water Directive	Municipalities, water utilities, companies	Wastewater treatment plants	Water quality monitoring

Source: European Commission 2001: 18

green infrastructure measures, such as reforestation, floodplains restoration, soil management, and sustainable urban drainage systems. Measures are to be integrated into the Common Agricultural and Cohesion Policies.

National plans and financing

Slovenia

The present state

Slovenia has various types of watercourses and a relatively dense hydrographical network. The amount of precipitation differs considerably between areas in the west and those in the east of the country: in some places there is regular or occasional flooding, while a few areas face a lack of water and drought. On average most Slovenian waters are in a good ecological state. There are two river basins districts in Slovenia: North Adriatic and Danube.

There is 922 million m^3 of available groundwater, or 759m^3 per inhabitant (2006 data). Karstic water accounts for almost half Slovenia's reserves of groundwater. Groundwater supplies as much as 97 per cent of the population with drinking water, thus its quality is of primary importance. Drinking water supply is mostly suitable and sufficient.

The quality in watercourses had improved significantly since 1992, due to construction of wastewater treatment plans and sewage systems. The quantity of water collected in the public sewerage systems has been increasing: in 2007 it amounted to 154 million m^3, 8 per cent more than in 2005. According to 2009 urban wastewater treatment assessment, 45 per cent of population equivalent[2] (p.e.) has its wastewater treated in treatment plants (up from barely fifth of population in 1998) and 56 per cent of wastewater is collected via sewerage systems.

Currently Slovenia has only water and wastewater contributions, which are collected by municipalities. These form negligible resources of municipalities' revenues. Instruments for determining economic prices of water for all types of use and the principle of recovery of costs for drinking water supply services and for the removal and treatment of municipal wastewater and rainwater have not yet been fully implemented.

Policy and regulation

Gradual alignment of the Slovenian water policy with the EU started in 1999, when the government adopted the Action Plan for Urban Wastewater Collection and Treatment with the Programme of Water Supply projects. This Programme provided for the first implementation phase of the Urban Wastewater Directive and the Drinking Water Directive. In the second phase, starting in 2001, the Action Plan for Urban Wastewater Collection and Treatment in Agglomerations between 2,000 and 15,000 p.e. and less than 2,000 p.e. was adopted.

The Water Act of 2002 (and amended in 2008) provided for alignment with the WFD. It sets a general regulatory framework for water management; defines operators of water management; territorial basis (river basin districts, catchment areas and river basins and their boundaries); types of water management acts; public participation by the preparation of management plans; and identifies water protection areas of surface water.

In order to achieve the objectives of the Water Act, the National Water Management Programme (for the period 2005–2012) sets deadlines for drafting and implementing operational programmes (OP) and determines their funding sources.[3] After 2012, emphasis will shift to the implementation of programmes of measures drawn up in the programmes on the basis of river basin management plans, or more detailed management plans.

In 2006, the government adopted the OP for Drinking Water Supply whose main goals are to increase the number of inhabitants connected to water distribution systems to 100,000 and to reduce the number (by 60,000) of those who are exposed to chemical and microbiological contamination of water to 40,000 in 2015, and to reduce the vulnerability of the Republic of Slovenia population to climatic changes. It is a priority to reduce water losses from mains water systems, which are still around 26 per cent, despite marked reductions.

The Water Management Plan (2009–2015) was adopted in 2010, which introduces separate measures for each river basin and each pressure (sector) in order to sustain quality and quantity of water resources.

The importance of improving water quality is stipulated in development documents (e.g. Slovenian Development Strategy 2006–2013) and environment action plans (National Environmental Action Plan 2005–2012). The Slovenian Development Strategy calls for alignment with WFD, while one of the strategic goals set by the National Environmental Action Plan was the finalization of river basin management plans by 2009. River basin management plans were expected to include all measures needed to prevent deterioration and help to achieve a 'good status' of all the Slovenian waters by 2015. However, by the deadline set by the National Environmental Action Plan (2009), Slovenia only had a proposal of the River Basin Management Plan. Delays in its adoption and a lack of financial resources might result in a failure to achieve a 'good status' of Slovenian waters by 2015.

Institutions

The main institutions responsible for implementing water policy include the government, the Ministry of Environment and Spatial Planning (MESP), local authorities, the Institute for Water of the Republic of Slovenia and Environmental Agency.

Central government and local communities have to ensure the maintenance of water and waterside land as a compulsory commercial public service. The government defines the method and conditions for the provision of other public services (e.g. the operation and maintenance of water infrastructure intended for the preservation and adjustment of water quantities; the operation, maintenance and monitoring of the condition of water infrastructure intended for the protection against the adverse effects of water; the implementation of emergency measures during periods of increased levels of risk due to the adverse effects of water).

MESP is responsible for water protection, use, management and tasks regarding the implementation of potable water supply and treatment of urban and drainage wastewaters.

In the area of water protection, the Ministry is in charge of programming documents relevant for the achievement of WFD goals (Directive 2000/60/EC), the Bathing Water Directive (2006/7/EC, 76/160/EEC), the Nitrates Directive (91/676/EEC) and the Marine Strategy Framework Directive (2008/56/EC) and the preparation and implementation of regulations concerning protection areas as regards the Water Act: water protection areas, bathing water protection areas.

Concerning the provision of the use of water, the Ministry deals with concessions, in particular for the production of electric energy in hydroelectric power stations; for the production of beverages; for the use of mineral, thermal and thermal-mineral water in bathing sites; for heating and similar uses; for the collection of debris, for aquaculture and production of freshwater organisms in still waters with a surface water greater than $0.5km^2$; and for the use of water space for ports and berthing facilities. The task of the sector is to ensure a use of water which is not contrary to the goals of the achievement and conservation of good water status and water ecosystems.

In the field of water regulation, the Ministry is responsible for the preparation of a detailed plan for the reduction of flood hazards in compliance with the Flood Directive (Directive 2007/60/EC) and management of the Water Fund. The Environment Cohesion Fund and Water Fund are in charge of the preparation and management of investments in the municipal and water infrastructure. The Water Fund is a special budgetary fund. The Fund's resources are made up from payments for water rights belonging to the state, and from water fees. The Water Fund's resources are used for water infrastructure including the requirements for the construction of national and local infrastructure and the acquisition of water and waterside (coastal) lands by local communities. The Environment Cohesion Fund co-finances infrastructure projects within the potable water sector, the collection and treatment of urban wastewater and the reduction of detrimental activities of water.

The preparation of investments financed with the environmental tax was centralized in order to foster the construction of a sewage system together with a treatment plant and sludge treatment. Before centralization municipalities preferred to construct treatment plants only but not sewage systems. A centralized approach enables an easier solution to problems in the acquisition of the approvals by different services.

The Institute for Water is responsible for the implementation of specific expert and developmental tasks, related to the formulation of water management plans; the granting of water rights and the issuing of water approvals; the determination of boundaries of water and waterside land; and the determination of plots of water land.

The Environmental Agency of the Republic of Slovenia and its regional offices (operating according to the territorial principle of river basin districts, river basins and sub-basins) are in charge of monitoring the quantitative, ecological and chemical status of water, and on the basis of this preparation, of administrative acts on water protection (environmental protection permits and licences in connection with water pollution); water use (water use licences); water regulation (water permits); public water regulation services; the forecasting of floods and landslides; and events that could have an adverse effect on water (droughts).

Financing

There are basically two types of financial sources for investment in water sectors: co-financing with EU financial instruments and national sources.

Since 1994 the EC has, through the PHARE programme, co-financed lower-cost infrastructure projects in the field of environmental protection.

In 1999 the Slovene government prepared the first strategy for harmonisation with EU environmental legislation and the EC launched the Instrument for Structural Policies for Pre-accession (ISPA). Costs of alignment in the field of water quality were estimated at €1,183 million, out of which most was for improving municipal wastewater treatment, followed by industrial wastewater treatment (World Bank, 1999).

For the period 2000–2006, the EC had earmarked non-repayable ISPA funds for the implementation of European environmental legislation relating to water supply and wastewater drainage and treatment, and financed a number of wastewater treatment projects in Slovenia (e.g. wastewater treatment plant Celje, wastewater treatment in the lower reaches of the Sava river) a sewage system and a couple of technical assistance projects (see Table 3.4).

The implementation of the strategy for harmonisation with the EU environment legislation was mainly financed from national sources. These included state budget (directly or through environmental taxes: water pollution tax and a tax on leakages from water supply system), municipal budgets (directly or through municipal tax or charges for water consumption and collection of wastewaters), the private sector (concession contracts, build-operate-transfer model) and environmental taxes, which are earmarked funds.

Table 3.4 Water projects financed through the ISPA fund

ISPA Fund
Waste water treatment plant Celje
Sewage system and the central waste water treatment plant Lendeva
Waste water treatment and upgrading potable water supply system in the Paka river basin
Water supply of Trnovsko-Banjiški plateau
Waste water treatment in the Mislinja river basin in Slovenj Gradec
Waste water treatment in the Mislinja river basin
Waste water treatment in the lower stream of the Sava river in Brežice, Krško and Sevnica
Technical assistance in waste water treatment in the middle of the Sava basin
Technical assistance in the preparation of the management plan in the Krka river basin

Source: National Strategic Reference Framework 2007–2013, 2007a

Water reimbursements were the main national source for investments in the water sector until 2005, when water pollution tax became effective. Since then it has raised annually more than €40 million (see Table 3.5).

Money raised by the water pollution tax was mainly invested in discharge and treatment of wastewater (see Table 3.6).

At the municipal level, however, water and wastewater charges did not provide sufficient revenue to invest in water infrastructure. In 2004 (which was the year of accession) and in 2005 €71 million was invested in water sector, which does not enable full implementation of the EU rules.[4] According to the Accession Treaty, Slovenia has to align its wastewater collection and treatment with applicable EU legislation by 2015.

Table 3.5 Financial effects of Slovenian environmental taxes for the period 2004–2008, in million euros

Environmental tax	*2004*	*2005**	*2006**	*2007**	*2008**
Water reimbursements	14.142	16.691	16.691	16.691	16.691
Reimbursement for water rights	3.755	3.755	4.172	4.172	4.172
Water pollution tax	0.069	48.823	48.823	41.729	41.729

Source: National Environment Action Programme, 2005

Note
* Estimate according to source

Table 3.6 Finance of key water programmes in Slovenia 2005–2008, in million euros

Programme	*Financial source*	*2005*	*2006**	*2007**	*2008**
Water regulation: • reducing effects of drought • reducing adverse effects of water • hydrological monitoring	Water reimbursements and payment for water rights	11.308	15.210	16.274	17.526
Water supply	Water reimbursements	1.418	1.481	1.251	1.251
	National budget	–	2.503	5.842	6.259
	EU	–	5.842	15.022	16.691
Protection of water from nitrate pollution from agricultural production	National budget	16.691	16.691	16.691	16.691
Discharge and treatment of waste water	Water pollution tax	43.815	39.642	31.296	31.296
	Budget	8.345	8.345	8.345	8.345
	Other sources	15.857	7.511	24.202	24.202

Source: National Environment Action Programme, 2005

Note
* Estimate according to source

Thus, to facilitate financing, in 2004 the government adopted the national OP for Wastewater Collection and Treatment which was extended in 2011.[5] Based on that programme, the OP for Environment and Transport 2007–2013 identified investment needs (€1,108 million, see Table 3.7) and an indicative list of major projects eligible for co-financing from the Cohesion Fund.

Financial needs for the period 2007–2013 are estimated between € 1,108–1,841 million (see Table 3.7). Investments planned to be financed from the Cohesion Fund and national sources in accordance with national strategic reference framework reach €530 million (on average €75.82 million annually), leaving a financial gap of between €578 and €1,144 million.

Full implementation of the polluter pays principle should help bridge the financial gap for investment in the water sector. The level of water price (both for water supply and treatment) in 2006 represented 1.2 per cent of average income, hence not causing an affordability problem (Gobec, De Sutter, 2006:11). Rising charges, despite negative impact of crisis on average income, should also not cause significant affordability problems.[6]

It was planned that out of the €75.82 million annually invested in the water sector for 2007–2013, €45.91 million (60%) will be financed from national sources (see Table 3.8).

Table 3.7 Estimates of Slovenian financial needs until 2013 for investment in water sector, in million euros

	Estimate 1	*Estimate 2*	*Estimate 3*	*Estimate 4*
Water supply	456	320	475	334
Wastewater treatment	1,175	884	1,175	589
Natural hazard (floods and droughts)	210	–	24	185
TOTAL	1,841	1,204	1,674	1,108
NSRF (2007–2013)	530	530	530	530
Financial GAP	1,135	674	1,144	578

Source: Estimates 1–3 Gobec and De Sutter, 2006: 6; Estimate 4 OP Environment and Transport and National Strategic Reference Framework 2007–2013, 2007a: 125

Table 3.8 Dynamics of investment in the Slovenian water sector 2007–2013, in million euros

	Total (national + EU)	*NSRF (EU)*	*NSRF (national)*	*Outside NSRF (national)*	*Total (national)*
Annual average	75.82	29.91	6.49	39.42	45.91
Total 2007–2013	530.74	209.39	45.44	275.91	321.34

Source: National Strategic Reference Framework 2007–2013, 2007

According to the Slovenian National Reform Programme (NRP) adopted in 2011, Slovenia plans to further increase the share of national sources for investing in the water sector, especially during 2011. During 2007–2010 planned investment (see Table 3.9) in water infrastructure, primarily water treatment facilities, but also in the improvement of drinking water supply and flood protection will reach €120 and €192 million in 2011 and 2012 respectively.

Maintaining this level of investment (around €200 million a year) until 2015 should be sufficient for alignment with the EU rules.[7]

Bulgaria

The present state

Due to the geographical location, specific atmospheric circulation and landscape structure, the water balance in Bulgaria is unfavourable. Bulgaria is among five of the poorest countries in Europe in terms of water (with Poland, Cyprus, Belgium and Czech Republic). Precipitation is moderate in quantity (the average is about 700mm, ranging between 450–1200mm) and unevenly distributed in terms of time and the position in the country.

The hydro-geographic network of the country is rather complex and in most of the regions quite dense, without big rivers, except for the Danube River forming the Bulgarian northern border. There are four river basin districts: Danube, Black Sea, East Aegean and West Aegean.

Surface water in Bulgaria as a whole is in good condition, except in specific regions. Nearly 75 per cent of the length of rivers in the country meets the standards for good quality. The basic pollutants of surface water are the domestic-faecal water from the urban sewerage system in the big settlements and the industrial wastewater which is discharged untreated into the rivers. The basic pollutants of groundwater in all river basin districts are the nitrates.

The water supply system covers 98.8 per cent of the population of the country (OP Environment, 2007: 12). Internal losses (between 40–80 per cent, on average

Table 3.9 Measures in the Slovenian water sector in 2011 and 2012, in million euros

Measure/project name	*2011*	*2012*
Waste water discharge and treatment	25.140	57.440
Drinking water supply	15.736	42.621
Provision of flood safety	2.731	3.787
Sustainable water use and management	56.463	59.409
SSSV–Water environment situation in Slovenia	4.056	9.576
Water management	16.194	19.560
Total	120.320	192.393

Source: National Reform Programme 2011–2012, 2011

60 per cent) in the distribution networks create the main problems for water supply, which in some places requires complete rehabilitation, and the lack of water reservoirs.

The share of population connected to sewerage networks (69 per cent) lags behind the share of population connected to water supply (99 per cent). Approximately 70 per cent of the towns in the country have sewerage networks, but only 2 per cent of the villages. In 2007, 34 per cent of people were connected to community wastewater treatment facilities offering at least secondary treatment. With regard to the sewerage network and wastewater treatment facilities, Bulgaria is lagging behind EU standards.

The price of water covers the operational costs of the Water Supply and Sewerage Companies, which have led to investment neglect during the transition period. The central government budget could not support rehabilitation, and the level of income of population did not allow significant increases in tariffs. This led to inadequate services, high water losses, environmental risks related to water quality and wastewater discharge, and financial difficulties for the utilities.

Therefore the EC requested that the Bulgarian Environment Minister should develop and adopt an urgent action plan for reforming the water sector infrastructure.

Policy and regulation

The gradual alignment with EU water policy started in 1999, when the National Programme for Priority Construction of Urban Wastewater Treatment Plants (1999–2010) was developed. The Water Act, enacted in January 2000, transferred the basic requirements and principles of the WFD. It has been amended, supplemented and corrected more than 30 times since (last time in 2009, when private participation in the water sector was allowed).

The purpose of the Water Act is to ensure an integrated and balanced management of water in the interest of the public, the protection of public health, and the sustainable development of Bulgaria. It provides for the implementation of the basic principles of effective environmental policy, such as polluter pays, public awareness regarding the state of the environment, shared responsibility, preventive action (control) and integrated management.

Since 2005 the price policy of the water supply and sewerage services has been regulated by the Water Supply and Sewerage Services Regulation Act. It regulates water tariffs, accessibility and quality of water and sewerage services provided by water and sewerage companies. It defines drinking water as a basic necessity of life and the activities for water supply and sewerage services as activities of public interest.

The basic principle for forming the price of the water supply and sewage services is the establishment of price levels that enable full coverage of operational costs. Profitability of up to 12 per cent is calculated into the costs. For some companies the percentage of profitability varies for households and legal entities. The elements included in this expenditure section comprise only tax-eligible expenditure and do not include investment costs other than those for depreciation. Investments are most often provided by governmental authorities in the form of subsidies. The price of water supply and sewerage services is determined on the basis of the costs estimated for $1m^3$ of water. They are calculated as a ratio between the overall costs and the predicted volume of water to be sold for the respective period. Due to the various parameters used in determining the tariffs, each company applies different tariffs for delivering water supply and sewerage services.

During negotiations for accession to the EU, several national strategies have been developed (e.g. National Strategy for Management and Development of the Water Sector 2004–2015, the Strategy for Management and Development of Water Supply and Sewerage in the Republic of Bulgaria) which should help the fulfilment of commitments under transition periods. Identified priorities include water supply for residential needs, protection of surface and groundwater sources, development of water infrastructure and services, as well as tackling regulatory and institutional reforms in the water and sanitation sector.

Institutions

At national level, the responsibility for water management is divided among five ministries:

- Ministry of Environment and Water, which is responsible for abstraction facilities for mineral waters constituting public state property.
- Ministry of Regional Development and Public Works, responsible for water supply and sewerage systems at national level and protection against water related damage and loss.
- Ministry of Agriculture and Food, for irrigation and land-reclamation systems and facilities in respect of protection against water related damage and loss beyond the limits of nucleated settlements.
- Ministry of Economy, Energy and Tourism, which is responsible for hydropower systems and facilities.
- Ministry of Health is responsible for the exercise of monitoring and control on the quality of surface water intended for drinking and household use, as well as bathing water.

At the basin level competent authorities include four Basin Directorates (Danube, Black Sea, East Aegean, West Aegean), district administrations and municipalities. The defined river basins do not follow the administrative divisions of Bulgaria. The main tasks of the municipalities include construction, maintenance and proper operation of the sewerage networks, the water industrial systems and small facilities for individual use of groundwater originating from the territory of the municipality.

The Regional Inspectorates on Environment and Water under the Ministry of Environment and Water ensure the state environmental policy at regional level and perform monitoring and controlling functions in reference to the fulfilment of the requirements under permits for wastewater discharge issued by the River

Basin Directorates. The Inspectorates control the emergency release of wastewater and maintain a database on the monitoring and control concerning the condition of wastewater.

The Executive Environmental Agency under the Ministry of Environment and Water organizes and guides the national system for surface water monitoring and controls quality of water by physical and chemical parameters through mobile laboratories.

The commercial water supply and sewage companies operate the facilities.

State Energy and Water Regulatory Commission to the Council of Ministers (under the Water Supply and Sewerage Services Regulation Act) regulates the price and the quality of water supply and sewerage services provided by the water supply and sewage companies.

Generally, Bulgarian environmental authorities lack both organizational and well-trained human capacity. Overlapping of the responsibilities and lack of coordination among key environmental authorities hinders implementation of the environmental legislation.

Financing

Bulgaria was not able to implement EU water related *acquis* by the date of accession. Transition periods (the longest expires in 2014) were necessary to ensure the public and private resources to fully comply with the requirements in this sphere, especially concerning 'heavy directives', primarily Drinking Water and Urban Wastewater Directives.

The Strategy for Management of the Water Supply and Sewerage (2004) estimated necessary investment at €9.06 billion including €2.8 billion for the rehabilitation of water supply infrastructure in settlements, €1.1 billion for building new water supply infrastructure and €2.1 billion for the collection and treatment of wastewater. The financial needs have been justified in a report by the World Bank from 2005 on the basis of the Strategy.

The World Bank report proposed two scenarios of cost recovery. Both include an EU grant component (37 and 40 per cent for Scenario 1 and Scenario 2 respectively), tax (budgetary support (2 per cent and 16 per cent respectively) and tariffs (61 per cent or 44 per cent, depending on the scenario).

From 2000–2006 the EU provided €378 million grants under ISPA funds, one of the EU pre-accession instruments which were designed to assist the candidate countries in reaching EU standards in environmental protection. Within the same period, Bulgaria invested about €144 million, or 0.2 per cent of its GDP in the improvement of water supply (Eurostat, 2010; see Table 3.10).

During the accession negotiations, necessary investment costs were connected with relevant directives. Costs of alignment with the Drinking Water Directive were estimated at €4 billion (€3,969 million in the period 2004–2014, recalculated for the financial period 2007–2013 at €3,800 million), and with the Urban Wastewater Directive almost €3 billion (€2,959 million up to 2014, see Table 3.11). According to the experts evaluation the investments costs are slightly underestimated and these amounts should be regarded as minimum needed by

Bulgaria to achieve compliance with the requirements (Tonchevski, Lust, 2006; see Table 3.11).

According to the National Strategic Reference Framework planned investments in the Bulgarian water sector for the period 2007–2013 amount to €1.5 billion, mainly from domestic sources (see Table 3.12).

To facilitate alignment EU has earmarked €1 billion from the Cohesion Fund in 2007–2013 under the financial framework for investment in the Bulgarian water sector (see Table 3.13). Together with necessary national contribution, this would provide for €1.3 billion investment until 2013. This is 15% lower than according to the National Strategic Reference Framework, requires less Bulgarian domestic sources and enables implementation of the OP Environment. The funds are foreseen for investment primarily in water supply and sewage infrastructure.

Table 3.10 Public investment expenditure in Bulgaria according to the water implementation programmes, in million euros

Sector	*Total investment*	*Investment till 2005*	*Investment expenditures for the period 2005–2009 (annual, cumulative)*						*Investment after 2009*
			2005	2006	2007	2008	2009	2005–2009	
Water	2,218	144	120	151	175	211	239	896	1,177
Total Environment	3,367	350	343	405	396	245	274	1663	1,353

Source: National Reform Programme 2011–2015 in implementation of 'Europe 2020' Strategy, 2011b

Table 3.11 Necessary investment in water supply and wastewater treatment in Bulgaria, in million euros (2004–2014)

	Indicative investment cost 2004–2014	*Indicative investment cost 2007–2013*
Water supply	3,969[a]	3,136[b]
Wastewater treatment	2,959[c]	2,487[d]
Total	6,928	5,623
NSRF – Water (2007–2013)	n.a.	1,461
Financial GAP		4,162

Source: Authors' calculations based on OP Environment 2007–2013, 2007; and Tonchevski, and Lust, 2006

Notes

a Based on the Implementation Plan for Directive 98/83/EC on the quality of water intended for water consumption, Romania 2004

b Re-calculated the values for the financial period 2007–2013

c National authorities' estimate

d Re-calculated the values for the financial period 2007–2013

Table 3.12 Planned dynamic of financing the Bulgarian water sector within the NSRF 2007–2013, in million euros

	TOTAL (national + EU)	*NSRF (EU)*	*NSRF (national)*	*Outside NSRF (national)*	*Total (national)*	
	Annual average in 2007–2013 NSRF					*Annual average 2004–2005*
Bulgarian water sector	208.86	44.14	Total	130.58	164.72	190.81
	Total for the period 2007–2013 NSRF					*Total for the period 2004–2005*
Bulgarian water sector	1,462.00	308.96	239.01	914.04	1,153.03	381.61

Source: National Strategic Reference Framework Programming Period 2007 2013, n.d.

Table 3.13 Structure of development priorities and priority orientation of the OP environment 2007–2013, in million euros

OP environmental and transport infrastructure	*ERDF resources*	*CF resources*	*Total (+national contribution)*	*%*
Total	439.059	1,027.366	1,800.748	100.0
Environmental protection – water sector		1,027.366	1,284.207	71.3

Source: Operational Programme Environment 2007–2013, 2007

However, in 2009, the Bulgarian absorption rate was just slightly above 1 per cent from the beginning of 2010 until February 2011 but the situation improved and financing under OP Environment amounted to €482 million (Dimitrova, 2011).

The majority of financed projects were related to the construction and improvement of water and wastewater sectors in Bulgarian municipalities. Since such projects are extremely investment intensive, the Bulgarian government has to mobilize significant domestic financial resources to co-finance projects. Full absorption of EU funds would enable covering 20 per cent of costs, i.e. approximately half of the necessary grant component according to both cost recovery scenarios of the World Bank proposal. This stipulates the need to rely on domestic sources coming from the budget and economic instruments (user charges, fees for the use of resources, concessions for natural resources, sanctions and market mechanisms) in order to meet EU requirements. The amount needed (in addition to EU support) to meet the requirements in the wastewater treatment sphere for cities with a population of more than 2,000 people is between €5–7 billion.

The domestic fund includes budgetary sources and economic instruments that regulate and guide the behaviour of the users of waters and water bodies:

- User charges: consumer fees for the services on water supply, sewerage and wastewater treatment.
- Fees for using resources like the fees for water use and/or permitted use of water bodies, differentiated according to the purposes and the related impact on water and water bodies as a natural resource.
- Concessions of natural resources like mineral water, which are applied for the exclusive use of state property.
- Sanctions for polluting water for wastewater discharge into surface water and input of pollutants into groundwater.
- Fees for water abstraction from surface water, groundwater and mineral water.
- Fees for the use of a water site for the extraction of alluvium deposits from surface water.
- Fees for the use of a water site for recreation activities and aquatic sports.
- The application of economic regulators leads to generation of considerable resources, part of which are redirected by the state and municipal budgets for investments in water sector.

Thus, the price of the water has constantly increased from €0.67 in 2004 and is planned to reach €2.18 in 2013, which should provide an incentive for consumers' behaviour.

Investments are supported by grants and low interest loans to public or private companies for environmental infrastructure improvements, in particular relating to water and waste sectors. The Enterprise for Management of Environmental Protection Activities (previously called the National Environmental Protection Fund) – whose sources of income are taxes and sanction revenues and funds at the municipal level – provides grants to municipalities. However, conflicts between local and national environmental interests slow down decentralization.

Romania

The present state

Romania is situated entirely within the Danube international river basin. Water resources are unevenly distributed throughout the country, with large seasonal and year-to-year variations. Romania is relatively poor in water resources, disposing of only 1,870m^3 water per inhabitant per year (European average: 4,000m^3). The main problem is not water scarcity, but pollution.

Approximately 68 per cent of population is connected to the drinking water supply network – 98 per cent of the urban population but only 33 per cent of the rural population (3.4 million inhabitants) (NSRF 2007–2013, 2007). From total population, 52 per cent benefit from the drinking water supply and wastewater sewerage systems, 16 per cent benefit only from drinking water supply system while 32 per cent of population do not benefit from either of them.

Around 11.5 million inhabitants benefit from a sewerage service, out of which 10.3 million are in the urban area (representing 90 per cent of the urban population) and 1.15 million inhabitants in the rural area (10 per cent of the rural population) (2004 data; OP Environment 2007:14). From the overall wastewater quantity, 25 per cent is adequately treated.

Water demand for households, industry and agriculture decreased considerably between 1990 and 2008, from 20.4 billion m^3 in 1990 to 9.44 billion m^3. The reasons for this included the reduction in industrial activity, the reduction in water consumption in technological processes, the reduction of losses and the implementation of an economic mechanism for water management. Furthermore, the introduction of water metering in cities led to a drastic downsize of water consumption as tariffs (ranging from €0.2–0.52 per m^3) are fairly large for Romanian family income. The levels of tariffs are lower in the smaller towns and rural areas with no wastewater treatment plans, while they increase with the size of town and the quality of water infrastructure.

The price of the wastewater is lower than the price of drinking water (generally between 1/5 and 1/3 of the price of drinking water services) and it is the same for both the population and for industry. It is determined at local level.

The prices for wastewater sewerage services have been gradually increasing. Price growth is slow, limited by affordability issues. The level of prices does not cover full cost and does not allow development, modernization or introduction of new technologies for the centralized water intake systems (GHK, Rojanschi and Lust, 2006).

Policy and requirement

Since 1970, water management in Romania has been based on the concept of integrated river basins management of water resources (both for surface and groundwater, quality and quantity). In the pre-accession period, Romania has gradually aligned its policy with European WFD and related daughter directives. The longest period of transition is obtained for the urban wastewater purification until the end of 2018, and it is in close connection with financial assessment required for the implementation of the Urban Wastewater Directive. This is the most expensive Directive to implement because Romania was declared, as a whole, a sensitive area, which creates large problems for wastewater treatment.

The conservation, development and protection of water resources in Romania are regulated by the Water Law (adopted in 1996 and amended in 2004 and 2006 to transpose the provisions of the WFD). Any water use is subordinated to obtaining a permit (before execution of all works on water or influencing water) and a licence (before exploitation begins). Water supply for human consumption prevails over other usages. Discharges of wastewater into groundwater are forbidden and only under strict conditions may wastewater and mine water be injected into very deep layers. The monitoring system based on the water protection objectives is established in accordance to the parameters and frequencies regulated by the *acquis*. Requirements include progressive reduction of discharges, emissions and losses of the dangerous priority substances in surface water, ceasing or phasing out of priority hazardous substance uses in industry, ensuring a good quality water supply for human consumption, the introduction of the combined approach using the pollution control through the establishment and implementation of the emission controls and of the quality standards for the aquatic ecosystems (environment).

Water sector strategies have been developed by the Romanian Water Association, Administration and Internal Affairs Ministry and Environmental and Water Management Ministry. These strategies are periodically updated (each 3–4 years) and cover both the field of investments and the problem of organization, as well as the good quality management of the sector.

The River Basin Management Plan, the main implementation tool of the WFD, has been finalized in 2010. It contains a summary of the measures required to bring the water bodies progressively to the required status by the extended deadline, setting out the reasons for any significant delay in making these measures operational and the expected timetable for their implementation.

Institutions

Key institutions responsible for water management in Romania are the Ministry of Environment and Forests, the National Administration 'Romanian Waters' and its 11 Water Directorates and the National Institute of Hydrology and Water Management.

According to the survey made in 2006 by the European Environment Office and World Wild Fund on the implementation of the Water Framework Directive, Romania is one of the three countries (with Ireland and Finland) which established water authorities with adequate competence to solve all hydrographic basin issues, as required by the EU law.

The Ministry of Environment and Forests is the national authority on water management. Its principal task is to draft policies, strategies and guidelines. The Water Policy Department is responsible for policy formulation and regulations in connection with the implementation of the WFD. As Romania is part of the international Danube River Basin, the Ministry contributes to an international Danube River Basin Management Plan for the Romanian territory (including for the coastal waters of the Black Sea).

It is the task of Romanian Waters to ensure the proper implementation of those policies and regulations, including approval of water extraction and water discharge. In that capacity, the Romanian Water established 11 departments (water management directorates) at river basin level.

The National Institute of Hydrology and Water Management provides scientific and methodological advice. Since 1970, groundwater quality is monitored by an extensive National Hydrogeological Network. Groundwater samples are analysed by 41 laboratories belonging to Romanian Waters, which also collects charges for the wastewater discharged from industrial platforms.

Local authorities are owners and investment managers of drinking and wastewater infrastructure.

Financing

Total investment required between 2002 and 2030 to rehabilitate the infrastructure of the water-sewerage services is estimated at €9.7 billion (€4.2 billion in urban areas and €5.5 billion in rural areas). These estimates are from the 'Government's Strategy concerning the Development of Local Public Services of Communal Husbandry' developed in 2001 by the Ministry of Public Administration on the basis of information from the 42 Environmental Protection Inspectorates (GHK, Rojanschi and Lust, 2006).

Estimates based on the detailed directive-specific implementation plan exceed €15 billion: total cost of the implementation of the Drinking Water Directive is about €5.6 billion and €9.5 billion for wastewater (out of which €5.7 billion for wastewater treatment and €3.8 billion for sewerage systems). Necessary investment over the period 2007–2013 for meeting the EU requirements within the negotiated deadlines are estimated around €9 billion (see Table 3.14).

This includes €4.8 billion investment in wastewater treatment and €5.6 billion in drinking water. About €500 million is needed for anti-flooding measures (and roughly half – €237 million – is expected to come from EU support).

Investment in the water sector, needed to comply with the relevant *acquis communautaire*, is higher than that which can be implemented within Sectoral Operational Plan Environment, for the period 2007–2013. According to the plan, €3.3 billion will be invested in the water sector (see Table 3.14). Out of this, 85 per cent is envisaged as EU support (form Cohesion Fund), and 15 per cent should be contributed from the national sources.

Thus, with a view to achieving ambitious water supply and wastewater treatment objectives and to finance the investment and sustainable operation, maintenance and replacement of Romania's water infrastructure

Table 3.14 Summary of investment cost in Romanian water supply and wastewater treatment, in million euros

	Indicative investment cost (2004–2015)	*Indicative investment cost (2007–2013)*
Water supply	5,600[a]	3,800[b]
Wastewater treatment	9,500[c]	4,800[d]
Total	15,100	8,600
OP Environment: water	n.a.	3,266
Financial GAP		5,334

Source: Authors' calculations based on GHK, Rojanschi and Lust, 2006

Notes

a Based on the Implementation Plan for Directive 98/83/EC on the quality of water intended for water consumption, Romania 2004

b Re-calculated the values for the financial period 2007–2013

c Based on the Implementation Plan for Directive 91/271/EEC concerning urban waste water treatment, Romania 2004

d Re-calculated the values for the financial period 2007–2013 improvement, additional sources have to be used. So far, most investment in the water supply sector in Romania was financed from EU funds (50–75 per cent of large investments), local sources (10–15 per cent), and rest from bank loans (primarily from EBRD and the World Bank) and international help in the form of twinning programmes (with Denmark, Holland, France, Germany, etc.). Over the period 2000–2006, PHARE, ISPA, SAPARD programmes were used for financing water projects. Under ISPA €1.2 billion (including national contribution) was invested: €397 million into 22 projects having a drinking water component and €823 million in 32 projects with a wastewater component (GHK, Rojanschi and Lust, 2006). During 2007–2013 Romania plans to attract additional sources of financing from the EU, the National Environmental Fund and private investors based on several national programmes:

- *National Rural Development Programme*, which includes investment in water infrastructure in rural areas. For the period 2007–2013, the Programme is coordinated by the Ministry of Agriculture and Rural Development and co-financed by the EU (EARDF).
- *Governmental Programmes for development of municipal water and environmental infrastructure 2006–2009* that include priority investments according to the National Plans for the implementation of the *acquis*.
- *Governmental Programme for development of infrastructure in the rural area in the period 2006–2008* has provisions for investments in water and wastewater infrastructure.
- *National Environmental Fund* provides co-financing of limited investments in the water sector.
- Foreign loans or various forms of public-private partnership (PPP) are also solutions considered in some of the urban agglomerations.

Croatia

The present state

Water availability in Croatia is sufficient, but its spatial and annual distribution is unfavourable (which is more evident in the Adriatic Sea basin district).

Following water management districts are defined:

1 Sava water basin, and basins of Drava and Danube, which form parts of the international Danube basin district, and
2 Primorje-Istria water basins and Dalmatian water basin, which are parts of international Adriatic Sea basin districts.

In 2006, the average population coverage rate for public water supply systems amounted to approximately 80 per cent (91 per cent in the Adriatic Sea basin district and 77 per cent in the Danube River Basin district). In 2008 there were 101 operational urban wastewater treatment plants with installed capacity of 3.48

million p.e., treating 27 per cent of wastewater from the total population and 62 per cent of collected domestic wastewater.

The connection rate of the population to public sewerage systems is 43 per cent, ranging from 74 per cent in agglomerations of more than 150,000 inhabitants to 7 per cent in small agglomerations of 2,000 inhabitants.

Prices for water and wastewater varied from €0.43–1.97 per m^3 for drinking water and from €0.04–0.57 per m^3 for wastewater in different towns of Croatia (2007 data). The average price for drinking water and wastewater in Croatia is around €1 per m^3 and for water services it amounts to approximately €3.3 per m^3. It is estimated that average affordability level (i.e. 4 per cent of household income) is €10, but there are significant differences among the regions (three times between Zagreb and poorest regions). Therefore, while increasing the water charges necessary to finance the maintenance and improvement of existing water sector infrastructure, affordability has to be considered.

Policy and regulation

The process of harmonizing the Croatian water management policy with EU *acquis* has led to the adoption of the Water Management Strategy in 2008, two key acts in 2009 (the new Water Act and the Water Management Financing Act) and several by-laws. In total, 35 by-laws have to be adopted by 2012 in order to complete the harmonization with the EU legislation. As regards the implementation, transition periods are defined by the Accession Treaty – until 2024 for alignment with the Urban Wastewater Directive (with intermediate targets in 2018, 2020 and 2023) and until 2019 with the Drinking Water Directive.

The strategic goal of the Water Management Strategy is the development of public water supply – the percentage of population supplied with water from the public water supply systems should increase from the current 80 per cent to 85–90 per cent and the percentage of population connected to public sewerage systems from the current 43 per cent to some 60 per cent by the year 2023, which is in line with European standards.

The Croatian Constitution defines water as a resource of public interest. Thus, direct privatization is explicitly excluded. According to the Strategy, the possibility of indirect privatization of the right to a water resource is excluded in public water supply activities. Licences for using water resources for public water supply are issued exclusively to local/regional self-government units at service areas. It is not possible to privatize the existing water utility infrastructure (public water supply systems, urban wastewater sewerage and treatment systems). The private sector is not denied the right to obtain licences for other aspects of commercial water use.

The Water Management Strategy and the Water Management Financing Act promote the user/polluter pays principle, i.e. an economic price of water, and an economic price of protection against floods and other adverse effects of water, but it is not fully implemented yet.

Institutions

Two institutions have direct responsibility for water management in Croatia. The first is the Ministry for Regional Development, Forestry and Water Management which is the competent authority for the implementation of a national policy of water management. The second is Croatian Waters, the national water agency, the legal body responsible for water management. Croatian Waters passes administrative and other acts and makes decisions on important issues for water management. These include the preparation of basic water management plans, maintenance of water related infrastructure, protection from the detrimental effects of water, water use, water pollution control, etc.

Water companies (mostly located in larger urban areas) provide water supply and wastewater treatment services. They are either founded by local authorities, or have emerged in the process of transformation of former public enterprises under the Municipal Services Act of 1995. As for the ownership structure, 99 per cent of these are limited liability companies, where local authorities hold at least 51 per cent of the shares. The share of private ownership in these companies may not exceed 49 per cent, and there are still no examples of fully privatized companies providing municipal services in the water sector.

The service providers, i.e. municipal service companies, determine the price for the provision of water and sewage services. There are no administrative or legal limitations on the price. In practice, however, the price set by the municipal service companies is controlled by the company's founders – local government units.

The local government and public utility companies have an obligation under the Public Utility Services Act, which defines sources of finance for the delivery of public utility services and, among others, also the funds required for the construction of public utility infrastructure. In the water supply, wastewater discharge and wastewater treatment sectors, infrastructure funds necessary for the construction of public utility infrastructure facilities and plants, and the purchase of equipment, shall be secured from public utility charges, charges for the connection to the system, budgets of local self-government units, concession fees and other sources as determined by separate laws. The representative body of the municipality that takes the decision on the connection to the water supply and wastewater and rainwater discharge infrastructure determines by the same decision the charge for the connection, the way of collecting charges and penalty clauses.

The Draft River Basin Management Plan for the period 2012–2015 was published in March 2011 by the Ministry and the Croatian Waters, and should be adopted by the end of 2011, according to the Action Plan.

Financing

The cost of alignment with EU water *acquis* is estimated at €4.5 billion: €2.75 billion for the Urban Wastewater Directive, €1.79 billion for the Drinking Water Directive (98/83/EC) (see Table 3.15).

Table 3.15 Summary of investment cost in Croatian water supply and wastewater treatment 2008–2023, in million euros,

	Indicative investment cost (2008–2023)
Water supply	1,790
Wastewater treatment	2,750
Total	3,540

Source: Authors' calculations

A combination of domestic and foreign sources has been and will be used in the future in Croatia to meet EU water policy requirements.

According to the Croatian Water Management Strategy the total costs of regular economic and technical maintenance of watercourses, water estate, and regulation and protective water works, which is the responsibility of water management, are estimated at around €120 million per year, while the total costs of carrying out technical tasks are estimated at around €35 million per year. It is planned that part of the necessary funds will be obtained from the current pre-accession and subsequent Structural and Cohesion Funds of the European Union.

Within the OP Environment (2007–2009) the amount earmarked for water management sectors was €35.267 million (including national contribution) (EC DG Regional Policy, 2011).

In the next period, according to the OP Environment and Energy (2011–2012) planned investments in water management sectors are €435 million, €370 from Cohesion Fund and €65 million from national contributions. It is estimated that these are the maximum planned investments in view of the financial potential of Croatia's citizens and its economy.

The main domestic sources of funding wastewater sector projects were the state budget and revenues of the Croatian Waters, as well as water and wastewater tariffs for water provision and wastewater collection respectively.

Direct revenue of the Croatian Waters comes partly from the water use charge and partly the water protection charge. These are paid like taxes on the basis of the statutory obligation and can be used as earmarked funds to co-finance the construction of facilities for the use or protection of waters. Croatian Waters' revenues cannot be used to finance the construction and maintenance of the sewerage network, but only for technical facilities (collectors, wastewater treatment plants, outlets into receivers and similar). These facilities are used to deliver public utility services and are owned by municipalities or legal entities providing public utility services. However, in practice it is frequently difficult to separate 'sewerage network' from the 'technical facilities'. In recent years, approximately €82 million have been used for funding of both drinking water and wastewater related activities.

Foreign sources include the EU pre-accession funds (PHARE, ISPA, IPA) and grants and loans of the international financial institutions (e.g. the World Bank, EBRD). According to the Country Assistance Strategy, the overall sum of assistance to the water sector from the World Bank amounted to approximately €24 million for the period 2005–2007. EBRD Assistance Strategy to Croatia published in 2005 indicates assistance to the water sector amounted to €38 million.

Only partial financing of water infrastructure has been through private capital, mostly through concession agreements, especially with respect to public wastewater discharge and waste disposal systems.

Compliance with the EU water policy requirements and implementation of the Water Management Strategy requires efficient use of domestic and foreign, public and private sources.

Turkey

The present state

Water resources are not distributed equally over the country. Their effective use and protection have become essential as a result of water quality degradation caused by population increase, rapid urbanization and industrialization and agricultural activities. Between 22–30 per cent of surface water in Turkey complies with the 'good status' norm.

There are 25 river basins in Turkey. Master plans on the improvement of water resources have been prepared for all of them and will eventually be converted into river basin management plans. These plans deal with water quality and water quantity, but according to the EC, the overall alignment to the EU water management standards is low and efforts in improving water quality are insufficient. (EC, 2010b: 90).

The coverage rate for public water supply systems in urban areas exceeds 98 per cent, while in rural areas it is 88 per cent. The connection rate of the urban population to the sewerage increased from 56 per cent in 1983 to 92 per cent in 2005. While sewerage connection is high, the proportion of people connected to community waste treatment facilities is low. Wastewater treatment must be promptly increased from its current level of 6–10 per cent. It is non-existent in many parts of the country, while it reaches 75 per cent in Istanbul and 100 per cent in Ankara. A system to finance priority wastewater investment and improve service efficiency and quality needs to be developed (Yapanoglu, 2010).

Policy and regulation

The main features of Turkey's water policy relate to the development of water resources, water transfer from Turkey to water-stressed countries, accession to the EU and transboundary water policy.

The Turkish Constitution provides the basic legislation for the water sector and states that water resources are the natural wealth of the country, are under the authority to the state and should be used for the benefit of the public. Thus, water related activities are planned at national level, within five-year development plans which aim to ensure optimal distribution of resources. The current,

Ninth Development Plan for the period 2007–2013 includes considerations based on the Law on Environment, adopted in 2006, which provides for adoption of specific by-laws defining protection of water and improvement of the existing water infrastructure.

The Ninth Development Plan calls for greater technical consultancy with municipalities in the realization of urban infrastructure investments. In this way municipalities would get the knowledge for improving cooperation with the private sector and international financial institutions (IFIs), thereby opening the water sector for private investment and unburdening public budget. In order to increase transparency and stability of financial resources earmarked for further water infrastructure investment, the Plan highlights the need to develop and adopt a clear financing strategy and an urban master plan for determining future investment in drinking water and wastewater infrastructure.

A number of water related directives are already incorporated into Turkish legislation, and the WFD announced that it should be transposed by the end 2011 and fully implemented (together with daughter directives) by 2027. Whereas transposition is seen as an unchallenging task for Turkey, the preparation of river basin management plans and implementation of their programmes could be difficult. Given the weak enforcement of existing legislation, lack of reliable data concerning the quality of water bodies and economic analyses, the declared deadline for full implementation of the EU rules (2027) remains ambitious.

The situation is further complicated by the inability of local governance to establish effective partnerships within the private sector which would facilitate necessary investment. Thus, there are significant subsidies in water management financing. The municipalities have traditionally been financed by the Bank of Provinces (Iller Bank) mostly in the field of water and wastewater management. It is estimated that from 2007–2023 the Bank will finance 12 per cent of water sector investments. However, the Bank's financing capacity has deteriorated. Thus, there is an even greater need for municipalities to attract additional financial resources for implementing water sector projects from private sector and lower public expenditures. While the World Water Forum recognized that 'the private sector has proven to be effective in driving better operational efficiencies which directly improves the financial viability of utilities', the PPP is still more discussed than implemented (Zachau, 2009).

Institutions

A number of governmental and non-governmental organizations are dealing with the development and conservation of water resources in Turkey. These include: the Ministry of Environment and Forests, the Ministry of Agriculture and Rural Affairs, the Ministry of Health, the General Directorate of State Hydraulic Works (DSI), the State Planning Organization, and the Bank of Provinces (Iller Bank).

At decision making level, relevant institutions include the Prime Ministry, the State Planning Organization and the ministries. The main executive level organizations responsible for the development of water resources are governmental organizations under the ministries (DSI, General Directorate of Bank of Provinces), and urban water and sewage administrations.

There are both governmental and non-governmental organizations at the water users' level for the operation and maintenance of projects (municipalities, utility agencies, irrigation cooperatives, etc.).

The State Planning Organization, under the Prime Ministry, is responsible for reviewing and approving the annual public investment programme and plans in the sector. Projects in water and sanitation are prepared and implemented through the central government organizations, like the DSI or the General Directorate of the Bank of Provinces (Iller Bank).

Under the Ministry of Environment and Forestry, the DSI is the main executive level organization responsible for the development of water resources at national level (groundwater and surface water). The specific responsibilities of the DSI include irrigation, energy (hydropower), drinking water and flood protection. The DSI is responsible for developing all stages of water supply and water treatment plants for municipalities with a population of more than 100,000.

The Iller Bank, under the Ministry of Public Works, is responsible for water supply development (including developing urban plans, supplying municipal water, constructing sewerage systems and treatment plants), and finance (providing loans) for cities with a population of less than 100,000, and sanitation development and financing for all urban areas, except metropolitan municipalities.

Urban water and sewage administrations in metropolitan municipalities are in charge of constructing, operating, and maintaining water supply and treatment facilities, and are responsible for the networks of industrial establishments within the boundaries of metropolitan municipalities.

There are a number of monitoring–supervising organizations performing under various legislative arrangements. Among them, the most important ones include the Ministry of Environment and Forestry, the Ministry of Agriculture and Rural Affairs, and the Ministry of Health.

The Ministry of Environment and Forestry is responsible, among other things, for setting policies, principles and rules, inspecting activities, coordinating studies and enhancing public awareness on environmental aspects of water resources.

Local administrations are formally responsible for financing drinking water services (on a polluter pays principle), but central government continues to support drinking water projects in municipalities with at least 55 per cent of financial resources from the central budget.

The responsibility of providing water and wastewater services in urban areas belongs to the municipalities together with the tariff setting, billing and collection services as a monopoly within the municipal boundaries and neighbouring zones.

The fact that there are many institutions working on water resources development, which are not organized at the river basin level, as well as their unclear responsibilities led to duplications, or partial coincidences and difficulties in application. To increase coordination among the relevant institutions and to develop strategies and policies for further alignment with the *acquis*, a high level steering committee for water quality management was set up in 2010.

One of the main problems is the absence of a regulatory authority for the water sector in Turkey. Under consideration, such an authority would set down the policies for the sector and coordinate relations among the various organizations at the national level of governance and numerous municipalities responsible for water management within their territory.

Financing

According to the EU Integrated Environmental Approximation Strategy the cost of alignment with water related heavy cost directives (Urban Wastewater Treatment Directive, Drinking Water Directive, Quality of Surface Water Intended for the Abstraction of Drinking Water Directive, Water Framework Directive, Directive on Dangerous Substances Discharged into Water, Nitrate Directive and Bathing Water Directive) is estimated between €33.97–37.87 billion (EU Integrated Environmental Approximation Strategy, 2006: 17, see Table 3.16).

The Urban Wastewater Treatment Directive was recognized as financially the most demanding EU water directive, followed by the Drinking Water Directive. Estimated implementation costs exceed €18 billion and €12.7 billion respectively.

It is estimated that initial investment and rehabilitation costs of the drinking water treatment plants and networks until 2023 will be €12.7 billion. On the other hand, the World Bank's estimated cost of alignment with water related heavy cost directives is significantly lower: about €14 billion (€215 per capita) from 1998–2020, or about €650 million annually. It is estimated that the sector

Table 3.16 Summary of investment cost in Turkish water supply and wastewater treatment 2004–2014, in million euros

	Indicative investment cost 2007–2023
Water supply	12,743
Wastewater treatment	18,083
Agricultural Nitrate and Bathing Water Directive	293
WFD and DSD	4,168[a]
Total	**35,287**
IPA EOP 2007–2009	179
IPA extension of programme years 2010–2011	179[b]
IPA extension of programme years 2012–2013	179[c]
Financial GAP	34,750

Source: Authors' calculations

Notes

a Based on ORSAM, 2011

b Authors estimation are based on Turkish Ministry of Environment and Forestry, 2007

c Same as above

had been investing at an annual rate of at least €540 million during 1995–2002, excluding reinvested internal cash (Yapanoglu, 2010). In the same period Turkey was receiving financial aid provided from IFIs to implement its environmental reforms. The average annual amount granted from IFIs and foreign direct investments to Turkish environmental sector amounted to around €25 million, out of which nearly 90 per cent was used for water sector (i.e. €180 million).

As stated in the Sectoral Environment OP, in the period between 2007–2009 priorities investments in the water sector include the establishment of wastewater treatment plans and the improvement of drinking water quality. Allocated financial sources from EU funds and national contribution for these investments are estimated to total €179 million (Turkish Ministry of Environment and Forestry, 2007).

In the period until 2013, EU financial support could cover roughly 6 per cent of the cost, as estimated by Turkey in the EU integration strategy. Even if the cost is halved (in line with the World Bank's cost estimate), a significant financial gap remains.

Thus, the regulation of the sector is one of the key prerequisites to stimulate private sector participation in financing large water sector projects and development of PPP. Turkish water and wastewater sectors were identified by the EBRD in 2009 as a high priority market for further investment. Increase in the flow of foreign capital in the Turkish water sector was also useful for promoting greater engagement of the private sector in helping municipalities to finance heavy water sector investments (Global Water Intelligence, 2011). In this respect it is also important to ensure sustainable financing of the operation costs. The inadequate level of tariffs and cross-subsidy between different groups of customers and also between departments/administrations create a severe bottleneck in the financial assessment of water services and the estimation of the necessary tariff level to enable cost recovery.

Tariff levels are set at the beginning of the financial year by the municipality and they vary considerably. On average, charges reached €1.16/m^3 in 2008 (Global Water Intelligence, 2009). Some customers pay for the inefficiencies of public management, while on the other side there are tariffs that do not recover costs and do not enable generation of the necessary funds for rehabilitation and new investment. Industrial and commercial consumers are generally charged with higher tariffs than households, whereas water use in agriculture is heavily subsidized.

In general, Turkey has been moving closer to European levels of water tariffs. Due to a constant increase in energy costs, as well as the threat of climate change, it is expected that water costs and water prices in Turkey will continue to rise and thus enable full alignment with the EU.

Conclusions

The EU water policy legislation is leading to a complete overhaul of the new EU member states' environmental legislation. Its full implementation requires significant investment (see Table 3.17). The new EU member states, as well as

Table 3.17 Assessed scale of water investment needs under EU water directives, in million euros

	Indicative investment cost			*NSRF (2007–2013)*	*Financial gap*
	Water supply sector	*Wastewater treatment sector*	*Total*		
Slovenia, 2005–2017	320	884	1,204	530	674
Bulgaria, 2004–2014	3,969	2,959	6,928	1,461	4,162
Romania, 2004–2015	5,600	9,500	15,100	3,266	5,334
Turkey, 2007–2023	17,204	18,083	35,287	n.a.	n.a.
Croatia, 2008–2023	1,790	2,750	3,540	n.a.	n.a.

Source: Authors' calculations

candidates, lack financial resources to implement EU water policy within the deadlines set by the EU rules. Thus transitional periods and external assistance are necessary for the alignment of the water sector with the EU.

While external assistance is necessary, most of the investments are to be financed from domestic financial resources. In this context, special attention is given to the implementation of the polluter pays principle and full cost recovery. Costs of improving water sector infrastructure should be financed from tariffs.

On the one hand, the adequate quality of infrastructure is crucial for attracting investment, generating new jobs and increasing the living standard of the local population. On the other, the increase of tariffs, which would reflect true costs, has to consider the matter of affordability.

Managing huge investments requires strong institutions and well-established coordination among relevant institutions, at national and regional level. Weaknesses of the local authorities, such as weak local budgets, lack of adequately trained workforce and low environmental infrastructure, slow down the decentralization process.

Privatization of the state owned water sector is controversial: water is a public resource, but there is an opportunity for the involvement of private sector and thus disburdening public budgets. There are still major reasons that impede effective use of private capital:

1 high poverty imposes a problem of affordability and full application of the polluter pays principle in the implementation of the pricing policy
2 ineffective systems of imposing and enforcing water charges, and
3 inefficient administrations which should facilitate investment.

Support from public funds, national, EU and bilateral assistance is thus necessary for the facilitation of investment and alignment with EU environmental regulations (see Table 3.18).

Table 3.18 Aggregate financial table of public or other equivalent structural expenditure in Slovenian, Bulgarian and Romanian water sector, in million euros

	Total (national + EU)	*NSRF (EU)*	*NSRF (national)*	*Outside NSRF (national)*	*Total (national)*
Annual average in 2007–2013 NSRF					
Slovenia	75.82	29.92	6.49	39.42	45.91
Bulgaria	208.86	44.18	34.14	130.58	164.72
Romania	n.a.	n.a.	n.a.	n.a.	n.a.
Turkey	n.a.	n.a.	n.a.	n.a.	n.a.
Croatia	n.a.	n.a.	n.a.	n.a.	n.a.
Total for the period 2007–2013 NSRF					
Slovenia	530.74	209.39	45.44	275.91	321.34
Bulgaria	1,461.00	308.96	239.01	914.03	1,153.03
Romania	3,266.51	2,776.53	489.98	n.a.	489.98
Turkey	n.a.	n.a.	n.a.	n.a.	n.a.
Croatia	n.a.	n.a.	n.a.	n.a.	n.a.

Source: National Strategic Reference Framework 2007–2013, 2007; National Strategic Reference Framework 2007–2013, 2007a; National Strategic Reference Framework Programming Period 2007–2013 (n.d.)

While significant financing is necessary in the water sector, key problems that hinder faster water sector reform are institutional: unclear division of responsibilities between various organizations and the lack of coordination. Increasing institutional capacity and decentralization is expected to contribute to the establishment of efficient management systems and enable engagement of available funds and alternative models (European funds, own budget, national or local budget, loans and in some cases different forms of private investment).

4 Waste sector

EU requirements

The European Union waste policy and legislation try to minimize adverse environmental impact caused by the generation and treatment of waste. They have developed substantially since 1975, when the very first legislation was adopted (Council Directive 75/442/EEC). The long-term goal of the EU waste policy, i.e. to become a recycling society, was set by the Thematic Strategy on the Prevention and Recycling of Waste or 'Waste Strategy' adopted in 2005 (EC, 2005a). The Waste Strategy identified seven key actions to achieve its objectives, and are still valid (EC, 2011b).

- Full implementation of existing legislation
- Simplifying and modernizing the existing legislation
- Introducing life-cycle thinking into waste policy
- Promoting more ambitious waste prevention policies, including an obligation to develop and make publicly available waste prevention programmes
- Improving knowledge and information
- Developing common reference standards for recycling and set a minimum EU standard to ensure a high level of environmental protection
- Elaborating the EU's recycling policy further.

EU waste policy is based on a concept called the waste hierarchy in which the waste treatment options are ranked from best (prevention) to worst (landfilling). Between prevention and landfilling there are several waste management options: reusing, recycling or composting the material, and recovering the energy by incineration.

Waste management options should be chosen in line with waste hierarchy: waste prevention should be used whenever possible, followed by reusing and recycling. If this is not possible, waste should be incinerated to recover energy. Landfilling should be used as a last solution. Such policy should increase resource efficiency and reduce the negative environmental and health impacts over the life cycle of resources.

The legal instruments underpinning this approach are the Waste Framework Directive (Directive 2008/98/EC), the Hazardous Waste Directive (Council

Directive 94/31/EC) and the Waste Shipment Regulation (Commission Regulation (EC) 308/2009). These framework directives are complemented by more detailed legislation setting standards for treatment options, such as landfilling (Council Directive 99/31/EC) and incineration (Directive 2000/76/EC) (see Table 4.1). Specific waste streams[1] are dealt with separately.

The reduction of the amount of waste created makes the disposal process simpler. It requires changes in industry, thus it is sector-specific. EU requirements and collection, recovery and recycling targets differ depending on the waste stream (waste oils; waste from titanium dioxide industry including the procedure for surveillance, monitoring, harmonizing and eventual elimination; agricultural use of sewage sludge, particularly soil; batteries and accumulators; packaging and packaging waste; disposal of polychlorinated biphenyls and polychlorinated terphenyls (PCB/PCT); and end-of-life vehicles (see Table 4.2).

The implementation of the principles of extended producer responsibility and polluter pays set by the Waste Framework Directive means that the cost of disposal must be borne by the holder or producer of the product. Waste management fees should enable full cost recovery, i.e. enable financing capital investment expenditure for the provision of waste management facilities and equipment and operational costs. Waste management, in accordance with waste hierarchy, should lead to decoupling of economic growth and waste production and reduce amounts of waste produced and share of waste landfilled. Targets set by EU legislation (see Tables 4.2 and 4.3) provide a basis for developing the national waste management plans.

Table 4.1 Selected EU Waste Framework and Waste Management Legislation

Directive 2008/98/EC	Waste Framework Directive, sets definitions, calls for national strategies, introduces concept of extended producer responsibility and polluter pay principle
Directive 2006/12/EC	On waste (codified version of Directive 75/442/EEC as amended)
Council Directive 91/689/EEC as amended	On hazardous waste (last amended by Directive 2008/98/EC
Regulation (EC) No 1013/2006	On the shipment of waste
Council Directive 1999/31/EC	On the landfill waste
Directive 2000/53/EC	On end-of-life vehicles
Directive 96/59EC	On the disposal of PCB and PCT
Directive 75/439/EEC	On the disposal of waste oil
Directive 91/157/EEC as amended	On batteries and accumulators
Decision 2000/532/EC	Establishing a list of wastes
Directive 2002/96/EC as amended	On waste electric and electronic equipment
Directive 94/62/EC as amended	On packaging and packaging waste
Directive 2000/76/EC	On the incineration of waste

Source: Authors' compilation

Table 4.2 EU targets on the treatment of waste

	Year	*Collection targets*	*Recovery targets*	*Recycling targets*
End-of-life vehicles	2006	100%	85%	80% including reuse
	2015	100%	95%	85% including reuse
	2005		Vehicles to be recoverable to a minimum of 95%	Vehicles be reusable and/or recyclable to a minimum of 85%
WEEE[a]	2006	Min. 4kg per inhabitant per year	70-80% depending on category of WEEE	50–80% including reuse, depending on category of WEEE
	2016 (prop)	65% of what is set on the market or 85% of waste arising		
Packaging waste	2008		60%	55% of which 50% metal, 60% glass, paper/cardboard, 22.5% plastics, 15% wood
Batteries and accumulators	2009			100% of collected batteries
	2011			65% for lead-acid batteries; 75% nickel-cadmium and 50% for others
	2012	25%		
	2016	45%		
Household paper, metal, plastic and glass waste and other similar waste	2015	Separate collection for at least paper, metal, plastics and glass		
	2020			50%
Construction and demolition	2020		70% by weight of non-hazardous waste to be prepared for re-use, recycled or recovered	
Biodegradable municipal waste	2006/2010	Reduction to 75% of 1995 landfill levels		
	2009/2013	Reduction to 50% of 1995 landfill levels		
	2016/2020	Reduction to 35% of 1995 landfill levels		
Tyres	2006		Zero landfill	

Source: European Commission, 2010

Note: (a) Waste electrical and electronics equipment

Table 4.3 Targets for landfill waste

Year (baseline 1995)	*Target*	*Biodegradable tonnes allowed in landfilling (baseline 2,247,500)*	*Biodegradable tonnes allowed in kg/person (baseline 268)*
2010	75%	1,685,625	224
2013	50%	1,123,750	152
2020	35%	786,625	109

Source: Council Directive 99/31/EC of 26 April 1999 on landfill waste

The national waste management plan/programme is the cornerstone of any national, regional or local policy on waste management. It takes stock of the existing situation (see Table 4.4), defines the objectives that need to be met in the future, formulates appropriate strategies and identifies the necessary implementation means, including sources of financing.

In principle, there are two broad ways of recovering costs of waste management: through tariffs (user charges) which are paid by users of the services, and through charges levied on a specific product or activity, where the resulting revenues are earmarked for waste management (Baltzar *et al.*, 2009: 72). Even though implementation instruments should enable covering the long-term costs of waste management, they should consider local economic conditions, primarily affordability.

National plans and financing

Slovenia

The present state

In the period 2002–2008 the quantity of waste generated in Slovenia increased by 55 per cent, reaching 7 million tonnes a year.[2] Despite this, there is significant progress towards prevention and recycling. According to the EEA, the recovery of waste has risen by 74 per cent since 2002. The system for breaking down end-of-life vehicles was established in 2004 and enabled reaching 80 per cent target levels of reuse and recycling of vehicles and 85 per cent reuse and recovery of tyres in 2006 and 2007. According to the EEA, 68 per cent of the waste was recovered in 2008.[3] The recovery rate varies depending on waste streams: 77 per cent of waste from manufacturing and services, 53 per cent of packaging waste, 47 per cent of hazardous waste and 29 per cent of municipal waste is recovered (EEA, 2010d). The greatest concern for Slovenia is municipal waste management, as more than 70 per cent of waste produced (900,000 tonnes per years, see Table 4.4) is still dumped (Vukadin and Polanec, 2009).

Table 4.4 GDP and generated waste of focus countries

Country	*Measure*	*2004*	*2006*	*2008*
Bulgaria	GDP (million euro)	19,614	24,770	32,677
	Generated waste (tonnes)	263,428,134	255,255,122	286,092,936
	Solid municipal waste (tonnes)	3,672,520	3,445,860	3,567,991
	Municipal waste generation per capita (kg/capita)	471	446	467
Romania	GDP (million euro)	57,040	86,086	133,895
	Generated waste (tonnes)	371,503,400	344,424,713	189,322,889
	Solid municipal waste (tonnes)	7,483,400	8,392,070	8,223,936
	Municipal waste generation per capita (kg/capita)	345	388	382
Slovenia	GDP (million euro)	26,956	30,412	35,817
	Generated waste (tonnes)	5,770,505	6,035,827	5,038,401
	Solid municipal waste (tonnes)	832,830	865,620	922,713
	Municipal waste generation per capita (kg/capita)	417	432	459
Croatia	GDP (million euro)	31,496	37,808	44,321
	Generated waste (tonnes)	7,208,688	n.a	4,172,152
	Solid municipal waste (tonnes))	1,311,450	1,655,179	1,789,279
	Municipal waste generation per capita (kg/capita)	295	373	403
Turkey	GDP (million euro)	293,454	413,610	446,335
	Generated waste (tonnes)	58,820,312	46,091,628	64,770,223
	Solid municipal waste (tonnes)	29,736,190	30,081,820	30,210,918
	Municipal waste generation per capita (kg/capita)	421	415	428

Source: Eurostat, 2011

Policy and regulations

Waste management policy and regulations are mostly based on the Environmental Protection Act which introduced polluter pays principle in 2004. The introduction of this principle has given rise to a significant source of financing environmental protection policy measures.

The Environmental Protection Act defines the responsibility of municipal authorities for the organization, management and maintenance of waste management facilities. Local communities are responsible for decisions on the management of solid waste (in accordance with strategies and legislative framework).

Based on the Environmental Protection Act, the National Environmental Action Plan (NEAP) 2005–2012 was developed and incorporates the provision of a strategic guidance for protecting the environment. Waste and industrial pollution is one of the four topics included in the NEAP.

The framework or basic regulation governing waste is the Decree on the Management of Waste, which regulates waste management, the conditions for carrying out collection, transport, trading, recovery, its disposal, classification list and the reporting obligations to the EC. These rules are supplemented by several subsidiary groups of regulations: regulations governing individual types of waste (e.g. management of waste oils, packaging and packaging waste, batteries), regulations governing facilities and equipment for waste management (disposal and incineration) and regulations on the transboundary shipment of waste. In 2011 a new legislative package for municipal waste management was prepared to redress the current state of municipal waste management. The package includes the Decree on the management of municipal waste, Decree on waste dumps, Decree dealing with the setting of prices for utility services in charge of environmental protection in individual municipalities and transferring the responsibility for waste management to municipalities, and an action plan. The Decree on the management of municipal waste deals with its collection, processing and disposal. It stipulates the responsibilities of the producer of municipal waste with regard to the separate collection at source. The new features include the provision on mandatory door-to-door separate waste collection for packaging waste and biological waste, using recycling bins only for collecting glass and paper, and the introduction of separate collections at least for paper, metal and plastic packaging and kitchen waste in public institutions and companies. The Decree also introduces quotas for separate waste collections for municipalities. The Decree on waste dumps sets limits for emissions resulting from waste disposal and outlines the rules for planning, construction and management of waste disposal facilities, as well as procedures after their closure.

The Public Utilities Act defines method, subject and conditions for the provision of the public utility service of waste management. More specific provisions are organized into three clusters: legislation concerning different kinds of waste; legislation on waste recovery/disposal, and legislation on monitoring of emissions from certain methods of waste disposal.

Institutions

The main actors in the field of solid waste are the Ministry of the Environment and Spatial Planning (MESP); local communities (municipalities); local public utilities and other companies; and the Environmental Agency of the Republic of Slovenia. The Nuclear Safety Administration is responsible for the issues concerning radioactive waste management. The Inspectorate for the Environment and Spatial Planning is responsible for waste management inspection and monitoring.

The responsibility of the MESP is to set up the legislative framework for waste management and national waste management plans for specific waste groups.[4] The MESP also supports regional cooperation among local communities and public local or regional utilities for building up regional waste management centres. Municipalities and municipal administrations in Slovenia are responsible for the organization, management and maintenance of waste management facilities. They play an important role in the management of public utilities and local public environmental protection services. Currently there is no regional administration, but Slovene territory is planned to be covered by 15 regional waste management centres with sorting, composting, processing and (regional) landfill facilities. In one (or two) regional centres municipal solid waste incinerator(s) will be constructed. Therefore it is of great importance that municipalities cooperate in addressing common problems. The introduction of an administration at a regional level will result in decentralization and transfer of responsibilities for solving environmental problems from the national to the regional level, so municipalities will have to transfer those tasks which they cannot or are unwilling to carry out to the regional level. Only a few municipalities have applied an active environmental protection policy and they continued to do so after the reform of local self-government. Municipal policy is generally restricted to the construction of local (public utility) infrastructure.

The Environmental Agency is responsible for the implementation of waste legislation, waste management information system development and maintaining, licensing in the waste management field including shipment of waste, monitoring and reporting of data on wastes and waste management. Municipalities manage municipal solid waste.

There are some specialized companies dealing with the preparation of waste and recycling of separately collected waste; there are also some publicly served private partners with concessions for the collection of waste for settlements and partly for the production sector. Most of the separately collected waste in such organized systems consists of: paper, cardboard, coloured and iron metal, some plastics and partly glass products.

Financing

The Costing Assessment for the Slovenian Environmental Approximation Strategy was prepared in 1998. The cost of achieving the environmental objectives in waste management sectors was estimated at €1,118 million (Slovenian Ministry of Environmental and Spatial Planning, 2003). The state budget was expected to cover 68 per cent of costs, municipal and private budgets 27.24 per cent, and 4.76 per cent was expected to be covered by EU funds. Table 4.5 shows financial plans for the management of waste in Slovenia listed in the NEAP of Slovenia for the period up to 2003, before its accession to the EU.

Table 4.5 Annual Slovenian budget for waste management 1999–2003

Measure	*Annual budget (million euros)*
Management of urban and similar waste	50
Management of waste generated in certain sectors	23

Source: Slovenian Ministry of the Environment and Physical Planning, 1999

According to the NEAP, it was planned to invest €365 million over the period 1999–2003, and €200 million during 2005–2008 (see Table 4.6). That is, in the period until 2008 about 50 per cent of necessary funds for waste management were planned. Income received from paid taxes and charges provided almost a half of sources for financing.

The waste taxes include waste water pollution tax (introduced in 1996), landfill tax (introduced in 2001) defined annually by municipalities for different types of waste (see Table 4.7), end-of-life vehicle tax (€0.04/kg, applied for new vehicles) or waste disposal tax.

Waste charges are applied in accordance with the polluter pays principle, proportionally to the amount of waste generated. Consistent with the increasing quantities of waste generated, increasing incomes received from paid charges

Table 4.6 Slovenian financial plan for programmes related to waste management 2005–2008, in million euros

Programme	*Financial source*	*2005*	*2006*	*2007*	*2008*
Waste disposal (excluding thermal treatment plants)	Waste dumping tax	14.61	16.69	25.04	25.04
	Budget	3.34	3.34	3.34	3.34
	EU	16.69	16.69	16.69	16.69
Management of waste oils (rehabilitation of old loads)	Waste oil tax	1.42	2.92	3.34	3.76
Management of end-of-life motor vehicles	Tax on end-of-life vehicles	2.30	3.76	5.00	5.84
Management of WEEE	Tax on WEEE	0.83	2.09	2.92	4.17
Total		39.19	45.49	56.33	58.84

Source: Resolution on the National Environmental Action Programme 2005–2012, 2005. Original currency is SIT, converted by author to EUR using the fixed rate of SIT239.64/€1 published in the Central Bank of Slovenia based on the decision of the Council.

Table 4.7 Waste charges in Slovenia

	Existing charges for handling/disposal by public service in Slovenia
Bio municipal waste	€0.04–0.09/kg
Other waste (organic and inorganic fractions)	€0.03–0.09/kg
households	€6.3–9.5/m^3
enterprises	€20/m^3
Processing of waste	
biowaste	€22.6/t
sludge	€62/t

Source: Gobec and De Sutter, 2006

and taxes were identified as a relevant source of financing programmes related to waste management in the period 2005–2008 (see Table 4.6).[5]

Table 4.6 presents the financial plan for several programmes in the waste management sector, financed from the national budget, EU funds and income from taxes and charges during 2005–2008. For the period 2007–2013 financial plans are developed on the basis of the Strategic Reference Framework and Operational Programme (OP) 'Development of environment and transport infrastructure'. According to the Strategic Reference Framework, the financially intensive priority investments – regional waste management centres and two incinerators for municipal waste – are planned to be co-financed from the EC programmes to the amount of €204 million, while the landfill issue is predicted to be solved by national funds amounting to only €98 million (in total €302 million).

The OP 'Development of environment and transport infrastructure' 2007–2013 will finance municipal waste management for €36 million (national contribution is included) (see Table 4.8).

With the implementation of the OP on eliminating waste aimed at the reduction of the quantity of biodegradable waste disposal, Slovenia, in terms of substance, created the right foundation for municipal waste management. This has enabled it to become a recycling society that is economically efficient and environment friendly. However, the instruments which were put in place within the programme and associated decrees were not in themselves efficient and clear enough to direct waste streams from disposal to recovery, to increase the recycling rate and improve its technology and to increase composting and energy recovery of waste. Necessary investment in the period 2007–2013 is estimated at €427 million (see Table 4.8), and together with €377.7 million invested in the period 1999–2006 (Table 4.9) reaches a total of €804.7 million, i.e. 72 per cent of 1999 estimate. This is also hard to reach, as the financial gap is estimated at €391 million (see Table 4.8).

Table 4.8 Summary of investment cost in waste sector 2007–2013, in million euros

	Indicative investment cost 2007–2013
Waste collection, sorting, recycling and composting	120
Disposal	302
Cooperation and capacity building for municipalities	5
Total	427
OP Environment: Waste, 2007–2013	36
Financial GAP	391

Source: Authors' calculations based on Tonchevski and Lust, 2006

Table 4.9 Priority investments in Slovenia, defined by the action plan in municipal waste management sector 1999–2006

Source of funding	*€ million*
PHARE and ISPA (1999–2003)	10.97
Cohesion Fund (2004–2006)	36.00
National funds	330.53
All sources of funding	377.50

Source: Gobec and De Sutter, 2006

Bulgaria

The present state

According to Eurostat, (2011) Bulgarian annual gross waste output amounts to more than 286 million metric tonnes. During the period 1999–2003, 3.23 thousand tonnes of municipal waste was collected and deposited in municipal landfills or approximately 500kg per capita. In 2008 the annual quantity of generated waste was 3.567 thousand tonnes and per capita amounted to 467kg (see Table 4.4).

Almost all (around 97 per cent in the period 2004–2008) waste generated is landfilled. In most cases landfill sites have already reached their maximum capacity. Of that, 20 per cent is disposed of in an uncontrollable way. Despite the efforts to build modern regional landfills meeting the European Union safety standards – adequate sealing, geological barrier, minimization of nuisances and hazards, etc. – the existing 3,000 illegal dump sites and areas polluted with waste are a serious problem for the country. Incineration is not a common practice and not used for municipal waste.

The municipal waste collection system covers 93 per cent of the population (up from 80 per cent in 2005 (EEA, 2010). Transportation of waste presents a problem for the municipal authorities that face serious challenges related to increased transport distances to the new regional disposal facility.

Bulgaria has reached the EU targets for recovery and recycling of end-of-life vehicles: in 2006 Bulgaria recovered a total of 87.24 per cent of the end-of-life vehicles (EU target 85 per cent) and recycled and reused 82.35 per cent of all waste vehicles (EU target 80 per cent).

Policy and regulations

Bulgarian waste management policy is based on EU requirements, with some transitional arrangements concerning electrical and electronic waste (until 2008), shipment of waste (until 2009), recovery and recycling of packaging waste (until 2014), landfill of certain liquid waste (until 2014).[6]

The national framework is set by the Environmental Protection Act and by secondary legislation in the field of waste. Policy implementation is governed by the National Strategy for Environment 2005–2014 and the Action Plan 2005–2009, national waste management programmes, specific strategies (National Strategic Plan for Gradual Reduction of Biodegradable Waste for Disposal 2010–2020, the National Infrastructural Sustainable Development Strategy and action plan for the period 2006–2015) and implementation plans for specific directives (e.g. Plan for Implementation of Directive 1999/31/EC on Landfill of Waste, the Implementation Programme for the Directive on packaging and packaging waste).

The First National Waste Management Programme (NWMP) was developed for the period 2003–2007 and the Second National Waste Management Programme for the period 2009–2013. It defines a long-term sustainable waste management strategy and a framework of decision making in compliance with the EU legislation and policy. Moreover, it applies a hierarchical cost for the financial plan of the treatment of different kinds of waste whose goal is to maximize the implementation of the low cost treatment and to minimize expensive treatments:

- low cost group treatments amount to less than €50 per tonne of waste (municipal green waste composting; paper collection; and agricultural use of sewage sludge)
- medium cost treatments amount to €50–90 per tonne of waste (biowaste collection and sewage sludge treatment by incineration)
- high cost treatments amount to more than €90 per tonne of waste (incineration of mixed waste).

It also introduced landfill tax which is calculated by the weight of the waste to be landfilled, increasing from €10 per tonne in 2008 to €20 per tonne in 2012. The income received from the landfill tax is to be used to promote various kinds of waste management activities and rectify improper landfill sites.

The National Strategic Plan for Gradual Reduction of Biodegradable Waste for Disposal (2010–2020) provides for an establishment of green yard waste composting systems – especially in bigger cities, establishment of paper collection systems, and the development of incineration systems. Introduction of green waste composting systems and paper recycling systems is necessary to meet quantitative targets imposed by the Landfill Directive for the period 2010–2013.[7] Thus, the development of backyard household composting is promoted and training provided. However, meeting the targets for 2020 will require more than composting. Introduction of incineration and/or biological treatment will be necessary.[8]

The National Infrastructural Sustainable Development Strategy and Action Plan for the period 2006–2015 set the following goals:

- practical implementation of EU standards for all operational waste treatment facilities and construction of new ones
- development and construction of national hazardous waste infrastructure

- separate municipal waste collection systems with subsequent reuse and recycling.

Obligations of the manufacturers and importers of batteries, vehicles, pneumatic tyres and packages to organize collection, use and/or disposal of waste from these products supports separate collection and subsequent reuse and recycling.

Institutions

The Ministry of Environment and Water is the competent authority responsible for the development and implementation of the national waste management policy. The mayors of 264 municipalities organize the management of the waste generated in their area according to the requirements of the Waste Management Act (adopted in 2003 and last amended in 2008). They are obliged to develop and implement waste management programmes for the respective municipality's region. The programmes are part of the municipal programmes for environmental protection and are developed, adopted and reported following the order defined in Environmental Protection Act (adopted in 2002 and last amended in 2007).

The Enterprise for the Management of Environment Protection Activities (EMEPA) (up to 2003 – National Environment Protection Fund) collects specific environmental fees (such as a fee for placing batteries or tyres on the market) which are used for financing separate waste collection.

Financing

In the pre-accession period (2000–2006) roughly €300 million was invested in the waste sector, mainly from national sources (state and municipal budgets); ISPA funding provided around €100 million and the European Investment Bank €90 million (see Table 4.10).

Almost €190 million was spent to comply with the Landfill Directive which was followed by investment in hazardous waste management (€7 million) (Sectoral OP Environment, 2007). Necessary investments for the implementation on NWMP for the period 2003–2007 were estimated at €407 million (see Table 4.11).

Table 4.10 Bulgaria's investments in the waste sector in the pre-accession period 2000–2006

Source of funding	*EUR (million)*
EU–ISPA	97.066
EIB	90.254
National funds	100.000
All sources of funding	287.320

Source: Authors' calculations, based on Tonchevski and Lust, 2006

Table 4.11 Bulgaria's waste sector investments and investment needs 2003–2007

Groups of investment projects		
1	Construction of regional landfills for municipal waste	136,609
2	Closure of existing landfills for municipal waste, served by organized municipal waste collection system	17,212
3	Cleaning up and elimination of illegal dump sites	9,625
4	Investments for treatment of construction and demolition waste	2,000
5	Construction of the National Hazardous Waste Treatment Centre	43,648
6	Healthcare waste	11,473
	6.1 Construction of incinerators	
	Sofia	2,150
	Plovdiv	3,413
	Varna	3,413
	Pleven	2,500
	6.2 Autoclave facilities	3,000
7	Completion of the national laboratory system for waste	1,275
8	Facilities for treatment of biodegradable municipal waste	
	Pre-treatment and composting	9,547
	Home composting	1,560
9	Past contaminations with hazardous waste at the territory of enterprises	20,443
10	Storage of obsolete pesticides	2,500
11	Organization of system for municipal waste collection and transportation	57,060
12	System for separate collection of packaging and packaging waste	70,000
13	Wood waste	1,500
14	End-of-life vehicles	
	Storage	4,750
	Dismantling	10,000
	Shredding	5,000
Total for the programme		407,203

Source: National Waste Management Programme 2003–2007

To a large extent, the NWMP 2003–2007 reduced the necessary financial resources: the implementation of the Landfill Directive (Council Directive 99/31/EC) alone would require investments of €737 million (compared with €407 million for the total programme). However, there were insufficient funds for implementation.

For the period 2009–2013, it is necessary to invest at least €930 million (according to the NWMP) (see Table 4.12).

Table 4.12 Bulgaria's required investment for waste management 2009–2013, in thousand euros

	Groups of investment projects	*Investments*					*Total NWMP*
		2009	*2010*	*2011*	*2012*	*2013*	
1	Construction of waste facilities	49,500	59,500	74,500	45,000	48,500	277,000
2	Closure of existing landfills	5,000	20,000	20,000	15,000	0	60,000
3	Cleaning and elimination of illegal dumps	5,000	0	0	0	0	5,000
4	Investment for the treatment of construction waste and waste from demolition	2,500	2,500	5,000	5,000	5,000	20,000
5	Construction of the National Centre for Hazardous waste disposal	0	1,000	1,000	18,000	17,500	37,500
6	Waste from hospitals	6,813	4,812	4,312	1,312	0	17,250
7	Completion of the national laboratory system for waste	2,000	0	0	0	0	2,000
8	Construction of facilities for treatment of biodegradable waste	3,229	2,324	2,324	2,029	2,034	11,938
9	Past contaminations with hazardous waste at the territory of enterprises	6,000	6,000	6,000	6,000	6,000	30,000
10	Storage of obsolete pesticides	500	500	500	500	500	2,500
11	Upgrading system for collecting and transport of waste	2,000	2,000	2,000	2,000	2,000	10,000
12	Completion of the management of specific waste streams	0	0	0	0	0	0
13	Wood waste	250	250	250	500	500	1,750
14	Construction of facilities for the integrated treatment of household hazardous waste	6,500	6,500	6,500	6,500	6,500	32,500
Total		189,150	215,230	189,190	173,000	158,036	929,149

Source: Authors' calculations based on National Waste Management Programme 2009–2013: 143–4, €1=BGN2

Based on the programmes for the implementation of key directives, investment needs are estimated at €1,600 million (OP Environment, 2007). These investments are mainly to be financed from national sources – €450 million is planned from state budget/EMEPA, €440 million from economic operators, based on the polluter pays principle, €336 million is programmed in OP Environment, and €26 million is expected to be financed from ISPA or other donors (see Table 4.13). Financing gap is €335 million, i.e. 20 per cent of investment needs.

Improvement and development of waste treatment infrastructure should enable compliance with the EU legislation. To this end, programmed investments include:

- 54 investment projects for reconstruction of existing and construction of new regional landfills for disposal of municipal waste
- optimize and enlarge existing systems for municipal waste collection and transportation
- develop the system of separate collection of packages and other recyclable waste

Table 4.13 Planned sources of funding in Bulgaria's waste sector until 2015, in million euros

	Investment needs 2007–2015	*Sources of funding*				
		ISPA/ Other donors	*OP Env*	*State/ EMEPA*	*Economic operators PPP*	*Total funding*
Implementation of Landfill Directive (Directive 99/31/EC)	862	24	353	253	233	863
Implementation of hazardous waste directive (91/689/EEC)	113	2	15	15	80	112
End of life vehicles (Directive 2000/53/EC)	141	0	0	0	0	0
PBD/PCT (Directive 96/59/EC)	185	0	0	0	185	185
Waste oils (Directive 75/439/EEC)	23	0	0	0	0	0
Accumulators (Directive 91/157/EEC)	21	0	0	0	0	0
Electric and electronic waste (Directive 2002/96/EC)	150	0	0	0	0	0
Packaging (Directive 94/62/EC)	128	0	0	1	128	129
Total	1,623	26	368	269	626	1,289

Source: Authors' calculations, based on OP Environment 2007–2013, 2007

- finalize construction of National Hazardous Waste Disposal Centre
- close all the incompliant landfills
- initiate a system for separate collection and utilization of green and food waste
- build up 1–2 incinerators for biological and hazardous waste.

The necessary investments for optimization and enlargement of the existing systems for municipal waste collection and transportation are estimated at €69 million. The amount of the investment is determined by the experience for investments at an average of €8 per inhabitant served population (Tonchevski and Lust, 2006). The necessary financing will be provided equally by the municipal budgets, EMEPA and by private investors.

Necessary financial resources for the construction of additional capacity for recycling and/or recovery of packaging waste should be provided by the private sector. The total amount of the necessary investments for supply and erection of equipment for recovery of wood waste is valued at €1.6 million. Installations will be financed through interest-free loans at 70 per cent of investments to be allotted by EMEPA through tendering. The regional composting installation will be part of the regional municipal waste landfills and investment for their construction will be provided by ISPA. The funding of the projects for home composting will be provided by EMEPA.

It is envisaged that the state budget will provide the necessary funding for the closure of existing landfills for municipal waste. According to evaluations made by the municipal administrations, the total costs for closing the dump sites and for the sanitation of past waste contaminations, are estimated at €10 million and these costs will be borne by the municipal budgets.

Investments for the construction of new regional landfills that meet the legal requirements are to be financed by grants, the state budget, EMEPA and bilateral projects. The state budget provided about €20–25 million annually up to 2007 and should also provide €13–16 million a year in the period 2008–2015 to finance the programme. While investments from the state budget are decreasing, participation of municipalities increases. Municipalities financed waste management with €4–6 million a year until 2007, and €9–10 million a year in 2008 and 2009. The state environment fund would be expected to provide a relatively small amount (€1–2 million per annum), as well as the private sector (see Table 4.12).

Romania

The present state

Uncontrolled dump sites, official landfills that do not comply with minimum environmental requirements (less than 10 per cent of the landfills respect the environmental regulations),[9] the discharge into waterways, rudimentary collection and transport of waste within the cities and uncontrolled burning of waste create major environmental and health problems in Romania. Moreover, hazardous waste is often not separated from inert or household waste, leading to serious pollution from inadequately protected landfills.

There is a general lack of adequate facilities to properly treat and dispose of existing waste streams. Waste recycling and recovery is almost non-existent (over 99 per cent of total municipal water is landfilled, 0.25 per cent of collected municipal waste is reused); and there is a lack of public awareness regarding household waste management. On the positive side, the amount of waste produced has not grown alongside the growth in GDP (see Table 4.4).

In 2008 the annual quantity of generated waste was 182 million tonnes, the majority being from mining. Municipal waste production was 8.2 million tonnes (382kg per capita). Recyclable materials account for about 40 per cent of the municipal waste, 20 per cent of which can be recovered provided it is not contaminated. However, only 2 per cent of the total recyclable materials generated is recovered and the rest is landfilled.

Biodegradable waste represents about 61 per cent of municipal waste generated in Romania. It is estimated that between 650,000 and 1,000,000 tonnes of biodegradable waste can be collected per year, and according to the Landfill Directive (Council Directive 99/31/EC), by 2013 Romania should treat 1,400 tonnes of biodegradable waste per year. Romania does not have the necessary experience for separate collection of organic waste and composting plants. Thus, pilot stations for biodegradable waste composting were set up, which should facilitate Landfill Directive targets to be met. Also, the system of separate collection of waste (primarily paper, cardboard, PET, and glass) is being established, enabling recycling and/or recovering the waste from the collection points.

Policies and regulations

In accordance with the EU waste framework requirements, the Ministry of Environment prepared the National Waste Management Strategy for 2003–2013 and the NWMP for 2004–2009. The NWMP presents analysis of waste management, prevention measures for waste production and for reducing its quantity, recycling methods and the list of monitoring indicators. Its aim is the establishment of the integrated waste management system, efficient from an economic and ecologic point of view. It deals with municipal and industrial (hazardous and non-hazardous) waste.

Each region (and each county within the region) had prepared regional waste management plans, dealing with municipal waste. All eight regional plans were adopted in 2006 (Joint Ministerial Order of MEWM and Ministry of Integration 1364/1499 from 2006). These plans transpose, at regional level, the objectives for the National Waste Management Plan. The plans provide for gradual alignment with EU legislation by 2017, in line with negotiated transition periods. This means that the percentage of population served by sanitation companies should increase to 84 per cent in 2013 and 100 per cent by 2017 (up from 54 per cent in 2009), increase the waste recovery and recycling to 60 per cent and 55 per cent respectively by 2012. The latest available data show that in 2008 less than 10 per cent of municipal waste was revered, one of the reasons being limited selective collection of 4 per cent (Larive Romania IBD SRL, 2011).

Institutions

Responsibility for waste management is shared between central government and local public administration authorities. The Ministry of Environment develops national strategies, policies and initiates or approves legal standards in the waste management field. Its specialized body, the National Environmental Guard is responsible for inspection and control.

The National Environmental Protection Agency (NEPA) is a technical body subordinated to the Ministry of Environment and is responsible for coordinating and monitoring the implementation of legislation in the waste management field. It provides technical support for the initiation of legal standards and norms. There are also eight regional and 42 county environmental protection agencies, subordinated to NEPA. County agencies collect primary information related to waste generation and management and carry out, at the county level, NEPA's responsibilities, while regional agencies accomplish NEPA's responsibilities at the regional level.

Municipalities are responsible for the collection and management of municipal waste. Industrial waste generators are responsible for the environmental sound management of their waste.

Financing

Compliance with the EU policy on waste management requires substantial investment and a long-term approach (the longest transition period for waste sector lasts until 2017). In the pre-accession period (2000–2006) significant investment (e.g. €147 million for nine projects with a solid waste component) was supported by EU programmes (primarily ISPA).

The investment needs for waste management in the 2007–2013 period is estimated between €1.7 and €2.4 billion, of which roughly €1 billion has been allocated (between €750 and €934 million from EU funds).[10] The investment will mainly target the improvement of municipal waste management practice, which was identified as the most critical area in the EU Accession Treaty (see Table 4.14).

Table 4.14 Indicative investment needs, waste sector Romania 2007–2013, in million euros

	Indicative investment cost 2007–2013
Waste collection	137
Waste sorting	0
Recovery	46
Disposal	1,400
Total	1,686
OP Environment: Waste (2007–2013)	1,167
Financial gap	520

Source: Authors' calculations, based on GHK, Rojanschi. and Lust, 2006: 75 and Sectoral OP: Environment 2007–2013, 2007: 100

The European Regional Development Fund (ERDF) is expected to support implementation of 15 counties' solid waste integrated management programmes. Estimated investment cost is €25–30 million per project. It is planned that €1,168 million will be invested until 2012 (80 per cent from the ERDF and 20 per cent national contribution) in development of integrated waste management systems and reduction of historically contaminated sites.

The total market for waste management equipment and technology was conservatively estimated at €50 million in 2008. After the crisis, the market is expected to increase to about €80 million by 2017 (Larive Romania IBD SRL, 2011). However, there is the significant matter of affordability that prevents more significant investment and full implementation of the polluter pays principle, e.g. waste charges in Romania are gradually increasing, having reached €8–12 per tonne, and are higher in more developed cities and areas with higher income per inhabitant (GHK Rojanschi and Lust, 2006). The charges are negotiated between the operator (mostly private companies) and the local administration. They are collected either directly by the operator from users of the services, or the operator is paid by the municipality, which collects taxes. The level of taxes is sufficient to cover the operational costs of the operator, but not for investments, and the collection of charges is also deficient. Also, environmental taxes (e.g. taxes for the use of land for storing recyclable waste, approximately €0.5 per kg of packages, eco-tax of €0.02 per unit for bags made of non-biodegradable materials, and €0.5 per kg of oil waste generated) (Danuletiu and Teiusan, 2007) collected by the Romanian Environmental Fund, do not present sufficient source of financing environmental problems.

Croatia

The present state

Despite growing awareness of the need to avoid and reduce increasing waste, the quantities of municipal waste (household waste and similar waste from manufacturing and services) continued to grow and in 2008 amounted to 1,788,311 tonnes or annually 403kg per capita (1.1kg per day, see Table 4.4).

The ratio of urban population covered by a solid waste management system was 93 per cent in 2009. Separate collection of municipal waste started to develop in Croatia in the second half of the 1980s using containers (paper, glass, PET, tin cans) and recycling yards. The amount of separately collected types of municipal waste is continually growing and in 2008 accounted for 14 per cent (247,252 tonnes). Only part of this quantity ends up being recovered, while the majority is landfilled.

The average percentage of municipal biodegradable waste amounts to about 70 per cent (42 per cent kitchen and biowaste and 20 per cent paper and cardboard). However, the system for further decreasing biodegradable waste deposited on landfills is not yet fully operational.

Policy and regulations

The Strategy for Sustainable Development (Croatian Ministry of Environmental Protection, Physical Planning and Construction, 2009) sets objectives, measures and activities by which the objectives of waste prevention should be achieved. Besides this Strategy, the main policy documents regarding waste management at the national level are the Waste Management Strategy 2005–2025 and the Waste Management Plan 2007–2015. Regional authorities (counties and City of Zagreb, towns, municipalities), as well as waste producers producing more than 150 tonnes of non-hazardous waste or more than 200 kilograms of hazardous waste per year, also have to prepare a waste management plan.

Rules governing implementation are defined by the Waste Act (last amended in 2009) and ordinances dealing with specific waste streams. A number of instruments have been established for the prevention/reduction of waste, including:

- Economic instruments for certain waste streams management or for burdening the environment (cars, tyres, household appliances, and electrical and electronic devices).
- Obligation to prepare waste management plans (national, regional, local level and selected waste producers).
- Construction/improvement of the separate waste collection and recycling systems for certain waste streams (biodegradable waste, paper, packaging paper, medical, construction waste, electronic waste, batteries, PET).
- Croatian waste exchange (within Croatian Chamber of Economy).
- Promotion of cleaner production projects and practices (mainly through activities of Croatian Centre for Cleaner Production and by co-financing activities by EPEFF).
- Education in the field of waste management (preschool, school, higher education programmes, scientific journals, international symposia).

Institutions

The Ministry of Environmental Protection, Physical Planning and Construction (MEPPPC) is the central body responsible for the waste sector at the national level, as well as for hazardous waste management and for incineration of waste. It is in charge of preparing waste management legislation, national waste management strategy and waste management plan, as well as the coordination of cooperation among all involved institutions in waste management in Croatia. The control over the implementation of the legal regulations and prevention of uncontrolled environmental pollution, including the Waste Act and by-laws, is conducted by the Environmental Protection Inspection at the MEPPPC.

Regional governments (20 counties and the City of Zagreb) are responsible for the management of all types of waste, apart from hazardous. They are obliged to draft waste management plans, alone or in cooperation with other counties, and form joint regional waste management companies to operate regional waste management centres. Locations in physical plans are determined at regional level.

Regional authorities also issue permits for non-hazardous and inert waste landfills, ensure conditions and implementation of measures for managing different waste streams, issue permits for municipal and non-hazardous waste management, and collect data on waste.

The Croatian Environment Agency is a public institution responsible for the collection and consolidation of waste data, developing and maintaining the waste management information system, enabling and facilitating access to information on waste to decision makers and the general public, developing reports on the status of the waste sector.

Croatian Environmental Protection and Energy Efficiency Fund is an extra-budgetary institution owned by the Republic of Croatia, the purpose of which is to finance environmental protection programmes and projects. Among others, it co-finances projects on waste prevention and projects for improving separate collections for certain waste types. The Fund collects different environmental charges as its own revenue, which includes charges for burdening the environment with hazardous and non-hazardous industrial waste and pays charges within specific schemes for waste streams collection/recovery.

Financing

The total investments needed in the waste sector for the period 2005–2025 are estimated at €3.25 billions (see Table 4.15). During the period 2007–2009, allocated financing sources for waste management amounted to €8.8 millions, out of which 75 per cent was financed from EU funds, and 25 per cent from national contribution.

Table 4.15 Croatia waste sector: investment needs and potential sources of financing 2005–2025, in million euros

	Indicative investment cost 2005–2025
Waste sector general measure	70
Municipal waste	2,262
Other type of waste	920
Total (2005–2025)	3,252
National budget	975
EPEEF[a]	325
County level budget	163
Municipality budget	163
IPA OP Environment waste (2007–2009)	8.8
Total (2006–2015)	1,634.8
Financial gap (2015–2025)	1,617.2

Source: Strategy of Waste Management in the Republic of Croatia, 2005

Note

a Environmental Protection and Energy Efficiency Fund (Croatia)

Depending on the number of regional waste management centres (21 or fewer), the assessed investments will range from €350–400 million in order to bring the landfills to operational level. The closing of old dump sites is a precondition for establishment of new waste management centres.

Financing the construction of regional waste management centres is envisaged through public sources (state budget, budgets of local and regional self-government units, EU funds, the Environmental Protection and Energy Efficiency Fund,[11] bank loans) as well as private sources (private investment in waste management centres, public-private partnership, concessions, primary separation and collection of waste, recycling and collecting plants/facilities).

It is planned that up to 80 per cent of costs for the construction of regional waste management centres (estimated at €20–60 million, depending on the size of the region) will be financed from EU funds and Environmental Protection and Energy Efficiency Fund, and 20 per cent by local authorities. Bank loans will be used for the establishment of a collection system and for the construction of the municipal waste disposal system at regional/local level. In the second phase, the cost of mechanical biological treatment plants is expected to be financed by the private sector (private public partnership) and if possible, the public sector.

The tariffs for collection, transportation, and disposal of municipal waste are based on living or commercial surface calculations. Tariffs for commercial spaces are higher than tariffs for households and intended to subsidize them. However, the current level of revenues is not sufficient and local authorities often co-finance waste management operational costs from their budget. Regional waste management centres, once operational, are expected to charge tariffs reflecting true costs and calculated on quantities of produced waste.

Turkey

The present state

Increasing waste volumes due to population growth, technological development, industrialization and urbanization present a potential threat for public health and the environment. The most common method of waste disposal, especially for municipal waste, is landfilling. In 2008 a total of 30.2 million tonnes of municipal waste was collected; 12.7 million tonnes was directly disposed into landfills and 300,000 tonnes were treated in composting facilities (see Table 4.4).

The production of municipal waste has increased (see Table 4.16) but the amount of municipal waste produced per capita has decreased from 1.21kg per person per day in 2005 to 1.15kg per person per day in 2008 (around 428kg per capita a year), indicating that population growth is a significant driver of environmental pressures. The ratio of overall population covered by solid waste management system was 82 per cent in 2009.

Separate collections are based on activities of individual collectors who buy used packages from sellers or collect them in the streets or from garbage containers. As a result, collection rates are rather limited and only glass and paper recycling are commercial activities.

Table 4.16 Percentage of recovery targets of Turkey

Type of package	*2007*	*2009*	*2010*	*2011*	*2012*	*2013*	*2014*
Glass	37	43	45	48	52	56	60
Plastic	37	43	45	48	52	56	60
Metal	35	42	45	48	52	56	60
Paper, cardboard	35	42	45	48	52	56	60
Batteries							
Group 1	35	65	80				
Group 2	25	35	40				

Source: Authors' compilation based on Turkish Court of Accounts, 2007: 24; and Turkish Ministry of Environment and Forestry, 2004

While formal rules are established, imposing in some cases more ambitious targets than the EU (e.g. for batteries: 25 per cent in 2006 in Turkey compared with 25 per cent in 2012 in the EU, see Tables 4.16 and 4.4) implementation is partial (in 2007 battery waste collection was below 5 per cent) indicating the need to improve monitoring and control.

Policies and regulation

Waste management strategy is based on the Five-year Development Plans, NEAP, and National Programme for the Adoption of the EU *Acquis* and the Turkish EU integrated environmental approximation strategy. Legal arrangements and national plans and programmes formed a sound basis for waste management strategy. The strategy called 'Regulation on General Principles of Waste Management' was prepared in 2008. General principles of waste management include waste hierarchy and the polluter pays principles, as well as waste prevention policies, policies on waste recovery, waste shipment and landfill policies, hazardous and medical waste policies and sanctions.

The primary goals of the waste management policy are to decrease waste production and to take necessary measures to ensure recycling, reuse and safe landfill. Special waste flows (hazardous, medical waste, waste oil, medical waste, batteries, etc.), as well as reuse, recycling, composting and generating energy from waste, is fostered by separate by-laws.[12] Quotas are introduced to producers who are liable to collect and recycle a certain percentage of these materials (see Table 4.16).

The sectors producing waste subject to quota application are encouraged to establish associations and organizations for the fight against waste and to encourage recycling (e.g. The Foundation for Environmental Protection and Reappraisal of Packaging Wastes (ÇEVKO) for packaging and Foundation of Transportable Battery Producers and Importers (TAP) for batteries).

The NWMP 2009–2013 outlines the current situation and management problems related to 12 examined waste streams and sets strategic targets. The plan includes:

- The waste legislation on which the Waste Management Action Plan is based
- Solid waste action plan for packaging wastes, medical wastes, organic waste oils, batteries and accumulators, the current situation in Turkey and targets for the period 2008–2012
- Hazardous solid waste action plan and the related legislation, the current situation, targets and disposal plan
- Solid waste action plans for different towns in Turkey.

The NWMP recognizes that it is very difficult to develop and implement a waste management model that fits all 2,951 municipalities. Thus, it suggests that the neighbouring small municipalities facing similar waste management problems collaborate on waste management. This model is called 'Union of Municipalities'. It is estimated that planning and running satisfactory solid waste management services with a sustainable cost service population shall not be less than a 300,000 within a service area of 50–60km transportation distances.

Municipality Unions develop plans regarding the establishment of landfills, reduction of solid waste, increase in recovery, reduction of the transportation cost and erecting waste transfer stations if necessary, and also to develop pilot projects for landfills and rehabilitation of old dump sites.

Institutions

The Ministry of Environment and Forestry has the power and responsibility to develop policies and strategy concerning waste management at the national level and to ensure they are implemented effectively. This includes preparation of regulations, by-laws, and national regulations, organization of nationwide actions on waste management, research, coordination of waste management plan preparation, taking precautionary measures, defining technical standards, licensing and monitoring. The Ministry also supervises institutions and establishments that dispose waste so that they do not pose a threat to the public and environment, and assesses the needs of these institutions and finds solutions for any insufficiencies. Ministry of Environment and Forestry tasks include: keeping track of given licences; data collection; exportation of wastes; release of permits regulating hazardous waste import and transportation of these wastes over Turkey; and ensuring the continuation of training. The Ministry of Health authorizes and issues licences for waste disposal areas and the Ministry of Interior directs monitors and controls local administrations. The Ministry of Finance makes arrangements related to the environmental cleanup tax. State Planning Organization is in charge of planning and programming waste. It manages investments and strategic solid waste projects and prepares sectoral plans. Moreover, the projects of central administrative institutions and the projects of municipalities that need foreign loans are appraised by State Planning Organization and those feasible are included in the public investment portfolio.

Local authorities (the metropolitan municipalities and municipalities) are responsible for implementation of the Solid Waste Management Plan. They have to ensure that solid waste is collected at source, recycled, reused or stored and removed accordingly; and to establish appropriate facilities, or to make sure that they are established by others, so that these services can be fulfilled. Producers of waste are involved in waste management: ÇEVKO is responsible for the provision of containers, boxes, collection bags and education materials to municipalities, and TAP is responsible for separate collection, storage and disposal of batteries in Turkey.

The Turkish Statistical Institute (TurkStat) is in charge of specifying standards in this sector. Iller Bank provides financing and implements projects on solid waste management. The distribution of authorities and responsibilities among institutions and organizations renders cooperation and coordination important. In practice, there is no sufficient cooperation. Also, waste management does not have an established institutional infrastructure authorized at both national and local levels. Thus, the core of the problem related to waste management is the inadequate institutional and technical capacity of responsible institutions and organizations.

Financing

Since municipalities are responsible for waste management, their financing must be provided from the municipal budget. Municipalities use 40 per cent of their budget for cleaning services including waste handling and landfilling. The tax and other revenues they receive are not adequate, thus environmental cleanup tax, applied to users of waste collection services, was introduced in 1993 (Waste Management Report, 2007). The tax per household is €11 a year.[13] It is estimated that an average household produces 1.5 tonnes of waste annually, thus €7.6 is collected per tonne, while cost per tonne is €30.4. Taxes, therefore, only cover a share of operational costs.

Full implementation of the polluter pays principle is necessary to enable financing investment. So far, the principle applies for medical waste and in areas where criminal sanctions are applied. As regards to medical waste, pricing criteria differs from one province to another. The penalty for polluting the environment ranges from TRY20 (around €8) for disposing household waste to TRY2 million (around €0.8 million) for importing or exporting hazardous waste without notification. However, despite the high level of environmental problems, the amount of fines accrued has remained low; in most of the provinces, no fine is imposed at all (Turkish Court of Accounts, 2007). As a result, investment in waste disposal facilities is expected to be financed from external sources (World Bank, Japan International Cooperation Agency, EU funds) and private sector based on build-operate and build-operate-transfer models.

In 2006 the cost of alignment with EU *acquis* for the period 2007–2023 was estimated at €9.6 billion (see Table 4.17), giving the basis for an investment plan of more than €1 billion. In 2007 the new cost estimate was published, identifying different investment priorities: €11 million for landfilling areas, €853 million for establishment of hazardous waste facilities, €74 million for the construction of shipment stations and €2.8 billion for incineration stations (Turkish Court of Accounts, 2007: 35).

In the period 2007–2009 €19 million (out of which 75 per cent was from EU funds) was earmarked for waste sector by the IPA OP Environment (see Table 4.18). For the period 2010–2013 it is expected that 30 per cent of EU Environmental Funds will be allocated to waste projects. Local administrations will co-finance the EU funded projects. Also credits from the Bank of Provinces and external institutions may be used as co-financing; 20 per cent of credits derived from the Bank of Provinces and 40 per cent of external credits will be used in waste projects.

Table 4.17 Estimated investment needs for alignment with EU acquis, 2007–2023, in million euros

	2006 estimate	*2007–2013*	*2014–2023*	*2007 estimate*
Landfill	7574	2,035	5,539	11
Packaging	655	245	409	
Incineration	1,257	317	940	2,800
Hazardous waste	74	17	57	853
Shipment stations				74
Total	9,560	2,614	6,946	3,738

Source: Turkish Ministry of Environment and Forestry 2006: 5

Table 4.18 Turkey: potential sources of financing 2007–2023, in million euros

	Indicative Investment Cost 2007–2023[a]
Solid waste sector	9,560
Total	9,560
National budget	1,128
Municipal budget	2,887
Iller Bank	1,396
External credits	398
EU+ other grants	3,751
Financial GAP	0

Source: Author's calculations

Note

a €1 is taken as TRY1.858

Conclusions

Dealing with waste management requires initially the development of organizational capacity. In all focus countries at national level, ministries of environment are responsible for policy development, while local authorities are responsible for implementation.

Local authorities often lack financial, institutional and technical capacities for effective waste management. Regional solutions are proposed but lack of coordination and cooperation among municipalities impedes implementation.

EU legislation transposed into national legal provisions requires a new approach to waste problems, based on the principles of waste hierarchy and polluter pays. While legislation on waste management has been improved, the implementation of these principles is challenging, burdened by the issue of affordability.

In all focus countries financial resources for waste sector investment are coming from various sources: national budget, local budget, private investments, EU funds and other external sources of financing. The EU support is relevant but not sufficient for financing investments.

The lack of reliable data on waste hinders estimates of necessary capacities. Thus, cost estimates and related investment plans vary considerably. To consolidate data, it is necessary to ensure a permanent and functional flow of information among organizations and entities at different levels of responsibilities.

The recycling business is recognized as an alternative source of financing waste management. However, selection of waste at source is still not sufficiently developed in focus countries to fully exploit its potential.

The involvement of the private sector will coincide with economic growth and will depend on the potential of the municipalities to reimburse all costs for collection, sorting, recovery and/or disposal of the waste. The realization of regional projects by joining the efforts of several municipalities for the construction of common waste treatment infrastructure, as well as the participation of the municipalities in joint ventures with national or foreign investors for the realization of such kind of projects, will play an important role in the achievement of new higher standards of waste management.

The opportunity for private companies to get involved in the waste industry is wide open and this might encourage private firms to invest more in this sector and create more profit as the new laws require more intensive and specific treatment for different kinds of wastes.

Figure 4.1 shows the data taken from Eurostat on the expenditure of Bulgaria and Slovenia on waste management sector. No such data for Romania and Croatia are available. The data for Turkey is taken from the national bureau of statistics.

From Figure 4.1, it seems that Turkey has invested massively more than Bulgaria and Slovenia. However, we must keep in mind that the population of Turkey is around ten times that of Bulgaria and over 30 times Slovenia's. Therefore, to give a clearer insight of the invested money on waste management, Figure 4.2 shows the expenditure per capita of the focus countries in euros.

See Table 4.19 overleaf.

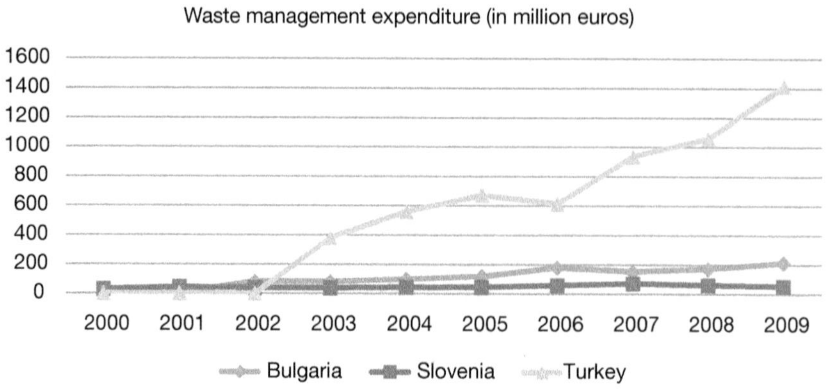

Source: Eurostat, 2011; and TurkStat, 2011

Figure 4.1 Waste management expenditure

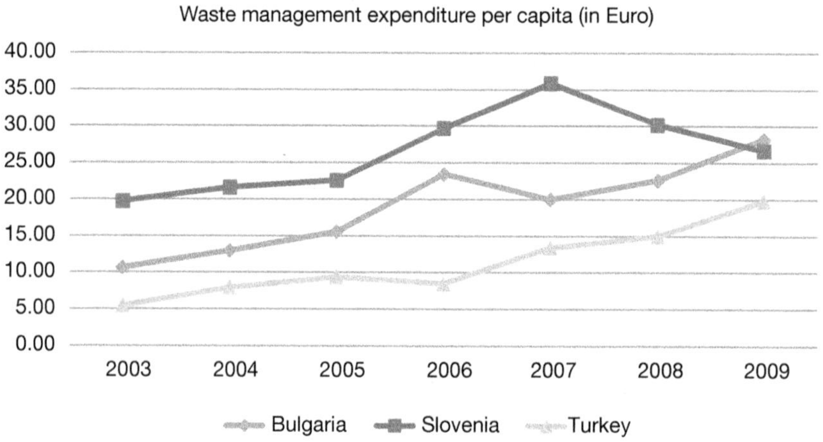

Source: Authors' calculation based on Eurostat, 2011; and TurkStat, 2011

Figure 4.2 Waste management expenditure per capita (in Euro)

Table 4.19 Summary of investment cost in the waste sector, in million euros

	Indicative investment cost – waste sector 2007–2013	*OP Env: waste 2007–2013 NB: Croatia/Turkey 2007–2009*	*National contribution*
Slovenia	427	36	n.a.
Bulgaria	912	366	n.a.
Romania	1,686	233	n.a.
Croatia	2,126	8.8	638
Turkey	2,614	19	5,411

Source: Authors' calculations based on Strategy of Waste Management in the Republic of Croatia, 2005; and Turkish Ministry of Environment and Forestry, 2006

5 Air sector

EU requirements

The EU has been working since the early 1970s to enhance air quality. The effort is made by controlling emissions of harmful substances into the atmosphere, improving fuel quality, and by integrating environmental protection requirements into the transport and energy sectors (Nilsson and Eckerberg, 2007). The EU has been acting in different stages to reduce exposure to air pollution: through European legislation, through work at international level to reduce cross-border pollution, through cooperation with sectors responsible for air pollution, through national, regional authorities and NGOs, and through research.

The EU air related legislation include rules on ambient air quality, rules related to stationary emissions, volatile organic compounds (VOCs), national emission ceilings, transport and environment (see Table 5.1). The mere list of relevant EU rules indicates that the improvement of air quality requires an integrated approach as it involves other sectors, such as energy (e.g. Large Combustion Plants' Directive), transport (through automotive fuel quality rules and emissions from ships), waste (incineration), or industry in general (e.g. Integrated Pollution Prevention and Control (IPPC), and VOCs).

The implementation of EU legislation led to a significant reduction in air pollution, especially by air pollutants such as sulphur dioxide, lead, nitrogen oxides, carbon monoxide and benzene. Despite a reduction in some harmful emissions, air quality continues to cause problems, especially summer smog and fine particulates.

Thus, building on achieved results, the 2005 Thematic Strategy on Air Pollution of the Commission, flowing from the Sixth Environmental Action Programme, provided a more comprehensive and ambitious EU policy framework for the period up to 2020. It defined air quality objectives: decrease sulphur dioxide (SO_2) emissions by 82 per cent, nitrogen oxide (NO_x) emissions by 60 per cent, VOCs by 51 per cent, ammonia (NH_3) by 27 per cent, and primary $PM_{2.5}$ (particles emitted directly into the air) by 59 per cent compared with the year 2000.

Based on the Thematic Strategy on Air Pollution, the existing air quality legislation was streamlined in 2008, new air quality limit values for fine particulate matter ($PM_{2.5}$) were introduced and emission limit values from different transport sources have been tightened (see Table 5.2).

Table 5.1 Selected EU air related legislation

Ambient air quality	
Directive 2008/50/EC	on ambient air quality and cleaner air for Europe; to merge most existing directives excluding the Fourth Daughter Directive
Council Directive 96/62/EC (*Air Quality Framework Directive*)	on ambient air quality assessment and management
Council Directive 1999/30/EC *(First Daughter Directive)*	relating to limit values for sulphur dioxide, nitrogen dioxide and oxides of nitrogen, particulate matter and lead in ambient air
Directive 2000/69/EC of the European Parliament and of the Council *(Second Daughter Directive)*	relating to limit values for benzene and CO in ambient air
Directive 2002/3/EC of the European Parliament and of the Council *(Third Daughter Directive)*	relating to ozone in ambient air
Directive 2004/107/EC of the European Parliament and of the Council *(Fourth Daughter Directive)*	relating to arsenic, cadmium, mercury, nickel and polycyclic aromatic hydrocarbons in ambient air
Council Decision 97/101/EC *(EoI Decision)*	establishing a reciprocal exchange of information and data from networks and individual stations measuring ambient air pollution within the member states
Commission Decision 2004/461/EC	laying down a questionnaire for annual reporting on ambient air quality assessment under Council Directives 96/62/EC *(Air Quality Framework Directive)* and 1999/30/EC *(First Daughter Directive)* and under Directives 2000/69/EC *(Second Daughter Directive)* and 2002/3/EC *(Third Daughter Directive)* of the European Parliament and of the Council
Commission Decision 2004/224/EC	laying down the obligation of Member States to submit within two years so-called *Plans and Programmes* for those air quality zones where certain assessment thresholds set in the Directives are exceeded
Council Directive 80/779/EEC amended by Directive 89/427/EEC	on air quality limit values and guide values for sulphur dioxide and suspended particulates
Council Directive 85/203/EEC amended by Council Directive 85/580/EEC	on air quality standards for nitrogen dioxide
Council Directive 2008/1/EC	concerning integrated pollution prevention and control

continued overleaf

Table 5.1 continued

Ambient air quality	
Stationary source emissions	
Directive 2001/80/EC	on the limitation of emissions of certain pollutants into the air from large combustion plants
Council Directive 94/66/EC amending Directive 88/609/EEC	on the limitation of emissions of certain pollutants into the air from large combustion plants
Directive 2000/76/EC of the European Parliament and of the Council of December 4, 2000	on the incineration of waste
Directive 94/63/EC of the European Parliament and of the Council	on the control of VOC emissions resulting from the storage of petrol and its distribution from terminals to service stations
Council Directive 1999/13/EC	on the limitation of emissions of VOC due to the use of organic solvents in certain activities and installations
Directive 1999/32/EC	on reduction of sulphur content of certain liquid fuels
Directive 2001/81/EC, as amended	on national emissions ceilings for certain atmospheric pollutants
Directive 98/70/EC of the European Parliament and of the Council of 13 October 1998 amending Council Directive 93/12/EEC	relating to the quality of petrol and diesel fuels
Commission Directive 2000/71/EC	to adapt the measuring methods as laid down in Annexes I, II, III and IV of Directive 98/70/EC of the European Parliament and of the Council to technical progress as foreseen in Article 10 of that Directive
Directive 2003/17/EC of the European Parliament and of the Council of 3 March 2003 amending Directive 98/70/EC	relating to the quality of petrol and diesel fuels (text with EEA relevance)
Marine Pollution Convention, MARPOL 73/78	

Source: European Commission DG Environment, 2011

Table 5.2 Limit values for the protection of human health

Pollutant	Averaging period	Limit value*	Date by which value is to be met
Benzene	Calendar year	5μg/m³ (1.54ppb)	1 January 2010
Carbon monoxide (CO)	8-hour, rolling basis	10mg/m³ (8.6ppm)	1 January 2005
Lead	Calendar year	0.5μg/m³	1 January 2005 or 1 January 2010 in specific cases
Nitrogen dioxide (NO_2)	1-hour	200μg/m³ (105ppb), not to be exceeded >18 times a calendar year	1 January 2010
Nitrogen dioxide (NO_2)	Calendar year	40μg/m³ (21ppb)	1 January 2010
Ozone (O_3)	Maximum daily 8-hour mean target value	120μg/m³ (60ppb), not to be exceeded >25 days a calendar year averaged over 3 years	1 January 2010
Particulate matter less than 10 microns in diameter (PM_{10}), Gravimetric**	24-hour	50μg/m³, not to be exceeded >35 times a calendar year	1 January 2005
	Calendar year	40μg/m³	1 January 2005
$PM_{2.5}$	Calendar year	25μg/m³	1 January 2015
	Calendar year, exposure reduction	20μg/m³	1 January 2015
	Exposure reduction	0–20% urban background reduction, to meet 18μg/m3 by 2020.	between 2010 and 2020
Sulphur dioxide (SO_2)	1-hour	350μg/m3 (132ppb), not to be exceeded >24 times a calendar year	1 January 2005
	24-hour	125μg/m³ (47ppb), not to be exceeded >3 times a calendar year	1 January 2005
Arsenic (As)	Calendar year	Target value 6ng/m³	1 January 2012
Cadmium (Cd)	Calendar year	Target value 5ng/m³	1 January 2012
Nickel (Ni)	Calendar year	Target value 20ng/m³	1 January 2012
Polycyclic Aromatic Hydrocarbons (PAH)	Calendar year	Target value 1ng/m³ (expressed as Benzo(a)pyrene)	1 January 2012
Limit values for the protection of vegetation (NO_x) and ecosystems (SO_2)			
Oxides of nitrogen (NO_x)	Calendar year	30μg/m³	19 July 2001
Sulphur dioxide (SO_2)	Calendar year and winter (1 October to 31 March)	20μg/m³	19 July 2001

Source: Low Emission Zone, 2011

Notes

* Limit Value is legally binding on member states. A target value is to be attained as far as possible by the attainment date and so is less strict than a limit value.

** Gravimetric refers to the method of measuring PM_{10}

Despite a reduction in some harmful emissions, air quality continues to cause problems. Summer smog – originating in potentially harmful ground level ozone – regularly exceeds safe limits. Thus, the EU member states have to divide their territory into a number of zones and agglomerations. In these zones air pollution level should be assessed based on measurements, modelling or using empirical techniques. Where levels are high, the air quality plan or programme should be prepared to ensure compliance with the limit value (see Table 5.2) before the limit value formally enters into force.

National plans and financing

Slovenia

The present state

Overall ambient air quality is satisfactory. Air pollution is largely linked to particles (PM_{10}) and, in summer, to ozone. The largest sources of outdoor air pollution are energy and transport sectors (which are responsible for 99 per cent of NO_x emissions), while agriculture is the main source of NH_3 emissions (97 per cent of emissions) (EEA, 2010b). A major contribution to the ozone pollution, which is more pronounced in the coastal Primorska region, comes long distance from the Po Valley in Italy. Compared to 1990, emissions of main pollutants have significantly decreased (see Table 5.3). Reduction of SO_2 is primarily a result from lowering emissions from thermal power stations (use of liquid fuels, implementation of the Large Combustion Plants (LCPs) and Integrated Pollution Prevention and Control (IPCC) Directive). Increased use of vehicles with catalytic converters led to a reduction of NO_x, non-methane volatile organic compounds (NMVOC) emissions and a fall of emissions of ozone precursors. As mentioned, agriculture is the main source of NH_3 emissions, which are directly linked to the number of animals: reducing cattle numbers led to decreasing emissions of NH_3 (36.5 per cent in 2006 relative to 1990). It is expected that implementation of reduction measures in cattle farming and promotion of pasture husbandry will cause further lowering of emissions after 2010.

It is expected that Slovenia will not exceed national ceilings (set by the Directive 2001/81/EC) for SO_2 emissions after 2010. According to the projections, NO_x emissions were expected to rise in the period 2007–2010 and start falling after 2010 as a result of the tightening of requirements on NO_x concentrations in vehicle exhaust gases. After 2015 a reduction is expected from the tightening of permitted NO_x concentrations in the flue gases of large thermal power facilities, the replacement of fuels in generating electricity and heat, and the continued tightening of requirements for NO_x concentrations in vehicle exhaust gases.

The projection of emissions from transport is very uncertain because of the influence of transit traffic that has increased markedly since Slovenia's entry into the EU in 2004. According to the projections, in 2010 emissions of NO_x should have exceeded the national ceiling set in the Directive 2001/81/EC. According to the projections, after 2010 VOC emissions should be below the limit value

Table 5.3 Main air pollutant emissions in Slovenia 1990–2007, in Gg

	1990	*1995*	*2000*	*2005*	*2006*	*2007*	*2008*	*2009*	*2010 Target*
SO_x	198	122	92	40	16	14	13	12	27
NO_x	60	57	50	47	46	48	53	45	45
NH_3	20	18	19	18	18	19	18	18	20
NMVOC	55	53	44	37	36	35	33	31	40
CO	107	125	101	84	108	99			
$PM_{2.5}$		9	7	7	6	5			
PM_{10}		11	9	9	8	7			

Source: Klein, *et al.*, 2011

set in this. The reduction in emissions is a consequence of replacing old boilers running on wood biomass with new ones featuring better combustion, and also the tightening of the requirements for VOC concentrations in motor vehicle exhaust gases.

Slovenia applied a countrywide 24 hour monitoring system for SO_2 and smoke through 49 stations. In addition there are eight automatic monitoring stations in larger cities and 11 monitoring stations in the most polluted areas near power plants. The highest ozone concentrations in Slovenia occur in the south-western part of the country. Slovenian transport is regarded to be the greatest source of ozone precursors, accountable for about two thirds.

Policy and regulation

As an EU member state since 2004, Slovenia has to implement legislations that demand high standards for the maintenance of air quality. At national level, in order to improve the quality of ambient air, the government adopted several operational programmes (for achieving national emissions ceilings for ambient air pollutants, to protect ambient air from PM_{10} pollution, for environment and transport infrastructure), and transport and energy sector resolutions.

According to the Operational Programme (OP) for the protection of air from PM_{10} in regions where PM_{10} concentrations exceed limit values, the development of infrastructure is foreseen. This includes arranging sufficiently large and free car parks at railway passenger stations linking the region and the urban environment. Tackling atmospheric pollution from transport is rather unmanageable due to the diffuse nature of transport. Other measures adopted in Slovenia include drafting an action plan for developing public passenger transport; formulating a comprehensive strategy for managing transit goods traffic on the roads; introducing carriageways intended exclusively for public passenger transport including along sections of national roads; introducing road tolls, taking into account external costs for goods vehicles for the use of toll roads; introducing environmental criteria in apportioning annual taxes for the use of vehicles on the road; taking the environmental aspect into account in determining the level of excise on motor fuels; introducing environmental criteria in public tenders for the purchase of personal vehicles (green public procurement); modernizing the railway network; and the construction of cycle lanes and support facilities, as well as the promotion of cycling.

At the local level, the majority of municipalities in areas with excessive air pollution adopted municipal environmental protection programmes. Such programmes include national and local measures to improve air quality.

Given the effect of polluted air on human health, especially children's, an action plan for the environment and children's health has been drafted. The aim of the plan is to prevent and reduce the incidence of respiratory diseases linked to the pollution of ambient and inside air among children. The plan envisages the following measures:

- ensuring areas of clean air around schools and educational institutions by limiting vehicle access, especially those with diesel engines, and by limiting sources of pollution in the vicinity – amending and implementing legislation.
- awareness raising/education of teachers, children and parents about the dangers of polluted air on health and education on preventive measures that need to be carried out on days when the pollution level is high – promoting educational programmes.
- introducing regular monitoring of ambient air quality and establishing a notification system on days when the air pollution level in urban areas is high, with the aim of notifying staff at schools and educational institutions so they will know that the risk to health is high – amending and implementing legislation, monitoring exposure to chemical substances in the environment.
- involving children, schools and local communities to spread information about the importance of clean air for human health – promoting the active participation of involved people, children, educators and health workers.

Institutions

The municipalities have the authority to regulate road traffic and the traffic regime on local roads of urbanized parts of an area with a degraded environment and in the area of an urban environment where the limit values of PM_{10} have been exceeded.

In view of the increasing concern of citizens over environmental problems, environmental education has also been incorporated into the school curriculum. Eco-schools and the UNESCO schools are actively involved in issues relating to the atmosphere. The Ministry of Education and Sport is providing education for teachers and the Slovenian Board of Education is publishing the magazine Environmental Education in Schools. Institutions dealing with sectors which are connected to air pollution or its consequences (e.g. such as transport, energy, health) regulate specific issues and also play a role in raising people's awareness of the necessity to reduce air pollution.

Financing

According to the National Environmental Action Plan, the costs of implementing air sector related measures in the period 1999–2003 were estimated at roughly €160 million (see Table 5.4). The private sector was expected to invest €158 million, and the public €2.5 million.

An additional €50 million is needed for the control of emissions in industry and for the reduction of risks. Estimated investment required for the protection of air quality in Slovenia for the period 2008–2012 is €241 million (Slovenian Ministry of the Environment and Spatial Planning, 2003). It is planned that 70 per cent of these costs will be borne by state budget, 1 per cent of necessary costs (€2.4 million) will be covered from EU funds and 29 per cent will have to be provided by local budgets.

Bulgaria

The present state

The introduction of emission control, the use of fuels with improved environmental performance and the reduction of production capacity led to decreased emissions of main air pollutants (SO_2, NO_x, NMVOC and NH_3) by 64 per cent in the period 1990–2009 (see Table 5.5).

Table 5.4 Review of costs for the implementation of NEAP air sector in Slovenia 1999–2003, in million euros

Year	*Cost*
1999	32.5
2000	32.4
2001	32.1
2002	31.4
2003	31.1
Total	159.5

Source: National Environment Action Programme 2005:102

Table 5.5 Emissions of main pollutants in Bulgaria 1990–2009, in Gg

Bulgaria	*1990*	*1995*	*2000*	*2005*	*2006*	*2007*	*2008*	*2009*	*2010 ceiling*
SO_2	1,767	1,350	1,080	1,142	1,144	1,278	1,238	658	836
NO_x	288	215	171	207	214	222	218	165	247
NMVOC	541	146	103	106	114	11	113	146	175
NH_3	144	99	109	57	55	58	58	51	108

Source: Eurostat, 2011

The main sources of air pollution are the energy sector (thermal power stations), transport and industrial processes. The energy sector is the main source of SO_2 emissions (97 per cent of total emissions) and is responsible for 37 per cent of NO_x emissions and 26 per cent of NMVOC emissions. Road transport is responsible for 50 per cent of NO_x emissions and 47 per cent of NMVOC emissions. Industrial processes are responsible for 10 per cent of NO_x emissions. Agriculture is the main source of NH_3 emissions (79 per cent) and 20 per cent of NMVOC (EEA, 2010).

The level of emissions of acidifying substance is 11.5 per cent below Bulgarian commitments under the relevant Directive (2001/81/EC). The National Automated System for the control of ambient air quality meets all requirements of national and European legislation in terms of number of points and controlled atmospheric pollutants. In 2009, the National Automated System for Monitoring Ambient Air Quality operated in 55 fixed points, including 11 points with manual sampling and subsequent laboratory analysis, 37 automatic measurement stations, 11 differential optical absorption systems and three automatic measurement stations monitoring forest ecosystems. Stations monitoring air quality are located in 34 cities.

Policy and regulation

Bulgaria has aligned its air quality legislation with the EU in the year of accession. Specific commitments were included in the accession treaty. National ceilings for emissions of four major pollutants: SO_2, NO_x, NMVOC and NH_3, as required by the Directive 2001/81/EC, were established by the National Programme for Restricting Overall Annual National Emissions of Sulphur Dioxide, Nitrous Oxide, VOCs and Ammonia (see Table 5.6). The National Programme advocates even lower levels for the emission of these substances than required by the Directive. These levels are to be met by bringing large thermal installations in line with statutory requirements.

Table 5.6 Annual trends in harmful substance emissions and accession negotiation commitments, in Gg

Atmospheric pollutants	*2007 emissions*	*Commitments under Directive 2001/81/EC 2010*	*Commitments under the NP set out in Bulgarian CMR No. 261 2010*	*Commitments under the NP set out in Bulgarian CMR No. 261 2015*	*Commitments under the NP set out in Bulgarian CMR No. 261 2020*
SO_x (as SO_2)	854	836	380	300	250
NO_x (as NO_2)	188	247	247	247	247
NMVOC	120	175	175	175	175
NH3	58	108	108	108	108

Source: EEA, 2010

The new Clean Air for Europe Directive (Directive 2008/50/EC had been transposed into Bulgarian law by the end of 2010. The legal framework for the air quality sector comprises the Environmental Protection Act, the Clean Ambient Air Act and secondary legislation. Since its accession to the European Union in 2007, Bulgaria has implemented the requirements of Regulation 2037/2000/EC on substances that deplete the ozone layer. Measures for the implementation of the Regulation are established as amended in 2006 by the Clean Air Act (promulgated SG. 99/8.12.2006) and amendments to the Decree 254/1999 for the management and control of substances that deplete the ozone layer (amended and supplemented by Decree 28/2007).

The Clean Ambient Air Act, which has been in force since 1996 and was last amended in 2009 (SG 6/2009), governs:

- Determination of indicators and standards for air quality, emission limitation, the rights and obligations of the authority, control, management and maintenance of air quality
- Limitation of emissions of pollutants from mobile and stationary sources
- Legal requirements relating to design, construction and operating facilities with sources of emissions
- Fees on liquid fuels for the National Fund for Environmental Protection
- Relevant administrative penal provisions.

In accordance with the national programme for phasing out the production and use of leaded petrol, as of year 2004, the use and production of leaded petrol in the country is forbidden.

In 2009, the desulphurization installations accounted for 461.9000 tonnes of SO_2. The emission levels of NO_x, NH3, NMVOC and SO_2 were significantly below the country's commitments for 2010, Annex I of the Directive 2001/81/EC. However, according to the country's commitments under the National Programme, measures to reduce emissions of SO_2 were insufficient. The programme for 2010 set the level of SO_2 from 380kt, which at the current level of 657kt is hard to reach.

During the negotiation process for the country's accession to the EU, the following transitional periods under several implementation programmes have been agreed:

- by the end of 2007 and 2009 for limitation of emissions from VOC, resulting from the storage of petrol and its distribution for terminals and service stations with 'average' and 'low' capacity pursuant to the Directive 94/63/EC. The investment plan for the implementation of the Directive does not envisage the use of external funding for providing the necessary investments for achieving compliance. It is agreed that the investments will be provided from the operators of the particular terminals, service stations and the transportation companies. The investments with regard to the fulfilment of measures in the Army, the Police and the State Reserve will be distributed equally between the state budget and the Enterprise for Management of Environmental Protection Activities (EMEPA).

- by the end of 2011 for limiting the sulphur content in boiler fuels to 1 per cent (mass) pursuant to the Directive 99/32/EC. In the implementation programme of this Directive, the existing situation is examined, the expenditures for achieving the requirements are calculated and the sources of funding are outlined. The total costs for ensuring compliance with the Directive are estimated as €1.5 million, which would be provided mainly through the state budget.
- by the end of 2011 and 2014 for achieving compliance (in terms of the permissible emissions limit values) for individual blocks of thermal power plants 'Rousse', 'Lukoil Neftochim – Bourgas', 'Varna' and 'Bobov dol' pursuant to the Directive 2001/80/EC. The implementation programme outlines the calculated expenditure and the sources of funding. Thermal power plants' funding is envisaged only from operator's own sources (i.e. the new owners of the facilities).

However, despite undertaken measures, by the end of 2009 Bulgaria had not fulfilled part of its obligations under the negotiation position of the Directive 2011/80/EC in relation to the total emissions of SO_2 and NO_x from LCPs.

The Bulgarian energy sector is regulated by several laws and more than 50 pieces of secondary legislation. There are three relatively differentiated regulatory subsystems:

1 general sector regulation provided by the Law on Energy 2003
2 nuclear energy and nuclear safety regulations, and
3 sustainable energy regulations – energy efficiency, renewable energy sources and biofuels.

The Energy Efficiency Law was adopted in Bulgaria in 2008 and in 2011 a specific Energy Efficiency Strategy will be adopted by the Bulgarian Parliament, with an emphasis on the energy efficiency of residential and public buildings, transport and industry. Financing opportunities include EU operative programmes, resources from the sale of emission units, the 'Kozloduy' International Fund and so on. In the meantime, various programmes and action plans have been adopted: the First National Action Plan for Energy Efficiency 2008–2010 in accordance with the Directive 2006/32/EC on energy end-use efficiency and energy services, the national long-term programme to promote the use of biomass for the period 2008–2020, the national long-term programme to promote the use of renewable energy sources 2005–2015 and the national long-term programme to promote the use of biofuels in the transport sector 2008–2020.

Bulgaria has been reforming its power sector and is working to urgently replace capacity that is inefficient, highly polluting and often in violation of EU environmental requirements. Private sector-led generation projects are an integral part of the country's energy sector reform.

The first Bulgarian Energy Strategy was adopted in 1999 and endorsed by the National Assembly under the title National Strategy for the Development of the Energy Sector and Energy Efficiency until 2010. Three years later, the new Energy Strategy until 2010 was adopted. A new concept for the Bulgarian Energy Strategy until 2020 was developed in 2008 and finally the Council of Ministers and the National Assembly adopted the Energy Strategy 2020 in June 2011. It outlines more clearly the national priorities, is more responsible in budget terms, and attempts the introduction of scenario planning in the development of the national energy sector. The proposed strategy provides a good basis for public discussion as it incorporates the main guidelines of the Energy Strategy for Europe 2020. As a member of the EU, and in accordance with the EU's Energy and Climate Change Package from January 2007, Bulgaria has undertaken a binding commitment to reduce its carbon emissions, reach a minimum share of renewable energy sources in final energy consumption and reduce its energy intensity.

Institutions

The Bulgarian Council of Ministers coordinates policy development. In communities with air quality problems, the main responsible authorities at the national level include the Ministry of Environment and Water, Ministry of Health, Ministry of Economy and State Standardization Agency. According to the Clean Air Act the Minister of Environment and Water, in coordination with the interested ministers, issues an order for the approval of a methodology for the calculation, with balance methods, of the emissions of harmful substances (pollutants), emitted in the ambient air. The national methodology is harmonized with CORINAIR methodology for the calculation of the emissions according to the UNECE/CLRTAP Convention.[1]

The Executive Environment Agency is the subordinate body of the Ministry which designs and manages the national system for environmental monitoring.

The Bulgarian municipalities play an important role in air quality improvement. In communities with air quality problems they are responsible for development programmes to cut air pollution levels in order to meet the required standards in line with the Directive 96/62/EC (Order No. 7/99). The programmes comprise short and long-term measures which are implemented by the municipalities. As regards other policies that are relevant for air quality, primarily the energy policy, a number of central government institutions are involved (e.g. Ministry of Energy, regulator).

Financing

Required expenditures in the air sector for the period 1998–2015 are estimated at €3,260 million. In the pre-accession period PHARE, ISPA and SAPARD supported the alignment with the EU. In 2009 it was estimated that about €209 million is necessary for air quality protection (which was 7.8 per cent lower than the amount in 2008). The EU support ensured about 10 per cent of necessary funds.

Romania

The present state

A change of economic structure – i.e. large-scale reduction of economic production in many industries and closure of many large pollutant installations – led to the decrease of the industrial emissions over 50 per cent in the period 1990–2004 and consequently to the improvement of air quality in many areas, especially where industry was the main polluter. Despite improvements, air quality is very low in many areas and the control of industrial emissions is still inadequate (see Table 5.7).

The energy sector is the main source of SO_2 emissions (99 per cent of total emissions) and is also significant for NO_x emissions (47 per cent) and NMVOC emissions (45 per cent). Transport is the main source of NO_x emissions (67 per cent) and significant contributor to NMVOC emissions (23 per cent). Agriculture is responsible for NH_3 emissions (90 per cent) and NMVOC (17 per cent) (EEA, 2011). The energy sector (i.e. thermal power plants using solid fuels) and industrial pollution (metallurgy, steel industries, cement) are the most significant sources of particulates, which are the main pollutants that significantly exceed the maximum admissible concentration.

The National System for Air Quality Assessment and Integrated Management was set up in 2004 to monitor the air quality and inform the public. It contains the national network for air quality monitoring and a national system for the inventory of air pollutant emissions.

Policy and regulation

Before accession to the EU, Romania has gradually aligned its policy with the EU rules. In 2004 it adopted the National Strategy for Atmosphere Protection. Its goals are:

- maintaining the quality of ambient air in the zones that comply with the limits set by the legal norms for quality indicators
- improving ambient air quality in the zones that do not comply with the limits set by the legal norms for quality indicators
- adopting necessary measures to minimize and finally eliminate negative environmental and/or cross-border impacts

Table 5.7 Emissions of main pollutants in Romania 1990–2009, Gg

Romania	*1990*	*1995*	*2000*	*2005*	*2006*	*2007*	*2008*	*2009*	*2010 ceiling*
SO_x	755	636	457	522	542	537	566	460	918
NO_x	459	386	304	332	344	348	280	247	437
NMVOC	335	280	336	539	601	1,056	466	432	523
NH_3	300	217	206	204	199	203	187	188	210

Source: EEA, 2010

- meeting the obligations assumed by international agreements and treaties to which Romania is a party (Convention on long distance cross-border atmosphere pollution, and the protocols of Convention on reduction of acidification, eutrophication and the level of troposphere ozone layer, the Gothenburg Protocol).

The achievement of set goals was foreseen in two periods: before accession (between 2004 and 2006) and after accession. As necessary investments exceeded Romania's potential, Romania obtained transition periods until 2013, respectively 2017 for certain emissions (sulphur dioxide, nitrogen oxides and particulates) and certain installations under the LCP Directive.

Institutions

As main pressures to the air quality originate in the energy sector, agriculture, industry and tourism, the relevant institutions (in addition to the Ministry of Environment) at national level are those in charge of sector-specific measures. For instance, responsibility for the implementation of the LCP Directive are separated between the Ministry of Economy and Finance (which owns 72 LCPs), the Ministry of Interior and Administrative Reform (which coordinates 80 LCPs belonging to 26 public local authorities) and public local authorities.

Municipalities are in charge of the development of air quality management programmes in areas where emissions of main pollutants exceed limit values.

The Environmental Fund Administration collects environmental taxes and directs money collected into environmental projects.

Financing

Air protection is not among priorities of the Sector OP Environment. However, the alignment with LCP Directive is seen as priority. In this respect, it is identified that €2 billion is needed for financing LCP Directive for the period of 2007–2013, and about €400 million of EU funds is foreseen for LCP Directive under Sector OP Environment and Sector OP Increase of Economic Competitiveness.

Taxes on pollutant emissions payable by companies and the pollution tax (registration fee) payable for new cars when they are first registered on Romanian territory are air pollution related environmental taxes. The money collected is directed to funding environment projects.

Croatia

The present state

The air is clean or slightly polluted (first category air) in 60 per cent of cities and settlements in Croatia (EEA, 2010a). Air is moderately polluted in 20 per cent of cities and settlements, and excessively polluted air is in 20 per cent of cities and settlements.

The energy production (emissions from fuel combustion and fugitive emissions) is the main source of a major part of the air pollution in Croatia. It contributes to 88.4 per cent of total SO_2 emissions, 89 per cent of NO_x, 27 per cent of NMVOC, 74 per cent of $PM_{2.5}$, 61 per cent of PM_{10}, 95 per cent of carbon monoxide (CO). Production processes are main sources of particulate matter (PM) (64 per cent of total emission), as well as significant source of NO_x emissions (10 per cent), heavy metal emissions (8–43 per cent). The use of solvents and solvent-based products is only relevant for NMVOC emissions (58 per cent). Agriculture is the main source of NH_3 emissions (83 per cent) (EEA, 2010a). Emissions of pollutants are decreasing, the exception being PM. For targets according to the Gothenburg Protocol see Table 5.8.

Policy and regulation

The EU accession process, as well as international obligations (from the Convention on Long-range Transboundary Air Pollution and eight associated protocols) provide general framework for Croatian air protection policy and regulation. The main targets for the protection and improvement of air quality and the long-term measures for the achievement of these targets have been adopted within the Environmental Strategy and the National Environmental Action Plan. The Air Quality Protection and Improvement Plan for the period 2008–2011, as an implementation document of the National Environmental Strategy, elaborates the targets and mid-term measures by sectors with priorities, deadlines and actors. The Programme for Gradual Reduction in Emissions of Certain Pollutants in the Republic of Croatia till the end of 2010 with Emission Projections for the period 2010–2020 specified measures by key sectors and emission projections

Table 5.8 Targets according to the Gothenburg Protocol and the regulation on emission ceilings compared to projected emissions in the no measures taken (NM) and additional measures (AM), 2010, 2015 and 2020

Pollutant	*Target emission 2010, kt*	*Relative target emission in relation to emission in 1990 (1990=100%)*	*Projections kt/year*								
			2010			2015			2020		
			NM	M	AM	NM	M	AM	NM	M	AM
NO_x	87	99%	81.8	80.5	74.2	81.8	89.0	82.4	98.7	91.5	84.9
SO_2	70	41%	47.5	45.9	n.a.	46.3	48.8	n.a.	53.5	42.5	n.a.
NMVOC	90	75%	103.7	88.8	80.5	103.7	46.7	38.3	118.3	44.4	34.5
NH_3	30	53%	41.4	41.4	41.4	46.0	38.7	36.9	49.9	42.0	40.3
	45	80%									

Source: EEA, 2010a

for the 2010–2020 period with measured proposals by key sectors, and sets 2020 pollutant emission ceilings for Croatia.

Under the Regulation on Emission Ceilings for Certain Pollutants, Croatia agreed to reduce ammonia emission to the limit value of 45 Gg (giga gram) by 2010. The commitment under the Gothenburg Protocol is more stringent, i.e. 30 Gg. The difference between the limit values prescribed by these two documents results from repeated calculations carried out for the 2003 Report on Emission of Air Pollutants on the Territory of the Republic of Croatia, which resulted in the increase in ammonia or NH_3 emission trend.

Institutions

At the national level, the Ministry of Environment is the key institution responsible for policy development and coordination. It is supported by various national or regional institutions/agencies in performing specific tasks, such as a state hydro-meteorological institute (for defining areas according to the air quality), Environment Agency (monitoring and reporting on air quality), Environmental and Energy Efficiency Fund (for implementation of national energy programmes).

Counties are responsible for adoption and implementation of their air quality protection and improvement programmes and biannually report on the status of the environment.

Financing

According to the Air Quality Protection and Improvement Plan for the period of 2008–2012 the average annual cost for air quality protection and improvement is estimated at €571 million per year (see Table 5.9).

The Plan was prepared under the assumption that the transition period for implementing the Directive on Industrial Pollution Prevention will last until 2020. According to the accession treaty it has to be implemented by the beginning of 2018 at the very latest, therefore, the annual investment needs are underestimated. It is planned that €1–1.3 million will be financed from the budget. Polluters are expected to bear other costs (through various charges or direct investments) (see Table 5.10).

Capital investments needed for approximation of Croatian legislation in line with the requirements of the European Union *acquis communautaire* in the field of industrial pollution with respect to air pollution reduction measures are estimated at round €1.97 billion.

Turkey

The present state

Turkey currently does not meet EU air quality standards. Air pollution makes itself felt, especially during the winter months, when pollution originates from heating (utilization of low grade fuel without improvement processing,

Table 5.9 Average annual cost of air quality protection and improvement of Croatia 2008–2012

No	*Type of cost*	*Annual average cost (million euros)*
1	Air quality management	1.8
2	Financing local air quality networks	1.3
3	Rehabilitation measures in Sisak and Kutina (H_2S) and in Rijeka and Mlaka refineries (SO_2 and H_2S) to reach air quality category II	20.1
4	Implementation of the UNFCCC and the Kyoto Protocol	53.7
5	Ozone depleting substances	0.5
6	Technical adaptation of equipment for the storage of petrol and its distribution from terminals to petrol stations – application of technical standards for reduction of volatile organic compounds emissions (Directive 94/63/EC)	22
7	Technical adaptation of existing large combustion plants (Directive 2001/80/EC)	125.5
8	Technical adaptation of oil refineries – production of liquid petroleum fuels of EU quality (Directive 2003/43/EC)	156.4
9	Technical adaptation of installations using organic solvents for certain activities (Directives 99/13 and 2004/42/EC)	10
10	Other IPPC installations (landfill, cement works, etc.)	165.9
	Total (million euros)	**571**
	Euro per capita	129
	Per cent GDP in 2006	1.67

Source: Air Quality Protection and Improvement Plan of The Republic of Croatia for the Period 2008–2011, 2008

application of inadequate burning techniques and lack of maintenance of the furnaces). It is estimated that using natural gas in air polluted urban centres could reduce health related problems caused by outdoor air pollution, and by doing so would save €150–240 million annually (Ozdilek, 2006).

Energy (production of electricity and heating during winter), transport, intensive urbanization and industrialization (including inappropriate location of industrial facilities) and rapid population growth are among the main pressures leading to deterioration of air quality: the energy sector is responsible for 61 per cent of NO_x emissions and 94 per cent of SO_2 emissions, transport contributes to 33 per cent of NO_x emissions, while industrial processing is responsible for 60 per cent of NMVOC emissions and road transport with 33 per cent (EEA, 2010c).

Policy and regulation

The Environment Law defines obligations for the measurement of air quality, and several by-laws determine specific issues on air quality control.

Table 5.10 Croatian plan for funds to be secured from the government budget

Relevant acquis activities (legislative and implementing) competent authority	*Source of Funds*	*Funds planned (EUR)*		
		2008	*2009*	*2010*
Preparation of planning documents in the field of air and climate protection (MEPPPC)	Government budget	242,153	228,700	228,700
Maintenance of stations and air quality measurement (MEPPPC)	Government budget	408,970	411,661	692,827
Setting up a national air quality monitoring network (MEPPPC)	Government budget	538,118	134,529	134,529
Current and investment maintenance services (MEPPPC)	Government budget	94,171	40,359	40,359
Establishment of an air quality monitoring and management system. PHARE 2006 (MEPPPC)	Government budget	67,265	470,854	n.a.
Annual reporting on GHG emission with corrections of a historical series from 1990 (NIR+CRF), including an overview (CEA)	Government budget	53,812	53,812	53,812
Report on implementation of measures and projections	Government budget	n.a.	26,906	n.a.
Development of an air protection information system (CEA)	Government budget	60,538	80,718	80,718
Maintenance of the Register (CEA)	Government budget	37,668	26,906	26,906
Purchase of equipment needed for maintenance of the Register (CEA)	Government budget	32,287		
Total amount	**Government budget**	**1,534,982**	**1,474,444**	**1,257,852**
PHARE 2006 – construction of stations in rural and protected areas	EU (PHARE)	161,435	67,265	n.a.

Source: Air Quality Protection and Improvement Plan of the Republic of Croatia for the Period 2008–2011, 2008

Turkish EU approximation strategy considers EU air related requirements (as presented in Table 5.1) within several sectors: air (which deals primarily with air quality, emission ceilings and fuel quality), industrial pollution control sector (which deals with IPPC, LCP, VOC emissions, and also waste and waters) and waste (incineration). Here we focus on air and industrial pollution, as investment needs for waste related air protection measures are presented in the waste chapter.

The implementation calendar for 13 different pollutants defined in the framework directive and daughter directives is defined by the by-law on air quality assessment and management in Turkey. The by-law covers necessary instruments, such as clean air and action plans, to improve air quality, while aiming at monitoring, sanctioning and institutional strengthening in the field of air pollution control and air quality.

The Turkish Industrial Strategy, prepared in 2010, includes goals related to environmental protection. Turkey believes that approximation with the EU Environmental *Acquis* will lay the basis for cleaner production. Within this context, approximation and implementation of the IPPC Directive will ensure the minimization of pollution at source and increase efficiency by use of best available technologies.

The Resource Efficiency Strategy identifies measures to be implemented for transformation towards a low-carbon economy and cleaner production, including measures in energy and transport sectors that are responsible for the majority of NO_x and SO_2 emissions. These include energy efficiency measures and utilization of renewable energy.

Institutions

The Ministry Environment and Forestry and the Ministry of Health are the main central governmental institutions dealing with air quality. The Ministry of Environment and Forestry determines methodology for measuring and monitoring air quality and defines limit values.

The Ministry of Health is responsible for monitoring the air pollution concentration in the country, and the State Institute of Statistics assesses and publishes the results of the concentration of SO_2 and PM by the city on a monthly basis, winter season and annual basis. Energy sector related measures can significantly contribute to improving air quality. As part of the efforts relating to energy efficiency, the Ministry of Energy and Natural Resources and the Ministry of Industry and Trade, the Ministry of Justice and the Ministry of Education have signed cooperation protocols involving joint action plans for the purpose of ensuring efficient and effective use of energy resources and energy, alleviating the burden of energy costs on the economy and protecting the environment.

The Ministry of Transport and Communication regulates transport related measures such as increasing efficiency standards in vehicles, expanding the use of public transportation vehicles, replacing signalling systems (converting systems run with acetylene butane gas into systems running on solar energy) as well as specific measures related to air transport.

Financing

Estimated costs for the implementation of air quality policies include the cost of establishing a monitoring system in line with the Air Quality Framework Directive and daughter directives (€11 million for 206 air quality stations), the maintenance and operational costs of the stations (€1.5 million) and the preparation of preliminary assessment studies for air quality (€6 million).

Additional costs include the setting up of the calibration laboratories and national calibration centre, the monitoring network management centre, national data centre, emission inventories, informing the public and reporting and related personnel costs (€3 million per year for 243 employees in the national and eight regional centres).

Fuel quality related investments costs necessary in the public sector are estimated at €39 million, but a significantly higher cost (between €885 and €1,135 million) is necessary to reduce sulphur rates in fuel oil and is expected to be borne by the industry, primarily TUPRAS (Turkey's largest industrial enterprise, with 28.1 million tonnes crude processing capacity).

Thus, the total investment requirement until 2023 for improving the air quality in Turkey reaches €15.8 billion (see Table 5.11). Harmonization and implementation of IPPC and LCP Directives will have high cost implications on Turkish economy, as shown in the Table 5.11. Significant investment is also necessary at a later stage, between 2020 and 2030, depending on the level of participation of the private capital.

The investment plan for the period 2007–2013 includes investments into air and fuel quality from central and local budgets (€27 million), from EU funds (€10 million) and from public enterprises (€1,187 million).

Table 5.11 Summary of investment needs in the Turkish air sector, in million euros

	2007	*2008*	*2009*	*2010*	*2011*	*2012*	*2013*	*2007–2013 total*	*2014–2023*	*Total*
Air quality	3	3	3	3	3	2	2	17	18	37
Fuel quality										1,172
IPPC*			370	406	445	485	520	2,226	10,412	12,638
LCP**	32	34	38	46	57	62	66	335	852	1,187
VOC		87	87	87	87	88	88	524	176	700
VOC emissions resulting from storing petrol		12	12	12	12	13	13	87	13	100
Total										15,834

Source: EU Integrated Environmental Approximation Strategy 2007–2023, 2006

Note

* The evaluation is based on values within the scope of High Cost Environmental Projects. From 2023 on, €1.4 billion a year additional investment is needed. Within the scope of the harmonization studies with the EU, investment period will be re-evaluated.

** The evaluation is based on values within the scope of High Cost Environmental Projects. From 2023 on, €697 million a year additional investment is needed. Within the scope of the harmonization studies with the EU, investment period will be re-evaluated.

Conclusions

Improvement of air quality requires coordination of measures in energy, transport, agriculture, and industry. Energy sector counts the most in air pollution, while agriculture is a dominant source of NH_3 emissions.

Air quality has improved in all focus countries since 1990 except Turkey. This is primarily the result of economic transition, downsizing of most polluting industry and improvement of fuel quality (for production of electricity and in transport sector).

It is projected that 2010 emissions of SO_2, NO_x and NMVOC will be below the emission ceilings as defined by the Gothenburg Protocol in all focus countries, while the NH_3 emission is expected to be above the emission ceiling in Slovenia by a small margin (less than 5 per cent).

Air protection is not among priorities for environmental financing in the period until 2013. The most significant investments relate to the implementation of LCP Directive and IPPC. The cost of aligning with these Directives is in the range of 0.3–0.6 per cent of GDP, and is expected to be borne primarily by industries.

6 Climate change

EU requirements

At the global level, the Kyoto Protocol is a first step to achieve the United Nations Framework on Climate Change's (UNFCCC) long-term objective 'to stabilize atmospheric greenhouse gas (GHG) concentrations at a level that would prevent dangerous anthropogenic interference with the climate system'. The Kyoto Protocol sets emission reduction targets depending on the status of the country within the UNFCCC. Annex 1 countries (including Bulgaria, Romania, Slovenia, Croatia and Turkey) had accepted the obligation of submitting annual reports and of reducing GHG emissions to a lower level than in 1990. The reduction emission targets were negotiated individually: the EU accepted the highest reduction target among the major industrialized countries (–8 per cent). The states which were members of the EU before 2004 must collectively reduce their GHG emissions by 8 per cent between 2008 and 2012. Member states which joined the EU after that date undertake to reduce their emissions by 8 per cent, i.e. Bulgaria, Romania and Slovenia have individual targets of 8 per cent reduction.

Croatia and Turkey acceded to the Protocol in 2007 and 2009 respectively, after intense pressure from both the European Union and international environmental organizations. Turkey does not have a binding reduction target while Croatia's reduction target is 5 per cent.

In addition to emission reduction obligation, countries listed in Annex 2 of the Climate Convention have obligation to provide financial resources for developing countries. The EU is listed in Annex 2.

Countries are expected to meet their targets mainly through domestic policies and measures. They are allowed to meet part of their emission reduction targets by investing in emission reducing projects in developing countries – Clean Developing Mechanism (CDM); or in developed ones – Joint Implementation (JI). The CDM is also meant to support sustainable development, e.g. by financing renewable energy projects. In order to meet the Kyoto Protocol requirements, the EU has developed legislation relating to monitoring and reporting GHG emissions and establishing national emission ceilings (see Table 6.1).

The Kyoto Protocol will expire in 2012. As the 15th Conference of Parties to the UNFCCC agreed in December 2009, the successor agreement of the Kyoto Protocol should limit the maximum temperature rise of less than two degree

Table 6.1 Key Pieces of EU legislation relating to GHG monitoring and reporting

Decision No 280/2004 EC	Concerning a mechanism for monitoring community GHG emissions and for implementing the Kyoto Protocol
Commission Decision No 2005/166/EC	Implementing Decision 280/2004/EC
Commission Decision 2006/944/ EC as amended (Decision 2010/778/EU)	Determining the respective emission levels allocated to the Community and each of its member states under the Kyoto Protocol
Council Decision 2002/358/EC	Concerning the approval on behalf of the European Community, of the Kyoto Protocol to the UNFCCC and the joint fulfilment of commitments thereunder
F-gas regulation (EC) No 842/2006 and regulations adopted pursuant to the F-gas regulation	Establishing the format for the report to be submitted by producers, importers and exporters of certain fluorinated GHG
MAC Directive 2006/40	Relating to emissions from air conditioning systems in motor vehicles, covers use of HFC in mobile air conditioning for passenger cars

Source: European Commission DG Climate Action, 2011

Celsius. Based on the current understanding of climate science, the two degrees limit will provide a measure of assurance that many negative climate impacts can be avoided.[1] The two degrees limit calls for global emission reductions of about 50 per cent by 2050. To achieve this goal developed countries have to reduce their emissions by 60–80 per cent which would require changes in energy, transport, agriculture, manufacturing and other industries.

To foster these changes, the EU pledged to reduce GHG emissions by 20 per cent by 2020 compared to 1990 levels, or by 30 per cent if other developed countries make similar commitments and developing countries contribute according to their abilities, as part of a comprehensive global agreement. According to the Commission's estimate (European Commission, 2010) a reduction of 30 per cent in emissions (including the costs related to the 20 per cent target) will cost €81 billion, representing 0.54 per cent of GDP.

Developed countries committed to provide US$30 billion short-term funding for immediate action till 2012. They pledged US$100 billion annually by 2020 in long-term financing, as well as mechanisms to support technology transfer and forestry.

At the Cancún climate talks in December 2010, the Copenhagen Agreement was formalized as part of the UN process, the Green Fund was created and the instruments for technology transfer provided. Still, the commitments from Cancún are not enough to keep the temperature increase below two degrees Celsius. A legal form of the agreement and ways to provide the long-term finance are still to be agreed upon. In order to avoid a regulatory gap following the expiration of the Kyoto Protocol on 31 December 2012, December 2011 negotiations in Durban should result with a concrete agreement – or protocol. This is highly unlikely. Thus alternative solutions at regional level are being put in place.

The EU endorsed an integrated approach to climate and energy in 2007. The 'climate–energy' package provides for cost-effective policies and measures to reduce GHG emissions in energy sector, which is the largest source of GHG emissions in the EU – 79 per cent in 2009 (EEA, 2011). The package sets climate and energy targets to be met by 2020, known as the '20–20–20' targets. They are:

- A reduction in EU GHG emissions of at least 20 per cent below 1990 levels
- 20 per cent of total primary EU energy consumption to come from renewable resource
- A 20 per cent reduction in primary energy use compared with projected levels, to be achieved by improving energy efficiency.

The core of the legislative package that makes these targets binding is presented in Table 6.2. By adopting legally binding provisions for the period after 2012, the basic requirements for EU member states were set, and by setting the climate policy which goes beyond the requirements of the Kyoto Protocol, EU tries to establish its role as a green leader and role model for other state actors.

The EU emissions trading system (EU ETS), launched in 2005, before the first commitment period, served as a model for voluntary schemes as it proved to be helpful in cutting emissions cost-effectively. The EU ETS is based on the 'cap and trade' principle. Cap is a limit on the total amount of certain GHG that can be emitted. Within this cap, companies receive emission allowances which they can sell to or buy from one another as needed.

The EU ETS is a tool for reducing industrial GHG emissions from power stations, combustion plants, oil refineries and iron and steel works, as well as factories making cement, glass, lime, bricks, ceramics, pulp, paper and board. Airlines will join the scheme in 2012. A single EU-wide cap on emission allowances will apply from 2013, when the third trading period will start. Cap will be cut annually, reducing the number of allowances available to businesses to 21 per cent below the 2005 level in 2020. The free allocation of allowances will be

Table 6.2 Key climate-energy legislation

Directive 2003/87/EC, its amendments and legislation adopted pursuant to this directive	Establishing EU ETS
Effort Sharing Decision (Decision No 406/2009/EC)	Establishes annual binding GHG emission targets for member states for the period 2013–2020
RES Directive (2009/28/EC)	Binding national targets for renewable energy which collectively will lift the average renewable share across the EU to 20% by 2020
Directive 2009/31/EC	Promotes the development and safe use of carbon capture and storage
Energy Efficiency Directive	Establishes binding energy efficiency target in 2020 (20%).

Source: European Commission DG Climate Action, 2011

progressively replaced by auctioning, and the sectors and gases covered by the system will be further expanded to the petrochemicals, ammonia and aluminium industries and to additional gases.

The EU implements the Rio Principle of common but differentiated responsibilities by the 'Effort Sharing Decision'. The Decision establishes binding GHG emissions targets based on the relative wealth of individual member states. Targets govern emissions for the period 2013–2020 from sectors not covered by the EU ETS, such as transport, housing, agriculture and waste. The targets range from an emission's reduction of 20 per cent by the richest member states to an increase in emissions of 20 per cent by the poorest. At the EU level, this will cut the emissions from the non-ETS sectors by 10 per cent by 2020 compared with 2005 levels. Implementation of policies and measures to limit emissions of sectors under the Effort Sharing Decision is the responsibility of member states and can include shifts away from transport based on fossil fuels, promotion of public transport, ambitious energy performance standards for buildings, more efficient heating systems, renewable energy for heating, more efficient farming practices, and the conversion of animal waste to biogas.

The EU legislation controls emissions but it is also expected to act as a driver for the development of innovative technologies, including renewable technologies and carbon capture and storage (CCS). CCS is a promising family of technologies that capture the carbon dioxide emitted by industrial processes and store it in underground geological formations where it cannot contribute to global warming. CCS technology might help reduce emissions provided that it is deployed safely and that risks are properly managed. Different components of CCS are already deployed on a commercial scale, but the technical and economic viability of its use as an integrated system has yet to be shown. Binding national targets for renewable energy to support deployment and commercialization of technology will collectively lift the average renewable share across the EU to 20 per cent by 2020 (more than double the 2006 level of 9.2 per cent). The national targets range from 10 per cent to 49 per cent.

The Energy Efficiency Directive, proposed in June 2011, will further strengthen the climate-energy package. Implementation is expected to add 5 per cent to EU's 20 per cent emission reductions, bringing the total reduction to 25 per cent.

The transport sector is the second biggest GHG emitting sector after energy. It is responsible for around a quarter of the EU GHG emissions. Road transport alone contributes to about one-fifth of the EU's total emissions of carbon dioxide (CO_2). While GHG emissions in other sectors decreased 15 per cent between 1990 and 2007, emissions from transport increased 36 per cent during the same period. GHG emissions have been increasing for most modes of transport, thus the EU has put a range of policies in place aiming to lower emissions from the sector. These include:

- inclusion of aviation in the EU ETS
- a strategy to reduce emissions from cars and vans, including emissions targets for new vehicles
- a target to reduce the GHG intensity of fuels

- rolling resistance limits and tyre labelling requirements and mandatory tyre pressure monitors on new vehicles
- requirements for public authorities to take account of lifetime energy use and CO_2 emissions when procuring vehicles.

Key legislation regarding the implementation of climate policy in the transport sector is presented in Table 6.3.

Climate change is a global problem having increasing effect at various levels. Decisions on how to fight climate change and on energy, transport and other necessary measures involve multiple levels of governance. Multilevel governance, characterizing the changing relationships between actors situated at different territorial levels, is therefore an essential element in sustainable energy policy making (Committee of the Regions, 2010). Thus, we present how the Kyoto Protocol is implemented at national level and which measures are foreseen for the period after it expires.

National plans and financing

Slovenia

The present state

Slovenia ratified the UNFCCC in 1995 and the Kyoto Protocol in 2002. Within the framework of the Kyoto Protocol Slovenia assumed a commitment to achieve an 8 per cent reduction in GHG emissions in the first commitment period 2008–2012, with 1986 as the base year. In the period 2008–2012 Slovenia will have to lower its emissions to 18.6Tg CO_2 equivalent (Česen, 2006) (see Table 6.4).

Table 6.3 Key legislation regarding implementation of climate policy in transport sector

Directive 98/70/EC	relating to the quality of petrol and diesel fuels
Directive 1999/94/EC	relating to the availability of consumer information on fuel economy and CO_2 emissions in respect of the marketing of new passenger cars
Directive 2009/30/EC	as regards the specification of petrol, diesel and gas-oil and introducing a mechanism to monitor and reduce greenhouse gas emissions
Regulation (EC) No 443/2009	setting emission performance standards for new passenger cars as part of the community's integrated approach to reduce CO_2 emissions from light-duty vehicles
Commission Regulation (EU) No 1014/2010	on monitoring and reporting of data on the registration of new passenger cars
Regulation No 510/2011	setting emission performance standards for new light commercial vehicles as part of the Union's integrated approach to reduce CO_2 emissions from light-duty vehicles

Source: European Commission DG Climate Action, 2011

Table 6.4 Indicators relevant to GHG emissions and removals for Slovenia

	1986 base year)	*1995*	*2000*	*2005*	*2006*	*2007*	*2008*	*2009*	*Change from base year to latest reported year (%)*
Population (million)	1.98	1.99	1.99	2.00	2.00	2.01	2.02	2.04	3
GDP (US$2000 billion market prices)	16.62	16.07	19.889	23.83	25.22	26.93	27.87	25.70	55
GHG emissions without LULUCF (Tg CO_2 eq)	20.23	18.45	18.8	20.23	20.45	20.57	21.29	19.33	–4,3 (Target: –8%, 18.7)
GHG emissions with LULUCF (Tg CO_2 eq)	12.54	11.16	11.57	11.78	12.21	12.10	12.80	10.88	–13.23
CO_2 emissions t/ capita	n.a.	7.05	7.26	7.45	7.55	7.48	n.a.	n.a.	n.a.
CO_2 emissions per GDP unit (kg/ US$2000)	n.a.	0.87	0.73	0.63	0.60	0.56	n.a.	n.a.	n.a.

Source: Kramar and Cegnar, 2010; and World Bank, 2011

Most recent GHG emission data show that emissions, despite the fall in 2009, are still well above the target of minus 8 per cent for the period 2008–2012. The decline in GHG emissions was sharper than the decline in GDP. Still, in the coming years, Slovenia needs to speed up the effort on climate change.

As regards reporting obligations, Slovenia submitted five national communications. It regularly submits its national emissions inventory and in 2006 reported on demonstrable progress under the Kyoto Protocol. As Slovenia was late in delivering its Second National Communication, it submitted it together with the Third National Communication in the single document in 2004.

Policy and regulation

One of the very first measures aimed at reducing GHG emissions in Slovenia was the adoption of the CO_2 tax in 1996. The tax was charged for the use of fossil fuels. At its introduction the tax amounted to SIT1/kg CO_2; in 1998 this was increased to SIT3/kg CO_2 (€15/t CO_2). The increase was followed by the introduction of partial exemptions for the purpose of enhancing the competitiveness of industry. Following an examination of consistency of the carbon tax with EU state aid rules, the carbon tax was revised in 2005. According to the new rules, partial tax returns became conditional upon signing an agreement on reduction of specific carbon dioxide emissions. Installations that participated in EU ETS were exempted from the carbon tax payment. Although it was never very successful in terms of emission reductions, it definitely brought attention to the problem. In 2000 the CO_2 tax contributed approximately 1 per cent to the total budgetary income (Paradiž and Kranjc, 2002).

The National Environmental Protection Programme adopted in 1999 included the reduction of GHG emissions as a priority and in 2000 the government adopted the Strategy and Short-term Action Plan of Reduction of GHG Emissions.

The main objective of the Strategy was to create conditions to enable the meeting of obligations from the first commitment period 2008–2012. It listed more than 120 measures for reducing emissions, although no time frame was given for the implementation of individual measures. In 2001 the Slovenian government started implementing measures from the short-term action plan, which was a part of the Strategy. In 2003 the Operational Programme (OP) for Limiting GHG Emissions was adopted and amended a year later. Environmental public finance reform (so-called green tax reform) was considered a key domestic instrument for GHG emission reduction. The reform provided for increasing taxes and excise duties for the use of environmental goods (Česen *et al.*, 2004: 40).

The OP for Limiting GHG Emissions until 2012 was adopted in 2006. The majority of measures in various sectors have been implemented, with the exception of the transport sector. Emissions have begun to increase rapidly in the transport sector since Slovenia entered the EU. Thus, a new OP that adapts the measures to reduce GHG emissions and contains measures in line with the EU climate policy was adopted in 2009.

For the period up to 2020, Slovenia is entitled to increase its GHG emissions by 4 per cent to the base year 2005 (see Table 6.4). The target relating to the share of energy from renewable sources in the gross final consumption is 25 per cent (which is a significant increase from 16 per cent in 2005).

A reduction of emissions in the energy sector is stimulated by replacing solid fossil fuels with natural gas, increasing the efficiency of plants and installations (in line with the Action Plan for Energy Efficiency adopted in 2008), replacing old boilers with new ones and increasing the proportion of combined heat and power generation, as well as by increasing the capacity for electricity and heat production from renewable energy sources, especially hydropower in the generation of electricity and wood biomass to produce heat (in line with the National Renewable Energy Action Plan, adopted in 2010). The main renewable targets are 25.3 per cent of final energy consumption from renewable sources (32.8 per cent of the heating and cooling sector and 39.4 per cent of electricity) and 10.7 per cent of the transport sector. Introduction of biodiesel, together with an increased efficiency of vehicles is expected to significantly contribute to the reduction of emissions in the transport sector. In the industrial sector, a further reduction in energy intensity is expected, along with a reduction in fluorinated gas (F-gas) emissions.

In the waste sector the reduction in quantities of waste disposed in landfills will contribute to lower methane emissions. In agriculture, the promotion of nature-friendly farming is expected, as well as the implementation of good agricultural practice in fertilizer use.

It is expected that national measures for reducing GHG emissions will not be sufficient to comply with the Kyoto target. Slovenia will have to purchase the rights to GHG emissions. In 2010 the Government Office of Climate Change drafted the Climate Change Act and started preparing the long-term low-carbon Strategy of Slovenia to determine the national policy of climate change mitigation and adaptation till 2050.[2]

Slovenia simply highlighted the significance of Slovenian forests that has been providing significant carbon sink. Based on this argument, Slovenia's position was to request more reward for parties that have been developing sustainable forest management under the Kyoto Protocol. Consequently, Slovenia also prioritizes projects on sustainable forest management when giving out funding.

Slovenia is still the country having the greatest percentage of forest area (see Table 6.5) compared to the total area of the country. This will lead to a reason of why, later in the Cancún Agreement, Slovenia insisted on requesting more appreciation from the Protocol toward countries who have been working on forest protection. In line with the effort to keep and extend forest area and in order to achieve the target of reversing the loss of environmental resources, countries are making sure to provide more and more renewable internal freshwater resources.

Institutions

The Ministry of Environment and Spatial Planning is responsible for the preparation and implementation of environmental policies and legislation. It defines strategically important long-term directions and goals concerning environmental protection, and preventing or mitigating threats to sustainable development. Climate change is defined as one of the key areas by the Resolution on the National Environmental Protection Programme.[3] The Ministry also submits national communications to the UNFCCC.

The Environmental Agency of the Republic of Slovenia implements environmental legislation and tasks in the field of environmental protection and monitoring. It also prepares inventories on national emissions.

The Government Office of the Republic of Slovenia of Climate Change, established in 2009, is a central body regarding climate change. It is in charge of drafting strategic and operational documents and legal acts in this area, providing the guidance of sectoral policies and also of reporting and monitoring its implementation.

Table 6.5 Forest area of Slovenia (percentage of land area)

	1990	*2000*	*2005*	*2010*	*Increase*
Bulgaria	30.07	30.51	33.61	36.16	20.23
Croatia	33.06	33.68	34.01	34.31	3.78
Romania	27.78	27.71	27.79	28.59	2.92
Slovenia	58.99	61.22	61.72	62.21	5.47
Turkey	12.58	13.18	13.95	14.73	17.09

Source: World Databank, 2011

The Ministry of Transport, the Ministry of Agriculture, Forestry and Food, the Ministry of the Economy and the Ministry of Finance also have a role in formulating climate policies.

Eko Sklad, the Environmental Fund of the Republic of Slovenia founded in 1995, provides grants and favourable loans to legal and natural persons for reducing environmental impacts.

Competencies of Slovenian municipalities in the field of reduction of GHG emissions are related to spatial development planning, local and public traffic regulations, preparing local energy use plans and waste collection and deposition. Urban municipalities are obliged to provide monitoring for emissions and adopt environmental protection programmes, as well as action plans.

Financing

In 2004, compliance costs for achieving the Kyoto target were estimated at around €15–33 million a year (Česen *et al.*, 2004: 43). In the period 2004–2008 it was planned that around €50 million a year would be collected from CO_2 tax (Resolution on the National Environmental Action Programme 2005–2012, 2005).

At the time, it was estimated that the tax policy together with market-based instruments (primarily emissions trading), loans and support for technology development would be sufficient. The National Strategic Reference Framework (NSRF) for the period 2007–2013 did not foresee any funding for climate change adaptation or mitigation.[4] However, as emissions continued to increase, new measures were foreseen and the implementation cost was estimated at €685 million for the period 2009–2012. Out of this, €604 million is necessary for the implementation of domestic measures and €80 million for buying emission permits. Out of €604 million, €80.4 million will come from the budget, €242.6 million from EU funds and €281.7 million from other sources (Operativni program zmanjševanja emisij toplogrednih plinov do leta 2012) (OPTgP-1, 2009).

The implementation of climate policy is expected to contribute to 0.1–0.3 per cent of the GDP by 2020 and to the creation of 0.3–0.5 per cent of additional jobs. Consistent implementation of climate policy will have a positive impact particularly on small and medium-sized high-tech companies. In the longer term, the implementation of law on fiscal revenues improves the competitiveness of the overall economy through the support for research and development and through reducing the burden of taxes and contributions (Zakon o podnebnih spremembah 3. Osnutek, 2011).

Previously, Slovenia used some external financing for its climate policy, mainly technical support.[5] Reaching high productivity and efficiency standards in the steel and metal industry enabled the Slovenian private sector to provide capacity building support to developing countries (Cisse *et al.*, 2003). Slovenia has recently launched programmes and activities to support and promote the development, application and diffusion and financing of the transfer and access to environmental technology to combat climate change (Kramar and Cegnar, 2010). For the post-Kyoto period, Slovenia pledged €8 million[6] for the 'fast-start finance', with a division of €0.5 million for 2010, €3 million for 2011 and €4.5 million for 2012. The financial support provided by Slovenia is dedicated mainly to western Balkan countries, in which the pilot project on energy rehabilitation was done in Montenegro.

The fast-start finance took 0.08 per cent of the annual GDP.[7] By 2020, according to UNFCCC, the developed countries have to mobilize US$100 billion or indicative of 1.5 per cent of its GDP, which means that Slovenia will have to save a much bigger part of its GDP to finance the developing countries. Although, basically, great global cooperation is required to solve the climate change issue, it is not very feasible considering the global crisis which has been causing deficit in most of the developed countries' budgets.

Bulgaria

The present state

The emission reduction target for Bulgaria under the Kyoto Protocol during the first commitment period (2008–2012) is 8 per cent of the base year (1998) emissions, to the level of 122Tg CO_2. Bulgaria is on track to meet its Kyoto commitments: it reports (regularly submits national emissions inventories, national communications on climate change and had submitted a report on demonstrable progress of the Republic of Bulgaria to achieve commitments under the Kyoto Protocol) and managed to reduce its emissions. Bulgaria's GHG emissions almost halved compared to the base year and are significantly below the level of 122Tg CO_2, the average annual level to which Bulgaria should limit its emissions during the Kyoto Protocol's first commitment period between 2008 and 2012[8] (see Table 6.6).

The main drivers of emission trends in Bulgaria are demographic developments, economic activity (including changes in the sectoral structure) and changes in energy use and transport patterns.[9] Following a sharp decrease in the 1990s, emissions rose in the period 2005–2007, but significantly slower than GDP. In 2008 GDP continued to rise, but at a slower rate, while emissions declined. The fall in emissions in 2009 was sharper than the GDP decline (Bulgarian Ministry of Environment and Water, 2010).

Policy and regulations

Despite the fact that the economic situation in Bulgaria did not allow for the allocation of extensive government funding for implementing climate change related policies, nor were the companies able to invest, climate change policy has been developing. Main drivers for implementing climate change measures were commitments under the Climate Convention, the Kyoto Protocol and the EU accession. In the pre-accession period Bulgaria had gradually aligned with the EU *acquis* on environment, including the climate change. Based on these commitments, the National Environmental Strategy was developed for the period 2005–2014 together with the Second National Plan on Climate Change (2005–2009).[10]

Table 6.6 Indicators relevant to GHG emissions and removals for Bulgaria

	Base year	*1995*	*2000*	*2005*	*2006*	*2007*	*2008*	*2009*	*Changes from base year to latest reported year (%)*
Population (million)	8.98	8.40	8.06	7.74	7.69	7.66	7.62	7.58	–15.5
GDP (const. US$2000 billion, market prices)	16.57	12.76	12.9	16.85	17.94	19.10	20.29	19.28	16.35
GHG emissions without LULUCF (Tg CO_2 eq)	132.61	88.01	67.7	67.1	68.3	71.7	69.02	59.49	–52.21
GHG emissions with LULUCF (Tg CO_2 eq)	110.33	67.98	53.10	55.77	56.89	61.51	57.46	47.71	–56.8
CO_2 emissions t/capita	8.79	6.93	5.34	60.7	6.24	6.75	n.a.	n.a.	
CO_2 emissions per GDP unit (kg per US$2000)	5.26	4.56	3.33	2.79	2.68	2.71	n.a.	n.a.	

Source: UNFCCC, 2010 and World Bank, 2011

The basic principles of the national policy on climate change were developed on the basis of Bulgaria's good will to join the efforts of the international community to solve the climate change problems according to the potential of the national economy and looking at the opportunity to attract foreign investments, which would facilitate their implementation (Bulgarian Ministry of Environment and Water, 2006). Bluntly, the key characteristics of Bulgarian climate polices were relying on measures that did not require significant financial support from the state (Second National Plan). Measures included the development of the Green Certificates Scheme under the Renewable Energy Directive and Emissions Trading Scheme and cost-effective measures that contribute to long-term cost savings in the energy sector, industry, residential and commercial/institutional buildings, transport, agriculture and waste management (Fourth National Report on Climate Change).

As regards investments, Bulgaria was trying to attract foreign investments and donor funds from multilateral financing institutions such as EBRD and the World Bank, EU structural funds such as ISPA, the EU ETS and financial sources directly linked to the Kyoto mechanisms, primarily JI.

High emission factors for electricity consumption in energy intensive industries (1.59kg CO_2/kWh) and in light industry (1.68kg CO_2/kWh) in the late 1990s enabled the implementation of the low costs of the GHG reduction measures. Potential for the reduction of energy intensity and hence for GHG mitigation, in the industrial sector of Bulgaria was estimated at more than 3Tg CO_2 annually.

Roughly half of the measures' costs were less than US$10 per tonne of CO_2 reduction and did not need a special programme. The companies that were to implement the remaining 50–60 per cent of measures had limited capital resources and were unable to finance investments, including those with a payback period less than three years. This made Bulgaria very attractive for JI projects.[11] Bulgaria ranked as the most attractive country for JI investments in 2006, but it fell to sixth place in 2008 and its rating further deteriorated in 2009 (Point Carbon, 2010).

For the period until 2020 Bulgaria adopted 40 per cent GHG reduction target[12] and a mandatory national target of a 16 per cent share of energy from renewable sources in the gross internal energy consumption, as well as a 10 per cent share of energy from renewable sources in transport by 2020.

Institutions

The Ministry of Environment and Water is responsible for overall climate policy and its implementation at national level. A subordinate body, The Executive Environmental Agency, monitors implementation, prepares GHG inventories, projections and registers and carries out the procedures on issuing GHG emission permits. The Energy Inter-ministerial Committee on Climate Change, Joint Implementation Steering Committee and Inter-ministerial Working Group for Development of the National Allocation Plan are established to facilitate the inter-ministerial coordination of climate related activities.

However, it should be noted that Bulgaria was suspended from participation in the flexible mechanisms from June 2010 to February 2011, because its national system for recording GHG emissions was not transparent and untrustworthy due to a lack of financial and human resources. Only one person (working in the Executive Environmental Agency) was in charge of the country's annual reports. The Bulgarian National Allocation Plan for the period 2008–2012, originally submitted in 2007, was twice rejected by the Commission before it was finally adopted in 2010. One of the reasons for rejecting this Plan was the fact that Bulgaria used an outdated model for its preparation instead of the latest version. These problems highlight challenges relating to institutional capacity, which go beyond mismanagement of national registries and extend to the political will to take the necessary measures to dedicate government funding, and build expertise and knowledge (Spassov *et al*., 2011).

In order to meet (existing) 2020 targets, institutional capacity has to be strengthened as it provides an important 'enabling environment' for climate action. Its absence increases the abatement hurdle. Following the update of regional development plans in 2011, the territorial context of climate change strategic planning is expected to be strengthened (Shirishtov and Stoyanoff, 2011).

Financing

According to the Kyoto Protocol, Bulgaria has much lower emissions than the admissible. The need for Bulgaria to undertake (and finance) emission reduction measures is thus limited, given the current GHG emission level and expected emission trends. However, it has potential for an additional decrease of GHG emissions. Implementation of such measures is driven primarily by economic and political development. The Bulgarian fiscal policy contains instruments to stimulate measures to reduce emissions of GHG and/or save energy. The Energy Efficiency Fund, State Agricultural Fund, Kyoto Protocol Mechanisms, JI, International Emission Trading, Green Investment Scheme and EU structural funds are among principal policy instruments applied to climate policy. The importance of these instruments can be illustrated by the fact that the estimated loss in revenue caused by suspension from the flexible mechanisms in 2010 is €250 million. The suspension might also have impact on surplus of allowed auction units in the first commitment period. They are estimated at around 200,000Gg CO_2 equivalent, which the government plans to sell. The income might be used for financing additional measures, which will be necessary if EU accepts 30 per cent reduction target. Accepting a 30 per cent reduction target would increase the burden on Bulgaria, but on the other hand, would result in significant public health benefits, in the range of €48–291 million compared to the 20 per cent target (Health and Environment Alliance, 2010).

Romania

The present state

Romania signed UNFCCC in 1922 and ratified it in 2004. Romania later signed the Kyoto Protocol in 1997 and was the first Annex I country that ratified it (in 2001).

The total GHG emission – excluding land use, land-use changes and forestry (LULUCF) – decreased by 54 per cent during 1989–2009 (see Table 6.7), while net GHG emissions (including LULUCF) decreased 62 per cent during the same period. The Romanian reduction target is 8 per cent. Based on these observations, there is a high probability that Romania will meet the commitments regarding the reduction of GHG emissions for the first commitment period, 2008–2012. It will actually achieve significant surplus emission rights.

Policy and regulations

Since 2005, when the Kyoto Protocol entered into force, the climate change policy framework in Romania has been based on the National Strategy on Climate Change and the National Action Plan on Climate Change.

The Strategy represented the general framework for implementing climate change policies and measures during 2005–2007 period, with the aim to meet the Kyoto Protocol and related commitments of the EU. The main instrument for implementing the Strategy is the Action Plan, which assigns tasks and responsibilities to stakeholders, provides deadlines and identifies potential funding sources. Regular update of both documents was foreseen (in 2007, 2008 and 2012) in order to reflect changing circumstances in the Romanian economy as well as the increased knowledge in the field.

Table 6.7 Indicators relevant to GHG emissions and removals for Romania

	Base	*1995*	*2000*	*2005*	*2006*	*2007*	*2008*	*2009*	*Changes from base year to latest reported year (%)*
Population (million)	23.15	22.68	22.43	21.52	21.59	21.57	21.50	21.50	
GDP (US$2000 billion, market prices)	46.4	43.99	39.5	37.05	48.9	52.76	55.93	61.2	
GHG emissions without LULUCF (Tg CO_2 eq)	292.92	187.88	142.12	155.74	160.40	156.21	153.42	130.83	–54.17
GHG emissions with LULUCF (Tg CO_2 eq)	250.56	148.90	104.12	118.56	123.21	120.1	117.0	94.30	–62.33
CO_2 emissions (t/capita)	6.84	5.66	3.90	4.24	4.56	4.37			
CO_2 emissions per GDP unit (kg per US$2000)	3.61	3.25	2.37	1.68	1.87	1.88	n.a.	n.a.	

Source: UNFCCC, 2010 and World Bank, 2011

Meeting the Kyoto target does not present a challenge for Romania. The EU membership and climate–energy policy are thus the main driving forces for climate policy. The goals of the climate policy, in addition to direct contribution to GHG reduction, are more efficient forms of energy production, improvement in the transport system and improved human health. The Romanian Strategy on Atmosphere Protection focused on policies and measures that require only a limited contribution from the state budget and that show economic side-benefits. Also, the policies and measures included in the National Action Plan were limited to those that have a large potential impact on emissions and that can realistically be implemented in the period 2006–2007. However, lack of financial measures has hampered implementation of measures (Romanian Ministry of Environment and Water Management, 2006).

Based on the objective of reducing GHG emissions by 20 per cent by 2020 compared to the 2005 level and according to the Effort Sharing Directive, Romania is entitled to increase its emissions by 17 per cent to the base year 2005, i.e. up to 140Tg CO_2 equivalent. In 2005 Romanian GHG emissions halved compared to 1990 level, thus Romania actually accepted a 44 per cent reduction target compared to 1990.

The energy sector is by far the largest contributor to the GHG emissions in Romania. It accounts for nearly 80 per cent of the total national GHG emissions.

Industrial processes follow with 14.5 per cent contribution to total national GHG emissions. The main Romanian policies to reduce GHG emissions include measures in the energy sector, industrial processes, transport, agriculture, waste management and forestry. Romania committed to increase the share from renewable sources from 18 per cent in 2005 to 24 per cent in 2020.

Romania uses market-based instruments to reduce emissions. Participation in the EU ETS and in JI is seen as a cost-effective way to reduce CO_2 emissions. In 2010 Romania created a legal framework for trading excesses of assigned amount units (AAU) and on the initiation and development of green investment schemes.

Institutions

The Ministry of Environment and Forests (until 2007 the Ministry for Environmental and Water Management) develops national policy on climate change and coordinates implementing activities at national, regional and local levels. It is technically supported by the National Environmental Protection Agency, established in 2005. The Agency is a specialized body responsible for ensuring the implementation of environmental protection related strategies, policies and legislation, including climate change. The main climate related responsibilities include maintaining and updating the GHG inventory, compliance with other reporting obligations, coordination of relevant activities developed at regional and local levels developed by regional and local environmental protection agencies.

The National Environmental Fund Administration manages the database of the GHG emissions reduction projects and administers green investment schemes funds.

The National Commission on Climate Change established in 1996 is a consultative body which aims to support the integration of climate policy into other sectoral policies. It also provides advice related to the approval of the National Communications and GHG inventories, as well as the approval of JI projects and emission trading activities. Almost all of the ministries have to implement environmental protection measures in sectoral policies, and provide input to annual reports on the implementation of the National Strategy on Climate Change and the National Acton Plan on Climate Change. The annual report is prepared by the Ministry of Environment and Forests and submitted to the National Commission on Climate Change.

The 42 local environmental protection agencies are used in some cases as a source of bottom-up data for the inventory (in the case of some HFCs, PFCs and SF_6 consumption).

The weaknesses of the Romanian system for evaluating its GHG emissions, in particular with respect to reports on LULUCF, in 2011 resulted in the decision of the Kyoto Protocol Compliance Committee to suspend Romania's right to trade on the carbon market. This means that, throughout the suspension period, Romania will be unable to sell its surplus AAU.

Financing

The National Action Plan on Climate Change of Romania estimated that additional €2.2 million was necessary for its implementation in the period 2005–2007. The measures foreseen are mainly for capacity building necessary for the creation of enabling conditions, such as improving the system for estimating GHG, development of the national registry, strengthening cooperation between agencies, institutions and other stakeholders. Lack of funds hampered implementation and led to the suspension of Romania from carbon trading.

As regard investment to ensure the reduction of GHG, Romania relies on flexible mechanisms provisioned through the Kyoto Protocol. The Ministry of Environment and Forests approved 17 JI projects with a reduction potential of approximately 21 million tonnes of CO_2 equivalent. Another important mechanism of the Kyoto Protocol is the International Trading of Emissions within green investment schemes by trading the excess of AAU.

According to official statistics, Romania has a surplus of 300 million AAU. By selling them Romania could raise between €1.5 and €3 billion (ICIS Heren, 2010).[13] The money raised from the sale of AAUs would be invested in green investment schemes, which include the rehabilitation and desulphurization of coal-fired power plants.

Croatia

The present state

Croatia has ratified the Kyoto Protocol in 2007 following the pressure from the EU and the decision of the Conference of Parties (COP 12) in Nairobi in November 2006, allowing Croatia 3500 Gg CO_2 emissions to the 1990 base year.[14] Croatia has to reduce its GHG emissions by 5 per cent in the first commitment period 2008–2012. The assigned amount has not yet been confirmed, thus Croatia cannot participate in flexible mechanisms.[15]

After an initial sharp decline in both GDP and GHG emissions (in the period 1990–1995) (see Table 6.8), the emission trends follow the pattern of the GDP development. GDP and emissions' projections before crisis indicated that Croatia would not be able to meet its commitments without flexible mechanisms. UNFCCC has reported that by the year 2008 Croatia had reduced by 0.9 per cent emission from the base year, far from its target of minus 5 per cent. The recession and the related economic downturn, and to some extent the implementation of emission reduction measures, resulted in a significant reduction in GHG emissions in 2008 and 2009. Thus, Croatia seems to be on track to meet the Kyoto target.

Policy and regulations

Capacity building activities and the establishment of a system of necessary institutional, legislative and organizational capacities were launched in conformity

Table 6.8 Indicators relevant to GHG emissions and removals for Croatia

	Base year	*1995*	*2000*	*2005*	*2006*	*2007*	*2008*	*2009*	*Changes from base year to latest reported year (%)*
Population (million)	4.77	4.66	4.42	4.44	4.44	4.44	4.43	4.43	–7.1
GDP (const, US$2000 billion market prices)	25.12	18.19	21.49	26.73	28.05	29.47	30.18	27.43	9.2
GHG emissions without LULUCF (Tg CO_2 eq)	31.44	22.98	26.02	30.27	30.66	32.21	30.98	28.85	–8.2
GHG emissions with LULUCF (Tg CO_2 eq)	24.51	16.11	18.80	22.17	22.44	23.7	22.31	20.15	–17.7
CO_2 emissions t/capita	n.a.	3.94	4.57	5.31	5.33	5.60	n.a.	n.a.	n.a.
CO_2 emissions per GDP unit (kg per US$2000)	1.01	0.94	0.88	0.84	0.84	n.a.	n.a.	n.a.	n.a.

Source: UNFCCC, 2010 and World Bank, 2011

with the recommendations of the First National Communication. The Action Plan for implementation of the Convention and Kyoto Protocol was included in the Air Quality Protection and Improvement Plan 2008–2011. The Plan also provides for measures in energy, transport, industry, agriculture, and forestry and waste sectors. These sectors are identified as the main drivers of emissions (Bašić *et. al.*, 2006: 35). The energy sector, which is responsible for 50 per cent of GHG emissions, also has the greatest potential for the reduction of GHG. The estimated potential for the reduction of CO_2 in the energy sector ranges between 2,168.2Gg and 5,586.5Gg CO_2 equivalent by 2020, depending on the investment in implementing measures. Comparable potential for reduction in other sectors (namely industrial processes, agriculture and waste management) does not exist. The policy measures that are so far put in place basically transpose EU rules in national legislation.

Monitoring and reporting obligations are considered to be a part of the air sector Regulation. Market-based mechanisms and incentives so far have not been successful. Due to the size of the Croatian economy, the national trading scheme was not foreseen. Inclusion into the European Union ETS is planned following Croatia's accession.[16] Thus, Croatia will not participate in flexible mechanisms in the first commitment period.[17]

For the period until 2020 Croatia officially pledged that it would accept a 5 per cent reduction target on the 1990 base year. However, the individual pledge is expected to be replaced by a common EU target if Croatia joins the EU in 2013 as planned. The Croatian commitments will thus be resolved at a bilateral level with the EU. Upon expiration of the first Kyoto period 2008–2012 the EU might loan Croatia additional needed emission allowances, from the future non-energy emission quotas, including, among others, the sectors of agriculture, waste management, household, transport, which are anticipated in the 2013–2020 period. In negotiating positions for EU accession with regard to these sectors, an increase in emissions by 11 per cent for the period 2013–2020 was determined. Such an arrangement would ensure the environmental integrity as it would not result in an increase in the total amount of allowed emissions of the EU and Croatia by 2020.

Institutions

At the national level, the Ministry of Environmental Protection, Physical Planning and Construction plays a major role in creating environmental policy, including those relating to climate change.[18] The Ministry is in charge of setting the strategic policy, coordinating and supervising its implementation, carrying out administrative work and providing technical assistance. The activities relating to climate protection fall within the competence of the Department for Atmosphere Protection and are operationally carried out by the Division for the Climate and Ozone Layer Protection.

The Croatian Environmental Agency collects and consolidates environmental data and manages the emission inventories at the national level.

The Environmental Protection and Energy Efficiency Fund supports the implementation of the UNFCCC and the Kyoto Protocol by financing projects and programs. Other line ministries, such as the Ministry of Economy, Labour and Entrepreneurship and the Ministry of Agriculture, Fisheries and Rural Development, are responsible for implementing sector-specific measures identified by the Air Quality Protection and Improvement Plan 2008–2011.

Financing

The costs of implementing the Kyoto Protocol in the first commitment period 2008–2012 are estimated at €40.5 million a year with an average reduction cost of €14 per Mg CO_2 equivalent. Reduction of emissions exceeding 2,800Gg CO_2 would require investments of €30 per Mg CO_2 equivalent. Thus it is expected that the implementation of the post-Kyoto targets would require participation in flexible mechanisms.

As regards financing sources, roughly half of necessary funds should be invested in the energy sector, as incentives for renewable and co-generation, and collected through electricity bills (Croatian Ministry of Environmental Protection, Physical Planning and Construction, 2007). It was estimated that €20–30 million per year would be collected and invested. However, the data show that while the collection is in line with the plan, the second largest sources of financing are CO_2 fees, collected by the Environmental Protection and Energy Efficiency Fund. Roughly €1.5–2 million annually is expected to be covered by the state budget (see Table 6.9).

In an effort to reduce emissions, Croatia has enjoyed assistance from the EU through the Community Assistance for Reconstruction, Development, and Stabilization since 2000, later on replaced by the Instrument of Pre-accession Assistance (IPA). Apart from the EU, financial assistance for environmental issues is also granted by the United Nations Development Programme (UNDP) as it encompasses the seventh MDG on sustainable development. UNDP assists Croatia in several ways: e.g. by demonstrating innovative practices for engaging local stakeholders in environmental planning; supporting integrated policy measures and drafting key environmental legislation; and increasing the level and type of predominantly commercial financing for investments, which promote energy efficiency and biodiversity. One significant project is also held in Croatia jointly by UNDP and the Global Environment Facility (GEF) entitled 'Climate Change Enabling Activity' that improves the implementation of biodiesel and energy efficient construction.

Turkey

The present state

Turkey ratified the Kyoto Protocol in 2009 and has a specific status vis-à-vis the current climate regime. When UNFCCC was adopted at the Rio Conference in 1992, Turkey was an OECD member. Thus, Turkey was included in Annex I and

Table 6.9 Main financing sources 2007–2012

	Time period	*Indicative amount €million/year*	*Collected amount*	*Invested*
State budget	2006–2012	1–1.5		
Incentives for renewable and co-generation	2007–2012	20–30	17	26%
CO_2 fee – stationary sources	2007–2010	10–20	15.5	
CO_2 Fee in transport and small sources	Starting in 2009 (with ETS)	10–15	n.a.	
CO_2 fee for foreign vehicles	2007–2012	2–3	Not implemented	
GEF	2005–2010	15.5		
CARDS	2007–2008	0.5–1		
LIFE – Third countries	2005–2007	0.56		

Source: Croatian Ministry of Environmental Protection, Physical Planning and Construction, 2007: 88

II of the Convention. In 2001 COP recognized special circumstances (Decision 26/CP.7) and Turkey was deleted from the list of Annex II countries. By the accession to UNFCCC in 2004, Turkey made the following main commitments:

- to submit regular reports, national communications and GHG inventories
- to implement policies and measures in climate change mitigation, adaptation, research, education and public awareness.

When the Kyoto Protocol was adopted in 1997, Turkey was not party to the UNFCCC. Turkey was, therefore, not included in Annex B of the Protocol which lists the individual targets for Annex I Parties to the UNFCCC. This enabled Turkey to become party to the Kyoto Protocol without taking any quantified emission limitations or reduction commitments within the first commitment period. On the other hand, Turkey cannot participate in flexible mechanisms as only non-Annex I Parties can host CDM, and only Annex B parties can participate in joint implementation and international emission trading.

Despite the fact that Turkey does not have a binding reduction target, the implementation of its commitments is a challenge. Turkey has not yet submitted (as of September 2011) its Fifth National Communication to the UNFCCC, which was due on 1 January 2010. Previous reports were not fully consistent with the structure outlined in the UNFCCC reporting guidelines. For instance, reporting the energy sector was not transparent enough: the calculation methodologies were not well documented and there was insufficient background information to enable the calculations (UNFCCC, 2007).

GHG emissions from fuel combustion increased by 73.1 per cent, from 130,698.13Gg CO_2 equivalent in 1990 to 226,200.42Gg CO_2 equivalent in 2004, mainly due to the increase in emissions from the energy and manufacturing industries and construction. Emissions from the transport sector increased by 55.5 per cent over the period 1990–2004. In 2008, the inventory for Turkey was partially in line with the guidelines. The expert review team noted that there were deficiencies of varying degrees in respect of all the inventory reporting principles (i.e. transparency, completeness, comparability, consistency, accuracy). The majority of these deficiencies are evidently due to the lack of proper institutional and organizational arrangements and an adequate allocation of resources for preparing and reporting the emission inventories (UNFCCC, 2009). The 2010 annual submission of Turkey contains a complete set of common reporting format tables for the period 1990–2008 and a National Inventory Report (NIR). The annual submission was submitted in accordance with the guidelines. Table 6.10 provides some data which illustrate specific national circumstances.

In the period since 1990 the Turkish population has increased by almost 18 million, or 32.2 per cent. It has had the highest population growth among the industrialized countries within Annex 1 of the UNFCCC. GHG emissions have also increased at the highest rate among Annex 1 countries since 1990, by 97 per cent. Ratification of the Kyoto Protocol was, therefore, debated for a long time over fears that it would cause economic and social problems. According to

Table 6.10 Indicators relevant to GHG emissions and removals for Turkey

	Base	*1995*	*2000*	*2005*	*2006*	*2007*	*2008*	*2009*	*Change from base year to latest reported year (%)*
Population (million)	55.12	59.76	64.23	68.58	69.42	70.26	72.52	72.90	32.2
GDP (const. US$2000 billion, market prices)	186.64	218.60	266.57	333.04	356.00	372.62	375.07	357.49	91.53
GHG emissions without LULUCF (Tg CO2 eq)	187.03	237.51	297.0	329.64	349.64	379.8	366.5	369.65	97.64
GHG emissions with LULUCF (Tg CO2 eq)	142.16	175.67	229.45	260.36	273.71	303.70	285.92	287.12	101.97
CO2 emissions t/capita	2.69	2.88	3.25	3.33	3.63	3.95	n.a.	n.a.	
CO2 emissions per GDP unit (kg per US$2000)	0.81	0.81	0.81	0.71	0.73	0.77	n.a.	n.a.	

Source: UNFCCC, 2010 and World Bank, 2011

the available estimates, a 5 per cent reduction target would lead to 59 per cent decrease of GNP. Flexibility, allowing 30 per cent increase of emissions to the base year, would lead to 16 per cent decrease of GNP (Bhutto *et al.*, n.d.).

Policy and regulations

The National Climate Change Strategy was adopted in 2010 as a framework for climate change policy. The Strategy will guide actions to tackle climate change during the 2010–2020 period. It will be updated as necessary, taking into account national or international developments.

The Strategy provides for GHG emission control of the following sectors: energy, transport, industry, waste, land-use, agriculture and forestry. It differentiates between short-term (to be achieved within one year), mid-term (undertaken or completed within one to three years) and long-term objectives (over a ten year period) but does not provide measurable targets. In the period until 2020, Turkey aims to limit GHG emission growth by 11 per cent compared to the business-as-usual scenario.

As Turkey is not eligible for flexible mechanisms, the voluntary carbon market is the principal instrument for cost-effective emission reduction. The number (109), volume (US$83.2 million in 2010) and results (annual emission reduction 8Tg CO_2 equivalent) of the voluntary carbon market make Turkey one of the first and most successful countries in the emerging voluntary markets. The relevance of the voluntary carbon market might support Turkey's negotiations to be considered as a carbon seller country by hosting clean development mechanisms or JI projects in the post-2012 period.

Institutions

The Ministry of Environment and Forestry coordinates activities related to climate policies. While the inter-ministerial Coordination Board on Climate Change was already established in 2001 (and restructured twice, in 2004 following Turkish ratification of the UNFCCC and in 2010 following Turkish accession to the Kyoto Protocol), the Climate Change Department within the Ministry was established in 2009.

The 2009 review report (par. 26) noted that Turkey was still lacking institutional capacity, but that the parties planned to allocate more human and financial resources (UNFCCC, 2009). The plan included the establishment of two additional working groups, as well as climate change focal points in all institutions represented in the Coordination Board on Climate Change and identifying a single national entity with responsibility for the inventory submission. The responsibility for the national inventory has been mainly shared between the Ministry of Environment and Forestry and the Turkish Statistical Office, TurkStat. Other ministries, organizations and institutions, as well as universities, are also involved in the preparation of the inventory.

TurkStat is the main organization responsible for the preparation of the national inventory. It collects activity data from the Ministry of Agriculture and Rural Affairs, the Ministry of Environment and Forestry, the Ministry of Transportation and the Ministry of Energy and Natural Resources. The Ministry of Agriculture and Rural Affairs and the Ministry of Environment and Forestry provide estimates for emissions and removals from the LULUCF sector. TurkStat is responsible for the processing of common reporting format tables and for the compilation of the NIR (UNFCCC, 2011).

Financing

Actually, signing the Kyoto Protocol has not put an additional burden on Turkey until 2012. The government estimated the cost of implementing climate policy until 2012 at €58 billion, out of which €15 billion investment will be made by the private sector (Yavuz and Altintas, 2009) to €100 billion (Yapanoglu, 2009) to adopt the Kyoto and EU environmental requirements in the first commitment period. Therefore, the environmental market will grow. This not only provides new business opportunities, but also opportunities for the adoption of new growth models which can foster changes in agriculture, manufacturing, transportation and other industries.

Despite the high price of compliance ratification, the Kyoto is seen as a positive economic step (Hattam, 2009) as it is expected to foster innovation and clean technology. While the National Climate Change Strategy contains a chapter on finance, it is rather vague about the size of necessary funds. It says that existing financial resources will be reassessed, and new funding explored in the short term. The capacity building activities, as well as the preparation of national inventories was funded from external sources.

Conclusions

The Kyoto Protocol is going to expire on 31 December, 2012. The successor treaty has not been agreed upon yet, but the goal is set to limit an increase of global temperature to two degrees Celsius.

There is no agreement on how to reach the agreed target, but there is an understanding that developed countries should finance domestic measures as well as adaptation and mitigation measures in developing countries.

As parties to the Kyoto Protocol, Bulgaria, Romania, Slovenia and Croatia have adopted binding reduction targets (8 per cent decrease of emissions; 5 per cent Croatia). Turkey has no commitment.

All the focus countries requested recognition of specific national circumstances under the Kyoto Protocol. They have relied of foreign assistance to build institutional capacity for climate policy creation and implementation.

The focus countries are either EU member states or candidates. According to their GNI per capita, they are considered as upper middle income (Bulgaria, Romania, and Turkey) or high income countries (Croatia, Slovenia). Thus, they are likely to be expected to participate in climate funds.

Climate policy has not been high on the agenda: institutions lack human and financial resources, capacities are developing with foreign help (financing national reports).

For the post-Kyoto period there are some commitments, but they mostly emerge from the need for alignment with the EU. Turkey insists on special circumstances.

EU integration has served as the main driver of the climate policies. The energy sector is the main source of GHG emissions in EU and all the focus countries. Thus, alignment with the EU energy policy is seen as a precondition for the implementation of climate related commitments.

Lack of staff and funding for climate policy implementation indicates that climate policies have not been high on the agenda of the focus countries. Climate change is seen as a technical, rather than policy issue, which can be illustrated by the fact that TurkStat was primarily in charge of climate policies.

Notes

Introduction

1 Several studies have shown that major failures of forecasting are related to incidence of slowdowns and contractions in general economic activity. For an overview see Loungani, 2000.
2 Nature can mean different things depending on cultural and language difference; we use the term as a synonym for biodiversity, which we consider a component of the environment.

1 Developing strategies, environmental protection and financing

1 The Rio Summit also known as Rio Conference, Earth Summit, the United Nations Conference on Environment and Development (UNCED), was a major United Nations conference held in Rio de Janeiro from 3 June to 14 June 1992.
2 E.g. for environmental and national resources, relevant documents identified by the Sustainable Development Strategy are: National Strategy and Action Plan for the Protection of Biological and Landscape Diversity of the Republic of Croatia, Environmental Protection Programmes of counties and the City of Zagreb, National Environmental Protection Strategy and National Environmental Action Plan, National Forestry Policy and Strategy, National Project for Irrigation and Management of Agricultural Land and Waters in the Republic of Croatia, Strategic Development Framework for 2006–2013, Physical Planning Strategy of the Republic of Croatia, Physical Planning Programme of the Republic of Croatia, Croatia in the 21st century – Agriculture and Fisheries Strategy of the Republic of Croatia, Strategic Coherence Framework 2007–2013. The relevant institutions include the Ministry of Culture, the Ministry of Environmental Protection, Physical Planning and Construction, the Ministry of Agriculture, Fisheries and Rural Development, the Ministry of Economy, Labour and Entrepreneurship, the Ministry of Sea, Transport and Infrastructure.
3 Education for Sustainable Development, Sustainable Production and Consumption, Environmental Protection Action Plan and the Protection of the Adriatic Sea, Coastal Areas and Islands: Action Plan. For more see <http://www.mzopu.hr/default.aspx?id=10347>
4 For more, see Nature protection chapter.
5 (i) The 1999 Protocol to Abate Acidification, Eutrophication and Ground-level Ozone – Gothenburg Protocol; (ii) The 1998 Protocol on Persistent Organic Pollutants; (iii) The 1998 Protocol on Heavy Metals; (iv) The 1994 Protocol on Further Reduction of Sulphur Emissions; (v) The 1991 Protocol concerning the Control of Emissions of Volatile Organic Compounds or their Transboundary Fluxes; (vi) The 1988 Protocol concerning the Control of Nitrogen Oxides or their Transboundary Fluxes; (vii) The 1985 Protocol on the Reduction of Sulphur Emissions or their Transboundary Fluxes by at least 30 per cent; and (viii) Protocol on Long-term Financing of the Cooperative

Programme for Monitoring and Evaluation of the Long-range Transmission of Air Pollutants in Europe – EMEP).

6 Air Pollution (European Commission, 2005c); Sustainable Use of Pesticides (European Commission, 2006; Prevention and Recycling of Waste (European Commission, 2005a); Sustainable Use of Natural Resources (European Commission, 2005d); Soil Protection (European Commission, 2006c); Protection and Conservation of the Marine Environment (European Commission, 2005c); and (Urban Environment (European Commission, 2006d).

7 Sector-specific laws, such as the Biological Diversity Act, the Plant Protection Act, the Waters Act, the Clean Ambient Air Act are presented in chapters dealing with these topics.

8 The MOEW has prepared the National Environmental Strategy 2009–2018 (can be found at <http://www.moew.government.bg/recent_doc/dialog/debate/strategy2008/MOSV_Strategia.doc>), the Strategy action plan (can be found at <http://www.moew.government.bg/recent_doc/dialog/debate/strategy2008/MOSV_NSOS_Plan.doc> and the Strategy for Sustainable Sevelopment (draft) (can be found at <http://www.moew.government.bg/recent_doc/dialog/debate/SDS_konsultper cent20-SHT.doc>

9 E.g. ratification of the Kyoto Protocol, which the EC in its Croatia 2007 Progress Report identified as progress regarding environmental chapter of accession negotiations.

10 See, for instance European Recovery Plan.

11 For more about this see EC DG Regional Policy, 2008.

12 The Rio Conference Secretariat estimated order of magnitude of costs of implementing Agenda 21 activities in developing countries. The average annual cost until 2000 was estimated to be over US$600 billion, including about US$125 billion on grant or concessional terms from the international community (UN Economic and Social Development, Division for Sustainable Development, 1992 par. 3318).

13 There are eight MDGs, one of which is ensuring environmental sustainability.

14 This paragraph is based on European Commission, 2011a.

15 These costs have been estimated (rounded up estimates) as follows:

- to the EU budget: €500,000 a year for setting up and running the International Panel; €1.5 million a year for the first three years for setting up the data centre and then €1 million a year to run it; €300,000 for studies and expert meetings per year; €800,000 administrative costs per year for Commission staff working on the follow-up to the strategy;
- to Member States' budgets: between €300,000 and €550,000 per year in administrative costs (staff needed for analysing existing data, gathering extra information, attending the high-level forum and other EU meetings devoted to the strategy, etc.) for small and big member states respectively.
- Follow-up costs, i.e. those arising from the implementation of the national measures were not estimated because they vary considerably across the EU member states and depend on number of factors (structure of the economy, prevailing environmental impacts, effectiveness and timeliness of actions, etc.). However, overall and in the long run the strategy's influence on environmental policy initiatives and legislation is expected to create major savings compared to the present situation.

16 The PHARE, ISPA and SAPARD are instruments for pre-accession. The PHARE programme focuses on institution building and *acquis* related investment. ISPA supports large-scale infrastructure projects in the fields of transport and environment, and SAPARD helps to prepare the countries for taking on the *acquis* in the fields of agriculture and rural development.

17 At an exchange rate of BGN1.942/€1.

18 E.g. Solidarity Fund, Marco Polo II, the Competitiveness and innovation programme, «Progress: Employment and Social Solidarity», Globalization fund, various Lifelong Learning Programmes such as «Comenius», «Erasmus», «Leonardo da Vinci»

and «Grundtvig», with an allocation of €6.97 billion; the Seventh Framework Programme, The programme for the Trans-European Networks).

19 The funds are mainly targeted on the strengthening of institutional and administrative capacity, and on projects for environment protection and training. The total financial allocation amounts to €50.5 million between 2008 and 2011, of which the share for grants varies between 60 per cent and 90 per cent.

2 Nature protection

1 For more about conventions, see chapter 1.

2 The Annexes to the Birds Directive have been adapted on a number of occasions in response to scientific and technical progress and to the successive enlargements of the European Union. The most recent adaption is in response to the Accession of Bulgaria and Romania to the European Union on 1 January 2007: Directive of 30 November 2009 on the conservation of wild birds.

3 The 'Man and Biosphere' is a UNESCO programme under which biosphere reserves are established. They are considered as (i) sites of excellence where new and optimal practices to manage nature and human activities are tested and demonstrated; (ii) tools to help countries implement the results of the CBD; and (iii) learning sites for the UN Decade on Education for Sustainable Development.

4 On the basis of the Commission's Communication from 2006 entitled 'Halting the Loss of Biodiversity by 2010 – and beyond' (European Commission, 2006).

5 Only a share of CO_2 tax is used for conservation of biodiversity and valuable natural features. According to the Taxes in Europe Database, revenue from CO_2 tax in 2005 was €46 million (US$57 million), decreasing to €33 million (US$42 million) in 2006 and €26 million (US$38 million) in 2007. Latest data show that the revenue has stabilized at around €30 million (US$42 million) (European Commission DG Taxation and Customs Union, 2011).

6 According to the International Union for Conservation of Nature, protected area categories are: Ia Strict Nature Reserve; Ib Wilderness Area; II National Park; III Natural Monument or Feature; IV Habitats/Species Management Area; V Protected Landscape /Seascape; Vi Protected area with sustainable use of natural resources. For more see Dudley, 2008. According to the Protected Areas Law of Bulgaria, (1998) categories are: strict nature reserve, national park, natural monument, managed reserve, nature park and protected site.

7 Recent consolidated data on the revenues raised on entrance fees are not available. OECD tax base revenues database provides data for 2001 and 2002 when €7 million and €6 million were raised, respectively.

8 For more detailed presentation, see (Turkish Ministry of Environment and Forestry, 2007).

3 Water sector

1 See Chapter 1 for overview of relevant regional agreements for focus countries. It is beyond the scope of this chapter to give a comprehensive view of the EU water policy, even the WFD. The authors have attempted to identify and focus on the key issues of the WFD.

2 Population equivalent (in wastewater monitoring and treatment) is a measure of pollution. It refers to the amount of oxygen-demanding substances whose oxygen consumption during biodegradation equals the average oxygen demand of the wastewater produced by one person. It is defined as the organic biodegradable load having a five-day biochemical oxygen demand of 60g of oxygen per day.

3 For example, 20 per cent of the costs should be borne by the municipalities' budgets, from the payments received from water sector utilities. As a possible source of funding, there are also loans from the Slovenian Eco Fund; (Petresin *et al.*, 2003: 11).

4 In 2004–2005 €35.7 million was invested annually, which is less than half of the necessary annual average according to the 1999 World Bank estimate. Covering costs of €1,183 million for 2000–2015 requires an annual investment of €73 million.

5 This problematic situation is also reported in the Urban Wastewater Treatment (CSI 024) – assessment, published by the European Environmental Agency in January 2009 (EEA, 2009).

6 Based on the estimate during 2007–2010, on average €75 million was invested annually (see Table 3.8) i.e. €300 million. With €120 and €192 millions of planned investments in 2011 and 2012, and €200 million a year until 2015, total investments in the period 2007–2015 would reach €1,200 million, just about enough for the alignment.

7 Most IFIs consider 4 per cent of household income as a limit for payment for water and wastewater related services.

4 Waste sector

1 A waste stream is the complete flow of waste from domestic or industrial areas through to final disposal. The intervention of recycling may act to lessen the content of a waste stream as it moves down the line.

2 There are significant differences between the European Environmental Agency data (7 million tons of waste produced) and Eurostat data presented in Table 4.4 (5–6 million tons, depending on the year).

3 According to Eurostat, recovery rate was 58 per cent in 2008.

4 According to 2009 EIONET edition of waste management plans, Slovenia has not developed a waste management plan.

5 The income from environmental taxes and charges are budget revenue, but amendments to the Public Finance Act in 2009 provided for earmarked revenue generated by environmental tax. Until then, each municipality was able to use such revenue at its own discretion.

6 Transitional periods were negotiated based on the assessments provided in implementing programmes for relevant directives, such as Implementation Programme for Directive 2004/12/EC, amending Directive 94/62/EC for packaging and packaging waste, September 2004.

7 According to the Regulation on the conditions and requirements for building and operation of landfills and other facilities and installations for waste recovery and disposal, Prom. SG No. 83/24.08.2004.

8 According to the Plan for Implementation of Directive 1999/31/EC on Landfill of Waste, Republic of Bulgaria, Ministry of Environment and Water, March 2003.

9 According to the Implementation Plan for Directive NO 1999/31/EC on landfill of waste.

10 The EU contributions of €2.4 billion and €750 million were provided in the context of Romania's negotiations in 2004. They are in constant prices (SOP Environment is in current prices) thus cannot be directly compared with financial plan presented in Table 4.13. For more see Sector OP Environment 2007: 137). The €1.6 billion is estimated by GHK, Rojanschi and Lust, 2006: 72 and the EU contribution of €934 million in Sector OP Environment, 2007: 100.

11 The Fund has so far approved co-financing recovery projects and separate collections in the amount of €6.35 million.

12 Between 2006 and 2010, Turkey has adopted 11 by-laws harmonizing the Turkish system with the EU laws on waste management.

13 US$1.32 and TRY 2.34 are equivalent to €1.

5 Air sector

1 Parties of CLRTAP should use the EMEP/CORINAIR Atmospheric Emission Inventory Guidebook both as a reference book on good emission estimation practice

and as a check-list to ensure that all relevant activities are considered and their emissions quantified. Parties should indicate where the Guidebook methodology has been used and where not. If another methodology has been used Parties are requested to provide additional explanatory information.

6 Climate change

1 The International Panel on Climate Change, a leading international body for the assessment of climate change, established by the United Nations Environment Programme (UNEP) and the World Meteorological Organization in its Fourth Assessment Report summarized the benefits of limiting the increase of global average surface temperature to around 1.6°–2.6°C relative to the pre-industrial level and risks of temperature rise above this level.

2 The Climate Change Act is expected to be adopted by the Parliament in 2011.

3 There were changes in the government structure and responsible ministries. While the First National Communication was prepared by the Ministry of Environment, Spatial Planning and Energy, the communications that followed were prepared by the Ministry of Environment and Spatial Planning. Further changes of the scope of work and distribution of authorities among the ministries took place in 2009.

4 The NSRF is the umbrella strategy document for programming EU structural funds and the Cohesion Fund. It links the community priorities with the national and regional priorities for sustainable development. It is developed on the basis of the priorities defined in the National Development Plan. It is the basis for further development of a number of sectoral or regional OPs. However, there were measures foreseen in the transport and energy sectors, which are the main contributors to GHG emissions, thus it might be a result of environmental integration.

5 Under UNFCCC financial mechanism, Slovenia received US$345,000 from the GEF for the preparation of its First National Communication. Other enabling activities supported by the GEF were the removal of barriers to biomass district heating projects (US$98,000) and the establishment of early warning systems for floods (US$95,000). Bilateral cooperation with neighbouring countries also facilitated implementation of some climate change related projects: Austria used innovative financing schemes for a natural gas co-generation system in Slovenia, and Italy supported coastal zone management projects and a co-generation development plan.

6 Based on the pledge issued by the government of Slovenia available at <http://www.faststartfinance.org/contributing_country/slovenia>

7 Total GDP of Slovenia in 2010 was €33.012 million according to IMF. The 0.08 per cent of the GDP was calculated by dividing €8 million in three equal instalments for the period of 2010, 2011, and 2012.

8 Available from <http://maindb.unfccc.int/public/country.pl?country=BG>

9 For more, see national communications (Republic of Bulgaria, 1996), (Republic of Bulgaria, 1998), (Republic of Bulgaria, 2002), (Republic of Bulgaria, 2006) and (Republic of Bulgaria, 2010).

10 The Third National Action Plan on Climate Change 2009–2013 is currently being implemented and mainly seeks funding at EU level. Preparation of 2013–2020 Action Plan is under way and is funded by the Norwegian government.

11 For more about projects see Second National Communication on Climate Change to the UNFCCC (Republic of Bulgaria, 1998).

12 According to the Effort Sharing Decision Bulgaria is entitled to increase its emissions by 20 per cent to the base year 2005, i.e. to 80.52Tg CO_2 equivalent. This is 40 per cent reduction to the Kyoto Protocol base year (1988) Bulgaria.

13 The price in 2009 was €10.00/tonne of CO_2 equivalent (tCO_2e) and in 2011 fell to €5–6/tonne.

14 Specific circumstances of Croatia were related to GHG emissions from the electricity generation sector of the former Yugoslavia (the use of coal fuel thermal power plants

in Bosnia and Herzegovina and Serbia of 650MW installed power and the use of 322MW from nuclear power plant Krško) (Bašić et al., 2006).

15 According to the initial report that Croatia submitted in 2008, the assigned amount for Croatia 2008–2012 is 171.1Tg CO_2 equivalent (Croatian Ministry of Environmental Protection, Physical Planning and Construction, 2009:13), i.e. 34,200Gg CO_2 equal annually. The expert team review questioned the assigned amount. The compliance committee declared Croatia's non-compliance. Croatia was required to submit a plan to address its non-compliance within three months. Instead of providing the plan, Croatia submitted an appeal against the final decision of the enforcement branch. Finally, in June 2011, Croatia withdrew its appeal. It is expected that the assigned amount would be 164.4Tg CO_2 equivalent or 32.9Gg CO_2 equivalents annually. The same amount can be calculated by adding 3.5Tg to the base year emission, as reported in the NIR.

16 Inclusion into the European Union emissions trading scheme requires coordination of Croatian GHG register with that of the EU. It is expected that coordination will be finalized one year after Croatia becomes an EU member.

17 For example, the Regulation on the criteria for joint investments in the projects for the decrease of GHG emissions, which is, according to the Ministry of Environmental Protection, Physical Planning and Construction, in the process of adoption (available at <http://www.mzopu.hr/doc/UREDBA_2810.pdf>) and the Plan for the distribution of GHG emissions quotas in the Republic of Croatia for the period from 2010 to 2012, which must be approved by European Commission (proposal available at <http://www.mzopu.hr/doc/HRV_NAP_1011.pdf>), Regulation on the criteria for joint investments in the projects for the decrease of GHG emissions, Plan for the distribution of GHG emissions quotas in the Republic of Croatia for the period from 2010 to 2012, Regulation on Carbon in fossil fuel tax.

18 In the period 2000–2004 the authorizing ministry was the Ministry of Environmental Protection and Physical Planning.

Bibliography

Adams, W. M., 2001. *Green Development, Environment and Sustainability in the Third World.* London: Routledge.

Air Quality Protection and Improvement Plan of the Republic of Croatia for the Period 2008–2011, 2008. Republic of Croatia: *Official Gazette*, No. 61/08. [Online] Available at <http://www.mzopu.hr/doc/Air_Protection_Plan_OG_61–08.pdf> [Accessed 2 May 2011].

Arslancan, A. C., Gracin, P., Jacobsen, M., Mols, A., Pavicic-Kaselj, A., Semeniene, A. and Tisma, S., 2008. Developing The Capacity of Environmental Authorities, through Transfer of Best Practice and Training to Support Effective Use of Financial Resources Environmental Investment and Financing Strategy – Croatia. COWI. [Online] Available at <http://www.cowiprojects.com/4CountryEnvironmentFinance/PDF/64400_HR_EFS_ver3.PDF> [Accessed 2 July 2011].

Baltzar, E., Petrovska, A., Sevic, D., Uzunov, D. and Varbova, V., 2009. *Speeding up Investments in the Waste Sector: A Manual For Waste Utilities in South Eastern Europe.* Szentendre, Hungary: Regional Environmental Center.

Bardarska, G., 2007. Access to Drinking Water and Sanitation in Bulgaria. In: Solidarity Water Europe's, *Equitable Access to Water.* 5–6 July 2007. Paris. [Online] Available at <http://www.oieau.fr/IMG/pdf/Bardarska.pdf> [Accessed 2 July 2011].

Bašić, F., *et. al.*, 2006. Second, Third and Fourth National Communication of the Republic of Croatia under the United Nations Framework Convention on Climate Change. Croatian Ministry of Environmental Protection, Physical Planning and Construction. [Online] Available at <http://klima.mzopu.hr/UserDocsImages/I_II_III_EN_29112007.pdf> [Accessed 2 July 2011].

Beaton, R. and Maser, C., 2012. Economics and Ecology, United for a Sustainable World. In: Maser, C. (ed.), 2012. *Social-Environmental Sustainability Series.* Boca Raton: CRC, Press.

Bešker, M., 2005. *Polika Okoliša.* Zagreb: OSKAR.

Bhutto, A., Cagatay, S. and Siddiqui, N. A., n.d. The Opportunity Cost of Ratifying Kyoto Protocol: An Input-Output Analysis for Turkey. [Online] Available at <http://www.iioa.org/pdf/17th%20Conf/Papers/492297253_090601_104626_NIAZAHMEDBHUTTO.PDF> [Accessed 2 July 2011].

Boer, A, 2008. Romanian Policy and Strategies in the Water and Wastewater Sector. *Doing Business. Ro*, [Online] Available at <http://rbd.doingbusiness.ro/ro/5/articole-recente/1/95/romanian-policy-and-strategies-in-the-water-and-wastewater-sector> [Accessed 8 August 2011].

Bojo, J. and Reddy, R. C, 2003. Poverty Reduction Strategies and the Millennium Development Goals on Environmental Sustainability. *Environmental Economics*

Series, No. 31219: 92. [Online] Available at <http://www.unep.org/civil_society/GCSF8/pdfs/poverty_red_mdgs.pdf> [Accessed 21 May 2011].

Bourguignon, F., Bénassy-Quéré, A., Dercon, S., Estache, A., Gunning, J. W., Kanbur, R., Klasen, S., Maxwell, S., Platteau, J. and Spadaro, A., 2008. Millennium Development Goals at Midpoint: Where do we Stand and Where do we Need to go? European Report on Development. [Online] Available at <http://ec.europa.eu/development/icenter/repository/mdg_paper_final_20080916_en.pdf> [Accessed 22 May 2011].

Brundtland, G. H., 1987. Our Common Future – Call for Action, *Environmental Conservation*, December 1987(14): 291–4.

Bulgarian Council of Ministers, 2009. *National Biodiversity Conservation Plan.* [Online] Available at <http://chm.moew.government.bg/modules_files/CONSERVATION%20 PLAN.doc> [Accessed 14 July 2011].

Bulgarian Executive Forest Agency, 2011. *Strategic Development Forestry Plan for 2007–2011.* [Online] Available at <http://www.nug.bg/lang/2/index> [Accessed 10 August 2011].

Bulgarian Ministry of Agriculture and Food, 2006. *National Strategic Plan for Agricultural and Rural Development 2007–2013.* [Online] Available at <http://prsr.government.bg/index.php/en/> [Accessed 26 July 2011].

Bulgarian Ministry of Environment and Water, 2005. *National Biodiversity Conservation Strategy and National Biodiversity Conservation Plans 2005–2010.* [Online] Available at <http://www.moew.government.bg/index_e.html> [Accessed 10 August 2011].

Bulgarian Ministry of Environment and Water, 2006. *Report on Demonstrable Progress of Republic of Bulgaria to Achieve Commitments under the Kyoto Protocol.* [Online] Available at <http://unfccc.int/resource/docs/dpr/bgr1.pdf> [Accessed 3 October 2011].

Bulgarian Ministry of Environment and Water, 2010. *National Inventory Report 2010 for Greenhouse Gas Emissions, Submission under the UNFCCC and the Kyoto Protocol.* Sofia: Executive Environmental Agency. [Online] Available at <http://eea.government.bg/eng/Output/UNFCCC/NIR–08-eng.pdf> [Accessed 4 October 2011].

Bulgarian Municipality of Haskovo, 2000. Regional Water Management in Bulgaria. *Public/Private Project for Water Treatment and Delivery to the Haskovo Municipality and Surrounding Municipalities.* [Online] Available at <http://archive.rec.org/ecolinks/bestpractices/PDF/bulagria_haskovo.pdf> [Accessed 22 September 2011].

Bulgarian National Statistical Institute, 2009. *Annual Data for 2009.* [Online] Available at <http://www.nsi.bg/EPDOCS/Environment2009_en.pdf> [Accessed 22 May 2011].

Bulgarian Protected Areas Fund Strategy, 2003. *Bulgarian EcoFund.* [Online] Available at <http://ecofund-bg.org/FZT/upload/paf_strategy_en.pdf> [Accessed 15 June 2011].

Česen, M., 2006. *Slovenia's Report on Demonstrable Progress under the Kyoto Protocol.* Ljubljana, Slovenia: Ministry of the Environment and Spatial Planning. [Online] Available at <http://unfccc.int/resource/docs/dpr/svn1.pdf> [Accessed 12 September 2011].

Česen, M., Kranjc, A. and Špendl, R., 2004. *Slovenia's Second and Third National Communication to the Conference of the Parties of the United Nations Framework Convention on Climate Change.* Ljubljana: Slovenian Ministry of The Environment, Spatial Planning and Energy. [Online] Available at <http://www.mop.gov.si/fileadmin/mop.gov.si/pageuploads/publikacije/drugo/en/drzavno_porocilo_spremembi_podnebja.pdf> [Accessed 12 September 2011].

Churchill, R. R. and Ulfstein, G., 2000. Autonomous Institutional Arrangements in Multilateral Environmental Agreements: a Little-noticed Phenomenon in International Law, *The American Journal of International Law*, 94: 4.

Cisse, M., Gaudioso, D., Pedisius, N. and Ren, X., 2003. *Slovenia: Report on the In-depth Review of the First National Communication of Slovenia*. UNFCCC. [Online] Available at <http://unfccc.int/resource/docs/idr/svn01.pdf> [Accessed 25 October 2011].

Commission Decision 2004/224/EC of 20 February 2004 laying down arrangements for the submission of information on plans or programmes required under Council Directive 96/62/EC in relation to limit values for certain pollutants in ambient air. [Online] Available at <http://eur-lex.europa.eu/LexUriServ/LexUriServ.do?uri=OJ:L:2004:068:0027:0033:EN:PDF> [Accessed 25 October 2011].

Commission Decision 2004/461/EC of 29 April 2004 laying down a questionnaire to be used for annual reporting on ambient air quality assessment under Council Directives 96/62/EC and 1999/30/EC and under Directives 2000/69/EC and 2002/3/EC of the European Parliament and of the Council. [Online] Available at <http://eur-lex.europa.eu/LexUriServ/LexUriServ.do?uri=OJ:L:2004:156:0078:0125:EN:PDF> [Accessed 26 April 2011].

Commission Directive 2000/71/EC of 7 November 2000 to adapt the measuring methods as laid down in Annexes I, II, III and IV to Directive 98/70/EC of the European Parliament and of the Council to technical progress as foreseen in Article 10 of that Directive. [Online] Available at <http://eur-lex.europa.eu/LexUriServ/LexUriServ.do?uri=OJ:L:2000:287:0046:0050:EN:PDF> [Accessed 26 April 2011].

Commission Regulation (EC) No. 308/2009 of 15 April 2009 amending, for the purposes of adaptation to scientific and technical progress, Annexes IIIA and VI to Regulation (EC) No. 1013/2006 of the European Parliament and of the Council on shipments of waste. [Online] Available at <http://eur-lex.europa.eu/LexUriServ/LexUriServ.do?uri=OJ:L:2009:097:0008:0011:EN:PDF> [Accessed 26 April 2011].

Committee of the Regions, 2010. Fighting Climate Change: Involving the Public in Sustainable Energy Solutions, Action Plan 2010 Of The Subsidiarity Monitoring Network Analysis Report. [Online] Available at <http://portal.cor.europa.eu/subsidiarity/SiteCollectionDocuments/AP1010_WGFightingclimatechange_Report_EN.pdf> [Accessed 27 April 2011].

Convention on Biological Diversity, 2005. *Third National Report*. [Online] Available at <http://www.cbd.int/doc/world/si/si-nr–03-en.pdf> [Accessed 15 August 2011]. Convention on Biological Diversity, 2011. *Country Profile: Romania*. [Online] Available at <http://www.cbd.int/countries/profile.shtml?country=ro#status> [Accessed 1 July 2011].

Convention on Biological Diversity, 2011a. *Fourth National Report to the United Nations: Romania*. [Online] Available at <http://www.google.com/url?sa=t&rct=j&q=fourth%20national%20report%20to%20the%20united%20nationsconvention%20on%20biological%20diversityromania&source=web&cd=1&ved=0CCIQFjAA&url=http%3A%2F%2Fwww.cbd.int%2Fdoc%2Fworld%2Fro%2Fro-nr–04-en.doc&ei=Zz2ETt6UlanM0QWhq4TxDw&usg=AFQjCNFj0jnvzsXlhJ32JvVlNLCVj0vDYQ&cad=rja> [Accessed 15 July 2011].

Convention on the Conservation of European Wildlife and Natural Habitats, 1979. [Online] Available at <http://conventions.coe.int/treaty/en/treaties/html/104.htm> [Accessed 1 July 2011].

Costanza, R., Cumberland, J., Daly, H., Goodland, R. and Norgaard, R., 1997. *An Introduction to Ecological Economics*. Boca Raton: St. Lucie Press.

Costanza, R., Limburg, K. and Kubiszewski, I. (eds), 2011. *Ecological Economics Reviews* Vol. 1219. Boston, MA: Blackwell Publishing.

Council Decision 97/101/EC of 27 January 1997 establishing a reciprocal exchange of information and data from networks and individual stations measuring ambient air pollution within the Member States. [Online] Available at <http://eur-lex.europa.eu/LexUriServ/LexUriServ.do?uri=CELEX:31997D0101:EN:HTML> [Accessed 1 July 2011].

Council Directive 75/439/EEC of 16 June 1975 on the disposal of waste oils. [Online] Available at <http://eur-lex.europa.eu/LexUriServ/LexUriServ.do?uri=OJ:L:1975:194:0023:0025:EN:PDF> [Accessed 16 May 2011].

Council Directive 75/442/EEC of 15 July 1975 on waste. [Online] Available at <http://www.wastexchange.co.uk/documenti/europeanorm/wfd_dr__859830.pdf> [Accessed 16 May 2011].

Council Directive 79/409/EEC of 2 April 1979 on the conservation of wild birds, OJ L103 (1979). [Online] Available at <http://eur-lex.europa.eu/LexUriServ/site/en/consleg/1979/L/01979L0409–20070101-en.pdf> [Accessed 19 June 2011].

Council Directive 85/580/EEC of 20 December 1985 adapting, on account of the accession of Spain and Portugal, Directive 85/203/EEC on air quality standards for nitrogen dioxide. [Online] Available at <http://eur-lex.europa.eu/LexUriServ/LexUriServ.do?uri=OJ:L:1985:372:0036:0036:EN:PDF> [Accessed 19 June 2011].

Council Directive 89/427/EEC of 21 June 1989 amending Directive 80/779/EEC on air quality limit values and guide values for sulphur dioxide and suspended particulates. [Online] Available at <http://eur-lex.europa.eu/LexUriServ/LexUriServ.do?uri=OJ:L:1989:201:0053:0055:EN:PDF> [Accessed 19 June 2011].

Council Directive 91/157/EEC of 18 March 1991 on batteries and accumulators containing certain dangerous substances. [Online] Available at <http://eur-lex.europa.eu/LexUriServ/LexUriServ.do?uri=OJ:L:1991:078:0038:0041:EN:PDF> [Accessed 19 June 2011].

Council Directive 91/271/EEC of 21 May 1991 concerning urban waste water treatment. [Online] Available at <http://eur-lex.europa.eu/LexUriServ/LexUriServ.do?uri=OJ:L:1991:135:0040:0052:EN:PDF> [Accessed 11 August 2011].

Council Directive 91/676/EEC of 12 December 1991 concerning the protection of waters against pollution caused by nitrates from agricultural sources. [Online] Available at <http://ec.europa.eu/environment/water/water-nitrates/directiv.html> [Accessed 19 June 2011].

Council Directive 91/689/EEC of 12 December 1991 on hazardous waste. [Online] Available at <http://eur-lex.europa.eu/LexUriServ/LexUriServ.do?uri=OJ:L:1991:377:0020:0027:EN:PDF> [Accessed 11 August 2011].

Council Directive 92/43/EEC of 21 May 1992 on the conservation of natural habitats and of wild fauna and flora. [Online] Available at <http://eur-lex.europa.eu/LexUriServ/LexUriServ.do?uri=CONSLEG:1992L0043:20070101:EN:PDF> [Accessed 11 August 2011].

Council Directive 94/31/EC of 27 June 1994 amending Directive 1991/689/EEC on hazardous waste. [Online] Available at <http://eur-lex.europa.eu/LexUriServ/LexUriServ.do?uri=OJ:L:1994:168:0028:0028:EN:PDF> [Accessed 27 May 2011].

Council Directive 94/66/EC of 15 December 1994 amending Directive 88/609/EEC on the limitation of emissions of certain pollutants into the air from large combustion plants. [Online] Available at <http://eur-lex.europa.eu/LexUriServ/LexUriServ.do?uri=CELEX:31994L0066:EN:HTML> [Accessed 27 May 2011].

Council Directive 96/59/EC of 16 September 1996 on the disposal of polychlorinated biphenyls and polychlorinated terphenyls (PCB/PCT). [Online] Available at <http://library.coastweb.info/536/1/PCBs_96.pdf> [Accessed 27 May 2011].

Council Directive 96/62/EC of 27 September 1996 on ambient air quality assessment and management. [Online] Available at <http://eur-lex.europa.eu/LexUriServ/site/en/consleg/1996/L/01996L0062-20031120-en.pdf> [Accessed 27 May 2011].

Council Directive 98/83/EC of 3 November 1998 on the quality of water intended for human consumption. [Online] Available at <http://eur-lex.europa.eu/LexUriServ/LexUriServ.do?uri=OJ:L:1998:330:0032:0054:EN:PDF> [Accessed 27 May 2011].

Council Directive 99/13/EC of 11 March 1999 on the limitation of emissions of volatile organic compounds due to the use of organic solvents in certain activities and installations. [Online] Available at <http://eur-lex.europa.eu/LexUriServ/LexUriServ.do?uri=CONSLEG:1999L0013:19990329:EN:PDF> [Accessed 27 May 2011].

Council Directive 99/30/EC of 22 April 1999 relating to limit values for sulphur dioxide, nitrogen dioxide and oxides of nitrogen, particulate matter and lead in ambient air. [Online] Available at http://eur-lex.europa.eu/LexUriServ/LexUriServ.do?uri=CELEX:52002DC0609:EN:HTML [Accessed 27 May 2011].

Council Directive 99/31/EC of 26 April 1999 on the landfill of waste. [Online] Available at <http://eur-lex.europa.eu/LexUriServ/LexUriServ.do?uri=OJ:L:1999:182:0001:0019:EN:PDF> [Accessed 27 May 2011].

Council Directive 1999/32/EC of 26 April 1999 relating to a reduction in the sulphur content of certain liquid fuels and amending Directive 93/12/EEC. [Online] Available at <httphttp://eur-lex.europa.eu/LexUriServ/LexUriServ.do?uri=CONSLEG:1999L0032:20090625:EN:PDF> [Accessed 11 August 2011].

Council Directive 2009/147/EC of 30 November 2009 on the conservation of wild birds. [Online] Available at <http://eur-lex.europa.eu/LexUriServ/LexUriServ.do?uri=OJ:L:2010:020:0007:0025:en:PDF> [Accessed 11 August 2011].

Countdown 2010, 2007. *Slovenia: a Green Leader of the European Union.* [Online] Available at <http://www.countdown2010.net/article/slovenia-a-green-leader-of-the-european-union> [Accessed 11 June 2011].

Croatian Ministry of Culture, 2010. Programi zaštite prirode i investicijski programi u 2010. godini za Državni zavod za zaštitu prirode (DZZP), nacionalne parkove (NP) i parkove prirode (PP). *Uprava za zaštitu prirode.* [Online] Available at <http://www.min-kulture.hr/userdocsimages/odobreni%20programi%20za%202010/np%20pp%20_financije_web%20_3_.pdf> [Accessed 11 August 2011].

Croatian Ministry of Culture, 2011. Programi zaštite prirode i investicijski programi u 2011. godini za Državni zavod za zaštitu prirode (DZZP), nacionalne parkove (NP) i parkove prirode (PP). *Uprava za zaštitu prirode.* [Online] Available at < http://www.min-kulture.hr/userdocsimages/financiranje/np%20pp%20_financije_web_11.pdf> [Accessed 11 August 2011].

Croatian Ministry of Environmental Protection, Physical Planning and Construction, 2007. *Prijedlog nacionalne strategije za provedbu Okvirne konvencije Ujedinjenih naroda o promjeni klime (UNFCCC) i Kyotskog protokola u Republici Hrvatskoj s planom djelovanja.* [Online] Available at <http://www.undp.hr/upload/file/208/104173/FILENAME/Croatia_Kyoto_strategy_hrv.pdf> [Accessed 3 October 2011].

Croatian Ministry of Environmental Protection, Physical Planning and Construction, 2008. *Initial Report of the Republic of Croatia under the Kyoto Protocol.* [Online] Available at <http://unfccc.int/files/national_reports/initial_reports_under_the_kyoto_protocol/application/pdf/initial_report_croatia_27_aug_2008.pdf> [Accessed 15 July 2011].

Croatian Ministry of Environmental Protection, Physical Planning and Construction, 2009. *Strategy for Sustainable Development of the Republic of Croatia.* [Online] Available at <http://www.mzopu.hr/doc/Strategy_for_Sustainable_Development.pdf> [Accessed 15 July 2011].

Cumberlege, S., 2009. Multilateral envioronmental agreements: from Montreal to Kyoto – a theoretical approach to an improved climate change regime. *Denver Journal of International Law and Policy*, 37: 2.

Danuletiu, D. and Teiusan, S., 2007. *A survey of the Romanian Environmental Fund*. MPRA Paper. [Online] Available at <http://mpra.ub.uni-muenchen.de/5983/1/MPRA_paper_5983.pdf> [Accessed 16 June 2011].

Darpo, J, 2011. *On Costs in the Environmental Procedure of the Aarhus Convention*. [Online] Available at < http://donanton.org/2011/02/01/jan-darpo-on-costs-in-the-environmental-procedure-of-the-aarhus-convention/#_ftnref7> [Accessed 11 June 2011].

Devarjan, S. Miller, M. J. and Swanson, E. V., 2002. Development Goals: History, Prospects and Costs, *World Bank Policy Research Paper*, 2891. Available at <http://papers.ssrn.com/sol3/Delivery.cfm/13269.pdf?abstractid=636102&mirid=1> [Accessed 9 May 2011].

DFID, EC, UNDP and World Bank, 2002. *Linking Poverty Reduction and Environmental Management: Policy Challenges and Opportunities*. Washington DC: World Bank. [Online] Available at <http://www.unpei.org/PDF/Linking-poverty-red-env.pdf> [Accessed 9 May 2011].

Dimitrova, M, 2011. Bulgaria Aims at Complete Absorbing of EU Funds for Environment Infrastructure. *Radio Bulgaria*. [Online] Available at <http://bnr.bg/sites/en/Lifestyle/BGEU/Pages/1705BulgariaaimsatcompleteabsorbingofEUfundsforenvironmentinfrastructure.aspx> [Accessed 12 May 2011].

Directive 98/70/EC of the European Parliament and of the Council of 13 October 1998 relating to the quality of petrol and diesel fuels and amending Council Directive 93/12/EEC. [Online] Available at <http://eur-lex.europa.eu/LexUriServ/LexUriServ.do?uri=CELEX:31998L0070:EN:HTML> [Accessed 11 August 2011].

Directive 1999/94/EC of the European Parliament and of the Council of 13 December 1999 relating to the availability of consumer information on fuel economy and CO_2 emissions in respect of the marketing of new passenger cars. [Online] Available at <http://eur-lex.europa.eu/LexUriServ/LexUriServ.do?uri=CELEX:31999L0094:EN:HTML> [Accessed 14 June 2011].

Directive 2000/53/EC of the European Parliament and of the Council of 18 September 2000 on end-of-life vehicles. [Online] Available at <http://eur-lex.europa.eu/LexUriServ/LexUriServ.do?uri=CONSLEG:2000L0053:20050701:EN:PDF> [Accessed 14 June 2011].

Directive 2000/60/EC of the European Parliament and of the Council of 23 October 2000 establishing a framework for community action in the field of water policy. [Online] Available at <http://eur-lex.europa.eu/LexUriServ/LexUriServ.do?uri=OJ:L:2000:327:0001:0072:EN:PDF> [Accessed 14 June 2011].

Directive 2000/69/EC of the European Parliament and of the Council of 16 November 2000 relating to limit values for benzene and carbon monoxide in ambient air. [Online] Available at <http://eur-lex.europa.eu/LexUriServ/LexUriServ.do?uri=OJ:L:2000:313:0012:0021:EN:PDF> [Accessed 14 June 2011].

Directive 2000/76/EC of the European Parliament and of the Council of 4 December 2000 on the incineration of waste. [Online] Available at <http://www.central2013.eu/fileadmin/user_upload/Downloads/Document_Centre/OP_Resources/Incineration_Directive_2000_76.pdf > [Accessed 14 June 2011].

Directive 2001/80/EC of the European Parliament and of the Council of 23 October 2001 on the limitation of emissions of certain pollutants into the air from large combustion plants. [Online] Available at <http://eur-lex.europa.eu/LexUriServ/LexUriServ.do?uri=OJ:L:2001:309:0001:0001:EN:PDF> [Accessed 14 June 2011].

Directive 2001/81/EC of the European Parliament and of the Council of 23 October 2001 on national emission ceilings for certain atmospheric pollutants. [Online] Available at <http://eur-lex.europa.eu/LexUriServ/LexUriServ.do?uri=OJ:L:2001:309:0022:0030:EN:PDF> [Accessed 14 June 2011].

Directive 2002/3/EC of the European Parliament and of the Council of 12 February 2002 relating to ozone in ambient air. [Online] Available at <http://eur-lex.europa.eu/LexUriServ/LexUriServ.do?uri=OJ:L:2002:067:0014:0030:EN:PDF> [Accessed 12 May 2011].

Directive 2002/96/EC of the European Parliament and of the Council of 27 January 2003 on waste electrical and electronic equipment (WEEE). [Online] Available at <http://eur-lex.europa.eu/LexUriServ/LexUriServ.do?uri=OJ:L:2001:309:0022:0030:EN:PDF> [Accessed 14 June 2011].

Directive 2003/17/EC of the European Parliament and of the Council of 3 March 2003 amending Directive 98/70/EC relating to the quality of petrol and diesel fuels. [Online] Available at <http://eur-lex.europa.eu/LexUriServ/LexUriServ.do?uri=OJ:L:2003:076:0010:0019:EN:PDF> [Accessed 14 June 2011].

Directive 2003/43/EC of 26 May 2003 amending Directive 88/407/EEC laying down the animal health requirements applicable to intra-community trade in and imports of semen of domestic animals of the bovine species. [Online] Available at <http://eur-lex.europa.eu/LexUriServ/LexUriServ.do?uri=OJ:L:2003:143:0023:0032:EN:PDF> [Accessed 14 June 2011].

Directive 2004/42/CE of the European Parliament and of the Council of 21 April 2004 on the limitation of emissions of volatile organic compounds due to the use of organic solvents in certain paints and varnishes and vehicle refinishing products and amending Directive 1999/13/EC. [Online] Available at <http://eur-lex.europa.eu/LexUriServ/LexUriServ.do?uri=OJ:L:2004:143:0087:0087:EN:PDF> [Accessed 14 June 2011].

Directive 2004/107/EC of the European Parliament and of the Council of 15 December 2004 relating to arsenic, cadmium, mercury, nickel and polycyclic aromatic hydrocarbons in ambient air. [Online] Available at <http://eur-lex.europa.eu/LexUriServ/LexUriServ.do?uri=CONSLEG:2004L0107:20090420:EN:PDF> [Accessed 14 June 2011].

Directive 2006/7/EC of the European Parliament and of the Council of 15 February 2006 concerning the management of bathing water quality and repealing Directive 76/160/EEC. [Online] Available at <http://eur-lex.europa.eu/LexUriServ/LexUriServ.do?uri=OJ:L:2006:064:0037:0051:EN:PDF> [Accessed 14 June 2011].

Directive 2006/11/EC of the European Parliament and of the Council of 15 February 2006 on pollution caused by certain dangerous substances discharged into the aquatic environment of the community (codified version) (Text with EEA relevance). [Online] Available at <http://eur-lex.europa.eu/LexUriServ/LexUriServ.do?uri=OJ:L:2006:064:0052:0059:EN:PDF> [Accessed 14 June 2011].

Directive 2006/12/EC of the European Parliament and of the Council of 5 April 2006 on waste (Text with EEA relevance). [Online] Available at <http://eur-lex.europa.eu/LexUriServ/LexUriServ.do?uri=OJ:L:2006:114:0009:0021:en:PDF> [Accessed 14 June 2011].

Directive 2006/44/EC of the European Parliament and of the Council of 6 September 2006 on the quality of fresh waters needing protection or improvement in order to support fish life (codified version) (Text with EEA relevance). [Online] Available at <http://eur-lex.europa.eu/LexUriServ/LexUriServ.do?uri=OJ:L:2006:264:0020:0031:EN:pdf> [Accessed 14 June 2011].

Directive 2006/113/EC of the European Parliament and of the Councilof 12 December 2006 on the quality required of shellfish waters (codified version). [Online] Available at <http://eur-lex.europa.eu/LexUriServ/LexUriServ.do?uri=OJ:L:2006:376:0014:0020:EN:PDF> [Accessed 14 June 2011].

Directive 2006/118/EC of the European Parliament and of the Councilof 12 December 2006 on the protection of groundwater against pollution and deterioration. [Online]

Available at <http://eur-lex.europa.eu/LexUriServ/LexUriServ.do?uri=OJ:L:2006:372:0019:0031:EN:PDF> [Accessed 14 June 2011].

Directive 2008/1/EC of the European Parliament and of the Council of 15 January 2008 concerning integrated pollution prevention and control. [Online] Available at <http://eur-lex.europa.eu/LexUriServ/LexUriServ.do?uri=OJ:L:2008:024:0008:0029:en:PDF> [Accessed 14 June 2011].

Directive 2008/50/EC of the European Parliament and of the Council of 21 May 2008 on ambient air quality and cleaner air for Europe. [Online] Available at <http://eur-lex.europa.eu/LexUriServ/LexUriServ.do?uri=OJ:L:2008:152:0001:0044:EN:PDF> [Accessed 14 June 2011].

Directive 2008/98/EC of the European Parliament and of the Council of 19 November 2008 on waste and repealing certain Directives. [Online] Available at <http://eur-lex.europa.eu/LexUriServ/LexUriServ.do?uri=OJ:L:2008:312:0003:0030:en:PDF> [Accessed 14 June 2011].

Directive 2009/30/EC of the European Parliament and of the Council of 23 April 2009 amending Directive 98/70/EC as regards the specification of petrol, diesel and gas-oil and introducing a mechanism to monitor and reduce greenhouse gas emissions and amending Council Directive 1999/32/EC as regards the specification of fuel used by inland waterway vessels and repealing Directive 93/12/EEC. [Online] Available at <http://eur-lex.europa.eu/LexUriServ/LexUriServ.do?uri=OJ:L:2009:140:0088:0113:EN:PDF> [Accessed 11 August 2011].

Directive 2009/147/EC of 30 November 2009 on the conservation of wild birds. [Online] Available at <http://eur-lex.europa.eu/LexUriServ/LexUriServ.do?uri=OJ:L:2010:020:0007:0025:en:PDF> [Accessed 11 August 2011].

Dudley, N. (ed.), 2008. *Guidelines for Applying Protected Area Management Categories.* Gland, Switzerland: International Union for Conservation of Nature. [Online] Available at <http://data.iucn.org/dbtw-wpd/edocs/PAPS-016.pdf> [Accessed 7 July 2011].

EEA, 2009. *Urban waste water treatment (CSI 024)* – Assessment published Jan 2009. [Online] Available at <http://www.eea.europa.eu/data-and-maps/indicators/urban-waste-water-treatment/urban-waste-water-treatment-assessment-1> [Accessed 13 May 2011].

EEA, 2010. *Air Pollution (Bulgaria).* [Online] Available at <http://www.eea.europa.eu/soer/countries/bg/soertopic_view?topic=air%20pollution> [Accessed 13 May 2011].

EEA, 2010a. *Air Pollution (Croatia).* [Online] Available at <http://www.eea.europa.eu/soer/countries/hr/soertopic_view?topic=air%20pollution> [Accessed 13 May 2011].

EEA, 2010b. *Air Pollution (Slovenia).* [Online] Available at < http://www.eea.europa.eu/soer/countries/si/soertopic_view?topic=air%20pollution> [Accessed 13 May 2011].

EEA, 2010c. *Air Pollution (Turkey).* [Online] Available at <http://www.eea.europa.eu/soer/countries/tr/soertopic_view?topic=air%20pollution> [Accessed 13 May 2011].

EEA, 2010d. *Waste (Slovenia).* [Online] Available at <http://www.eea.europa.eu/soer/countries/si/soertopic_view?topic=waste> [Accessed 28 June 2011].

EEA, 2011. *Annual European Union Greenhouse Gas Inventory 1990–2009 and Inventory Report 2011 Submission to the UNFCCC Secretariat.* Technical report No.2/2011. [Online] Available at <http://unfccc.int/files/national_reports/annex_i_ghg_inventories/national_inventories_submissions/application/zip/euc-2011-nir-27may.zip> [Accessed 28 June 2011].

EEA Grants–Norway Grants, 2011. *Slovenia Concentrates Funding on Public Health.* [Online] Available at <http://www.eeagrants.org/id/2484> [Accessed 13 May 2011].

EEA Grants–Norway Grants, 2012. *Key Achievements 2004–2009 in Bulgaria.* [Online] Available at <http://eeagrants.org/id/2896.0> [Accessed 3 January 2012].

EU Integrated Environmental Approximation Strategy 2007–2023, 2006. Ministry of Environment and Forestry of the Republic of Turkey. [Online] Available at <http://www.delta-eko.org/_docs/f6e6cf8efd_uces_eng.pdf> [Accessed 13 May 2011].

European Bank for Reconstruction and Development, 2010. Overview by Business Sector 5. *Sustainability Report 2010.* [Online] Available at <http://www.ebrd.com/downloads/research/sustain/sr10ef.pdf> [Accessed 7 July 2011].

European Bank for Reconstruction and Development, 2011. *Romania.* [Online] Available at <http://www.ebrd.com/downloads/research/factsheets/romania.pdf> [Accessed 14 June 2011].

European Commission, 2001. *Green Paper on European Union Consumer Protection.* COM(2001) 531 final. 2 October 2001. [Online] Available at <http://eur-lex.europa.eu/LexUriServ/site/en/com/2001/com2001_0531en01.pdf> [Accessed 13 May 2011].

European Commission, 2004. *Financing Natura 2000.* Communication from the Commission to the Council and the European Parliament. Brussels: COM(2004) 0431 final. [Online] Available at <http://eur-lex.europa.eu/LexUriServ/LexUriServ.do?uri=COM:2004:0431:FIN:EN:PDF> [Accessed 13 July 2011].

European Commission, 2005. *Comprehensive Monitoring Report on the State of Preparedness for EU Membership of Bulgaria and Romania.* Communication from the Commission. Brussels: COM(2005) 534 final. [Online] Available at <http://eur-lex.europa.eu/LexUriServ/LexUriServ.do?uri=COM:2005:0534:FIN:EN:PDF> [Accessed 13 May 2011].

European Commission, 2005a. *Taking Sustainable Use of Resources Forward: a Thematic Strategy on the Prevention and Recycling of Waste.* Communication from the Commission to the Council, the European Parliament, the European Economic and Social Committee and the Committee of the Regions. Brussels: COM(2005) 666 final. [Online] Available at <http://eur-lex.europa.eu/LexUriServ/LexUriServ.do?uri=COM:2005:0666:FIN:EN:PDF> [Accessed 18 July 2011].

European Commission, 2005b. *Thematic Strategy on Air Pollution.* Communication from the Commission to the Council and the European Parliament. Brussels: COM(2005) 446 final. [Online] Available at <http://eur-lex.europa.eu/LexUriServ/site/en/com/2005/com2005_0446en01.pdf> [Accessed 18 July 2011].

European Commission, 2005c. *Thematic Strategy on the Protection and Conservation of the Marine Environment.* Communication from the Commission to the Council and the European Parliament. Brussels: COM(2005) 504 final. [Online] Available at <http://eur-lex.europa.eu/LexUriServ/LexUriServ.do?uri=COM:2005:0504:FIN:EN:PDF> [Accessed 18 July 2011].

European Commission, 2005d. *Thematic Strategy on the Sustainable use of Natural Resources.* Communication from the Commission to the Council, the European Parliament, the European Economic and Social Committee and the Committee of the Regions. Brussels: COM(2005) 670 final. [Online] Available at <http://eur-lex.europa.eu/LexUriServ/LexUriServ.do?uri=COM:2005:0670:FIN:EN:PDF> [Accessed 18 July 2011].

European Commission, 2006. *A Thematic Strategy on the Sustainable Use of Pesticides.* Communication from the Commission to the Council, the European Parliament, the European Economic and Social Committee and the Committee of the Regions. Brussels: COM(2006) 372 final. [Online] Available at <http://ec.europa.eu/environment/ppps/pdf/com_2006_0372.pdf> [Accessed 1 July 2011].

European Commission, 2006a. *Halting the Loss of Biodiversity by 2010 – and Beyond Sustaining Ecosystem Services for Human Well–being.* Communication from the Commission. Brussels: COM(2006) 216 final. [Online] Available at <http://eur-lex.europa.eu/LexUriServ/site/en/com/2006/com2006_0216en01.pdf> [Accessed 1 July 2011].

European Commission, 2006b. *Summary of Progress in Delivery of Objectives of EU Biodiversity Action Plan: Slovenia*. [Online] Available at <http://ec.europa.eu/environment/nature/biodiversity/comm2006/pdf/profiles/si.pdf> [Accessed 17 September 2011].

European Commission, 2006c. *Thematic Strategy for Soil Protection*. Communication from the Commission to the Council, the European Parliament, the European Economic and Social Committee and the Committee of the Regions. Brussels: COM(2006) 231 final. [Online] Available at <http://ec.europa.eu/environment/soil/pdf/com_2006_0231_en.pdf> [Accessed 1 July 2011].

European Commission, 2006d. *Thematic Strategy on the Urban Environment*. Communication from the Commission to the Council and the European Parliament. Brussels: COM(2005) 718 final. [Online] Available at <http://ec.europa.eu/environment/urban/pdf/com_2005_0718_en.pdf> [Accessed 1 July 2011].

European Commission, 2008. Report from the Commission to the European Parliament and the Council on the Management of EU funds in Bulgaria. Brussels: COM(2008) 496 final. 23 July 2008. [Online] Available at <http://ec.europa.eu/environment/nature/biodiversity/comm2006/pdf/profiles/si.pdf> [Accessed 9 July 2011].

European Commission, 2008a. *Sustainable Consumption and Production and Sustainable Industrial Policy Action Plan*. Communication from the Commission to the European Parliament, the Council, the European Economic and Social Committee and the Committee of the Regions. Brussels: COM(2008) 397 final. [Online] Available at <http://ec.europa.eu/environment/eussd/pdf/com_2008_397.pdf> [Accessed 16 June 2011].

European Commission, 2009. *Enlargement Strategy and Main Challenges 2009–2010*. Communication from the Commission to the European Parliament and the Council. Brussels: COM(2009) 533 final. 14 October 2009. [Online] Available at <http://eur-lex.europa.eu/LexUriServ/LexUriServ.do?uri=COM:2009:0533:FIN:EN:PDF> [Accessed 16 June 2011].

European Commission, 2009a. Report from the Commission to the European Parliament and the Council in accordance with article 18.3 of the Water Framework Directive 2000/60/EC on programmes for monitoring of water status. Brussels: COM(2009) 156 final. 1 April 2009. [Online] Available at <http://eur lex.europa.eu/LexUriServ/LexUriServ.do?uri=COM:2009:0156:FIN:EN:PDF> [Accessed 16 June 2011].

European Commission, 2009b. *Turkey 2009 Progress Report*. Commission Staff Working Document. [Online] Available at <http://ec.europa.eu/enlargement/pdf/key_documents/2009/tr_rapport_2009_en.pdf> [Accessed 16 June 2011].

European Commission, 2009c. *Status of Implementation of EU Funds in Romania on 31 July 2009*. [Online] Available at <http://ec.europa.eu/budget/library/biblio/documents/2007/disch_status_funds_inRO_en.pdf> [Accessed 16 June 2011].

European Commission, 2010. *Analysis of Options to Move Beyond 20% Greenhouse Gas Emission Reductions and Assessing the Risk of Carbon Leakage*.: Communication from the Commission to the European Parliament, the Council, the European Economic and Social Committee and the Committee of the Regions. Brussels COM(2010) 265 final. 26 May 2010. [Online] Available at <http://eur-lex.europa.eu/LexUriServ/LexUriServ.do?uri=COM:2010:0265:FIN:EN:PDF> [Accessed 10 October 2011].

European Commission, 2010a. *Cohesion Policy: Strategic Report 2010 on the Implementation of the Programmes 2007–2013*. Communication from the Commission to the European Parliament, the Council, the European Economic and Social Committee and the Committee of the Regions. Brussels: COM(2010) 110 final. 31 Mar 2010. [Online] Available at <http://ec.europa.eu/regional_policy/sources/docoffic/official/communic/reporting2010/com_2010_110_en.pdf> [Accessed 10 October 2011].

European Commission, 2010b. *Energy 2020 A Strategy for Competitive, Sustainable and Secure Energy*. Communication from the Commission to the European Parliament, the Council, the European Economic and Social Committee and the Committee of the Regions. COM(2010) 639 final. [Online] Available at <http://eur-lex.europa.eu/LexUriServ/LexUriServ.do?uri=COM:2010:0639:FIN:EN:PDF> [Accessed 16 June 2011].

European Commission, 2010c. *Enlargement Strategy and Main Challenges 2010–2011*. Communication from the Commission to the European Parliament and the Council. Brussels: COM(2010) 660. 9 November 2010. [Online] Available at <http://ec.europa.eu/enlargement/pdf/key_documents/2010/package/strategy_paper_2010_en.pdf> [Accessed 16 June 2011].

European Commission, 2010d. *EU 2020 Integrated Guidelines for the Economic and Employment Policies of the Member States*. Brussels: SEC (2010)448 final. 27 April 2010. [Online] Available at <http://ec.europa.eu/eu2020/pdf/Brochure%20 Integrated%20Guidelines.pdf> [Accessed 16 June 2011].

European Commission, 2010e. *Europe 2020 –Public Consultation First Overview of Responses*. Brussels: SEC(2010)116 final. 2 February 2010. [Online] Available at <http://ec.europa.eu/eu2020/pdf/eu2020_public_consultation_preliminary_over-view_of_responses.pdf> [Accessed 16 June 2011].

European Commission, 2010f. *Turkey 2010 Progress Report*, Commission staff working document accompanying the communication from the Commission to the European Parliament and the Council: Enlargement Strategy and Main Challenges 2010–2011. Brussels: SEC(2010) 1327. 9 November 2010. [Online] Available at <http://ec.europa.eu/enlargement/pdf/key_documents/2010/package/tr_rapport_2010_en.pdf> [Accessed 16 June 2011].

European Commission, 2011. *A Budget for Europe 2020 – Part II: Policy Fiches*. Communication from the Commission to the European Parliament, the Council, the European Economic and Social Committee and the Committee of the Regions. Brussels: COM(2011) 500 final. 29 June 2011. [Online] Available at <http://ec.europa.eu/budget/library/biblio/documents/fin_fwk1420/MFF_COM–2011–500_Part_II_en.pdf> [Accessed 16 July 2011].

European Commission, 2011a. *A Budget for Europe 2020: the Current System of Funding, the Challenges Ahead, the Results of Stakeholders Consultation and Different Options on the Main Horizontal and Sectoral Issues*. Accompanying the document communication from the Commission to the European Parliament, the Council, the European Economic and Social Committee and the Committee of the Regions. SEC(2011) 868 final. 29 June 2011. [Online] Available at <http://ec.europa.eu/budget/library/biblio/documents/fin_fwk1420/SEC–868_en.pdf> [Accessed 16 July 2011].

European Commission, 2011b. *A Roadmap for Moving to a Competitive Low Carbon Economy in 2050*. Communication from the Commission to the European Parliament, the Council, the European Economic and Social Committee and the Committee of the Regions. COM(2011) 112 final. [Online] Available at <http://eur-lex.europa.eu/LexUriServ/LexUriServ.do?uri=COM:2011:0112:FIN:EN:PDF> [Accessed 16 July 2011].

European Commission, 2011c. *Energy Efficiency Plan 2011*. Communication from the Commission to the European Parliament, the Council, the European Economic and Social Committee and the Committee of the Regions. COM(2011) 109 final. [Online] Available at <http://eur-lex.europa.eu/LexUriServ/LexUriServ.do?uri=COM:2011:010 9:FIN:EN:PDF> [Accessed 16 July 2011].

European Commission, 2011d. *Our Life Insurance, Our Natural Capital: an EU Biodiversity Strategy to 2020*. Communication from the Commission to the European Parliament, the Council, the European Economic and Social Committee and the Committee of the Regions. COM(2011) 244 final. [Online] Available at <http://ec.europa.eu/environment/nature/biodiversity/comm2006/pdf/2020/1_EN_ACT_part1_v7%5B1%5D.pdf> [Accessed 16 July 2011].

European Commission, 2011e. *Rio+20: Towards the Green Economy and Better Governance*. Communication from the Commission to the European Parliament, the Council, the European Economic and Social Committee and the Committee of the Regions. COM(2011) 363 final. [Online] Available at <http://eur-lex.europa.eu/LexUriServ/LexUriServ.do?uri=COM:2011:0363:FIN:EN:PDF> [Accessed 16 July 2011].

European Commission, 2011f. *Roadmap to a Single European Transport Area – Towards a Competitive and Resource Efficient Transport System*. White Paper. Communication from the Commission to the European Parliament, the Council, the European Economic and Social Committee and the Committee of the Regions. COM(2011) 144 final. [Online] Available at <http://eur-lex.europa.eu/LexUriServ/LexUriServ.do?uri=COM:2011:0144:FIN:EN:PDF> [Accessed 16 July 2011].

European Commission, 2011g. *Roadmap to a Resource Efficient Europe*. Communication from the Commission to the European Parliament, the Council, the European Economic and Social Committee and the Committee of the Regions. COM(2011) 571 final. [Online] Available at <http://ec.europa.eu/environment/resource_efficiency/pdf/com2011_571.pdf> [Accessed 16 July 2011].

European Commission, 2011h. *Thematic Strategy on the Prevention and Recycling of Waste*. Report from the Commission to the European Parliament, the Council, the European Economic and Social Committee and the Committee of the Regions. Brussels: COM(2011) 13 final. [Online] Available at <http://eur-lex.europa.eu/LexUriServ/LexUriServ.do?uri=COM:2011:0013:FIN:EN:PDF> [Accessed 13 June 2011].

European Commission, 2011i. The Sixth Community Environment Action Programme. Final Assessment. Communication from the Commission to the European Parliament, the Council, the European Economic and Social Committee and the Committee of the Regions. Brussels: COM (2011) 531 final. Brussels, 31.8.2011. [Online] Available at <http://eur-lex.europa.eu/LexUriServ/LexUriServ.do?uri=COM:2011:0531:FIN:EN:PDF > [Accessed 18 July 2011].

European Commission DG Agriculture, n.d. *Rural Development Programmes 2004–2006: The Republic of Slovenia*. [Online] Available at <http://ec.europa.eu/agriculture/rur/countries/sl/slovenia_en.pdf> [Accessed 5 October 2011].

European Commission DG Climate Action, 2011. *Climate Law – Acquis of the European Union*. [Online] Available at <http://ec.europa.eu/dgs/clima/acquis/index_en.htm#Monitoring> [Accessed 5 October 2011].

European Commission DG Environment, n.d. *LIFE Projects in Romania*. [Online] Available at <http://ec.europa.eu/environment/life/countries/documents/romania_en_oct06.pdf> [Accessed 5 May 2011].

European Commission DG Environment, 2009. *Ex-post Evaluation of Projects and Activities Financed under the LIFE Programme Country-by-country Analysis Slovenia*. LIFE. [Online] Available at <http://ec.europa.eu/environment/life/publications/lifepublications/evaluation/documents/eval_slovenia.pdf> [Accessed 5 May 2011].

European Commission DG Environment, 2010. *EU Waste Legislation*. [Online] Available at <http://ec.europa.eu/environment/waste/legislation/index.htm> [Accessed 11 June 2011].

European Commission DG Environment, 2011. *Legislation Ambient Air Quality.* [Online] Available at <http://ec.europa.eu/environment/air/legis.htm> [Accessed 5 June 2011].

European Commission DG Environment, 2011a. *Water Framework Directive.* [Online] Available at <http://ec.europa.eu/environment/water/water-framework/index_en.html> [Accessed 5 June 2011].

European Commission DG Environment, 2011b. *The Economics of Environmental Policy.* [Online] Available at <http://ec.europa.eu/environment/enveco/economics_policy/index.htm> [Accessed 5 June 2011].

European Commission DG Regional Policy, 2008. *Guide to Cost-benefit Analysis of Investment Projects, Structural Funds, Cohesion Fund and Instrument for Pre-accession.* [Online] Available at <http://www.sk-at.eu/sk-at/downloads/EN/CBAguide2008_en.pdf> [Accessed 5 June 2011].

European Commission DG Regional Policy, 2011. *Instrument for Pre-accession Assistance (IPA).* [Online] Available at <http://ec.europa.eu/regional_policy/thefunds/ipa/croatia_environment_en.cfm> [Accessed 5 June 2011].

European Commission DG Taxation and Customs Union, 2011. *Taxes in Europe Database.* [Online] Available at <http://ec.europa.eu/taxation_customs/tedb/taxSearch.html> [Accessed 5 June 2011].

European Community, 2009. *Nature & Biodiversity Projects 2008.* [Online] Available at <http://ec.europa.eu/environment/life/publications/lifepublications/compilations/documents/natcompilation08.pdf> [Accessed 3 June 2011].

European Council, 2010. *Conclusions, 17 June 2010.* [Online] Available at <http://ec.europa.eu/eu2020/pdf/council_conclusion_17_june_en.pdf> [Accessed 5 June 2011].

European Parliament and Council Directive 94/62/EC of 20 December 1994 on packaging and packaging waste. [Online] Available at <http://eur-lex.europa.eu/LexUriServ/LexUriServ.do?uri=OJ:L:1994:365:0010:0023:EN:PDF> [Accessed 5 June 2011].

European Parliament and Council Directive 94/63/EC of 20 December 1994 on the control of volatile organic compound (VOC) emissions resulting from the storage of petrol and its distribution from terminals to service stations. [Online] Available at <http://www.vaporec.gr/files/94_63_ec.pdf> [Accessed 5 June 2011].

European Sustainable Development Network, 2008. *Single Country Profile, Bulgaria.* [Online] Available at <http://www.sd-network.eu/?k=country%20profiles&s=single%20country%20profile&country=Bulgaria> [Accessed 5 June 2011].

Eurostat, 2010. *Public and Private Specialised Producers Environmental Protection Expenditure, 2006.* European Commission. [Online] Available at <http://epp.eurostat.ec.europa.eu/statistics_explained/index.php?title=File:Public_and_private_specialised_producers_environmental_protection_expenditure,_2006_%281%29_%28%25_of_GDP%29.png&filetimestamp=20101215163323> [Accessed 8 August 2011].

Eurostat, 2011. *Your Key to European Statistics.* European Commission. [Online] Available at <http://epp.eurostat.ec.europa.eu/portal/page/portal/eurostat/home/> [Accessed 5 May 2011].

Final Report on Financing Natura 2000. Working Group on Article 8 of the Habitats Directive. [Online] Available at <http://chm.moew.government.bg/nnps/upload/Common/Baurle_literature_NOF/Local%20Publish/WG_Art._8_2002._final_report_en.pdf> [Accessed 5 July 2011].Fondacija Heinrich Boell, 2007. *Forumi o regionalizaciji I održivom življenju.* Zagreb: Tiskara Varteks.

Francis, P., 2000. Financing Environmental Protection in Economies in Transition: the Role of Environmental Funds. *Environment and Planning B: Planning and Design* 27(3) 365–77.

FRD Center Market Entry Service, 2011. *Water and Wastewater Management in Romania.* [Online] Available at <http://static.globaltrade.net/files/pdf/20110307130809262.pdf> [Accessed 5 July 2011].

Gantioler, S., Bassi, S., Kettunen, M., McConville, A., ten Brink, P., Rayment, M., Landgrebe, R. and Gerdes, H., 2010. *Costs and Socio-Economic Benefits Associated with the Natura 2000 Network.* London and Brussels: Institute for European Environmental Policy. [Online] Available at <http://ec.europa.eu/environment/nature/natura2000/financing/docs/natura2000_costs_benefits.pdf> [Accessed 21 July 2011].

GHK, Arecadis, Milieu, Institute for European Environmental Policy, 2011. *Combined Impact Assessment and Ex Ante Evaluation of the Review of the LIFE+ Regulation: Options Development* [Online] Available at http://ec.europa.eu/environment/life/about/documents/LIFE_IA_ghk_full.pdf > [Accessed 19 January 2011].

GHK, Rojanschi, V. and Lust, A., 2006. *National Evaluation Report for Romania.* Brussels: European Commission.[Online] Available at <http://ec.europa.eu/regional_policy/sources/docgener/evaluation/pdf/evalstrat_env/ro_main.pdf> [Accessed 24 June 2011].

Global Water Intelligence, 2009. *EBRD Eyes First Investment in Turkish Water Sector.* [Online] Available at <http://www.globalwaterintel.com/archive/10/8/general/ebrd-eyes-first-investment-turkish-water-sector.html> [Accessed 5 July 2011].

Global Water Intelligence, 2009a. *No Let Up in Pressure on Water Tarriffs.* [Online] Available at <http://www.globalwaterintel.com/archive/10/9/market-insight/no-let-pressure-water-tariffs.html> [Accessed 5 July 2011].

Global Water Intelligence, 2011. *Market Leading Analysis of the International Water Industry.* [Online] Available at <http://www.globalwaterintel.com/> [Accessed 5 July 2011].

Gobec, S. and De Sutter, R., 2006. *National Evaluation Report for Slovenia.* Brussels and London: GHK. [Online] Available at <http://ec.europa.eu/regional_policy/sources/docgener/evaluation/pdf/evalstrat_env/si_main.pdf> [Accessed 13 June 2011].

Grimes, A. Myers, G. and Ploetz, J, 2002. *Assessment of Natural Resources and the Environment: Issues and Opportunities for USAID/Sofia.* Washington DC: USAID. [Online] Available at <http://pdf.usaid.gov/pdf_docs/PNACQ170.pdf> [Accessed 13 June 2011]

Guler, S., 2011. *The UN Joint Programme on Enhancing the Capacity of Turkey to Adapt to Climate Change.* MDG Achievement Fund Turkey. [Online] Available at <http://www.iklimmdgf-tr.org/default-en.asp> [Accessed 14 July 2011].

Guven, C., 2007. *Climate Change & Turkey: Impacts, Sectoral Analyses, Socio-Economic Dimensions.* Ankara: UNDP Turkey. [Online] Available at <http://europeandcis.undp.org/environment/show/6C27F762-F203-1EE9-B6E081020AABCDE7> [Accessed 13 October 2011].

Haukioja, T, 2007. *Sustainable Development and Economic Growth in the Market Economy.* Tampere: Turku School of Economics. [Online] Available at <http://info.tse.fi/julkaisut/vk/Ae6_2007.pdf> [Accessed 13 May 2011].

Hattam, J., 2009. *Turkey Finally Gets on Board with Kyoto.* Treehugger. [Online] Available at <http://www.treehugger.com/files/2009/02/turkey-finally-ratifies-kyoto.php> [Accessed 13 October 2011].

Health and Environment Alliance, 2010. *Climate Report: How Bulgaria Could Improve Health and Save Money.* [Online] Available at <http://www.env-health.org/spip.php?article126> [Accessed 12 October 2011].

ICIS Heren, 2010. *Romania Could Begin AAU Sale Within Year.* [Online] Available at <http://www.icis.com/heren/articles/2010/02/17/9335657/emissions/edcm/romania-could-begin-aau-sale-within-year.html> [Accessed 12 October 2011].

IISD, Najam, A., Papa, M. and Taiyab, N., 2007. *Global Environmental Governance: Key Challenges to Effective Global Environmental Governance*. Encyclopedia of Earth. [Online] Available at <http://www.eoearth.org/article/Global_Environmental_Governance:_Key_Challenges_to_Effective_Global_Environmental_Governance> [Accessed 12 October 2011].

ISPA Implementing Agency, 2010. *ISPA Programme*. [Online] Available at <http://ispa-mrrb.org/en/?id=108#id1> [Accessed 12 October 2011].

Jehlička, P. and Tickle, A., 2004. Environmental Implications of Eastern Enlargement: The End of Progressive EU Environmental Policy? *Environmental Politics*, 13: 1.

Kampa, E., Ward, J. G. and Leipparand, A., 2008. *Convergence with EU Water Policies: Short Guide for ENP Partners and Russia*. Brussels: European Communities. [Online] Available at <http://ec.europa.eu/environment/enlarg/pdf/pubs/water_en.pdf> [Accessed 12 June 2011].

Kettunen, M., Carter, O., Gantioler, S., Baldock, D., Torkler, P., Arroyo Schnell, A., Baumueller, A., Gerritsen, E., Rayment, M., Daly, E. and Pieterse, M., 2011. *Assessment of the Natura 2000 Co-financing Arrangements of the EU Financing Instrument*, Institute for European Environmental Policy. [Online] Available at <http://www.ieep.eu/assets/791/Assessment_of_Natura_2000_Co-financing.pdf> [Accessed 12 June 2011].

Klein, H., Gauss, M., Nyiri, A. and Steensen, B. M., 2011. *Transboundary air pollution by main pollutants (S, N, O3) and PM: Slovenia*. Norwegian Meteorological Institute. [Online] Available at <http://emep.int/publ/reports/2011/Country_Reports/report_SI.pdf> [Accessed 12 June 2011].

Knill, C. and Liefferink, D., 2007. *Environmental Politics in the European Union*. Manchester and New York: Manchester University Press.

Kolk, A. and Van der Weij, E, 1998. Financing Environmental Policy in East Central Europe. In: Baker, S. and Jehlička, P., (eds), *Dilemmas of Transition. The Environment, Democracy and Economic Reform in East Central Europe*. London: Frank Cass.

Kramar, H. and Cegnar, T., 2010. *Slovenia's Fifth National Communication under the United Nations Framework Convention on Climate Change*. Ljubljana, Slovenia: Ministry of Environment and Spatial Planning. [Online] Available at <http://unfccc.int/resource/docs/natc/svn_nc5.pdf> [Accessed 12 September 2011].

Kraus, H. H., 1998. *Environment Policy In Slovenia*. European Parliament: [Online] Available at <http://www.europarl.europa.eu/workingpapers/envi/pdf/brief6en_en.pdf> [Accessed 12 September 2011].

Langeveld, H., Sanders, J. and Meeusen, M. (eds), 2010. *The Biobased Economy, Biofuels, Materials and Chemicals in the Post-oil Era*. London and Washington DC: Earthscan.

Larive Romania IBD SRL, 2011. *Waste management research in Romania*. Den Haag: Agentschapt NL. [Online] Available at <http://www.dutchromaniannetwork.nl/pdf_files/Waste%20management%20research%20in%20Romania_0.pdf> [Accessed 14 June 2011].

Liarikos, C., Schubert, D., Lang, S., Beckmann, A., Aulotte, E. and Torkler, P., 2005. *EU Funding for Environment: A handbook for the 2007–13 programming period*. Brussels: World Wide Fund for Nature. [Online] Available at <http://www.google.com/url?sa=t&rct=j&q=eu%20funding%20for%20environment&source=web&cd=1&ved=0CFEQFjAA&url=http%3A%2F%2Fwww.panda.org%2Fdownloads%2Feurope%2Feufundingforenvironmentweb.pdf&ei=IlCpTpSUINLS4QST2LkM&usg=AFQjCNGBiqVPHXuq7BY507nWJGi6NLLdvw&sig2=0HrCIHPf7NQ3wcFj4BZ21w&cad=rja> [Accessed 14 June 2011].

Loungani, P., 2000. *How Accurate are Private Sector Forecasts? Cross-country Evidence from Consensus Forecast of Output Growth*. International Monetary Fund. [Online]

Available at <http://www.imf.org/external/pubs/ft/wp/2000/wp0077.pdf> [Accessed 14 June 2011].

Low Emission Zone, 2011. *EU Air Quality Targets.* [Online] Available at <http://www.lowemissionzones.eu/what-are-lezs--othermenu–32?start=10> [Accessed 14 June 2011].

Markovič-Hribernik, T. and Murks, A., 2006. The Long Road from Ljubljana to Kyoto: Implementing Emissions Trading Mechanism and Co_2 Tax. *Financial Theory and Practice*, 30 (1): 29–65. [Online] Available at <http://www.google.com/url?sa=t&rct=j&q=t.%20markovi%C4%8D-hribernik%2C%20a.%20murks&source=web&cd=1&ved=0CBkQFjAA&url=http%3A%2F%2Fhrcak.srce.hr%2Ffile%2F9207&ei=D32mTqjWJK7a4QS5r5XxDw&usg=AFQjCNH1XmCOcid40gyfZtFxf40CFsWrFw&cad=rja> [Accessed 14 July 2011].

Martin, J. and Henrichs, T., 2010. *The European Environment, State and Outlook 2010 Synthesis.* Copenhagen: EEA.

Morales, A. and Efstathiou Jr., J., 2010. *Bank Tax, CO2 Auctions Recommended by Soros Panel to Help Climate Efforts.* Bloomberg: [Online] Available at <http://www.bloomberg.com/news/2010–11–05/soros-panel-draft-says-bank-taxes-c02-auctions-can-fund-climate-aid.html> [Accessed 19 July 2011].

McCormick, J., 2008. *Environmental Policy in the European Union.* Basingstoke, Hampshire: Palgrave.

National Development Plan 2007–2013, 2005. Government of Romania. [Online] Available at <http://www.fsenordest.ro/BIBLIOTECA/ndp0713_en.pdfdf> [Accessed 4 July 2011].

National Environment Action Programme, 2005. Government of the Republic of Slovenia. [Online] Available at <http://www.mop.gov.si/fileadmin/mop.gov.si/pageuploads/publikacije/drugo/en/okolje.pdf> [Accessed 4 July 2011].

National Reform Programme 2011–2012, 2011. Government of the Republic of Slovenia. [Online] Available at <http://ec.europa.eu/europe2020/pdf/nrp/nrp_slovenia_en.pdf> [Accessed 4 July 2011].

National Reform Programme 2011–2013, 2011a. Government of Romania. Bucharest. [Online] Available at <http://ec.europa.eu/europe2020/pdf/nrp/nrp_romania_en.pdf> [Accessed 4 July 2011].

National Reform Programme 2011–2015, 2011b. In: *Implementation of 'Europe 2020' Strategy.* Government of the Republic of Bulgaria. [Online] Available at <http://ec.europa.eu/europe2020/pdf/nrp/nrp_bulgaria_en.pdf> [Accessed 4 July 2011].

National Strategic Reference Framework 2007–2013, 2007. Government of Romania. [Online] Available at <http://www.fonduriadministratie.ro/pictures/CSNR_final_EN%5B1%5D%281%29.pdf> [Accessed 5 May 2011].

National Strategic Reference Framework 2007–2013, 2007a. Government Office for Local Self-Government and Regional Policy of Slovenia. [Online] Available at <http://www.svlr.gov.si/fileadmin/svlsrp.gov.si/pageuploads/KOHEZIJA/kohezija–200207/National_Strategic_Reference_Framework.pdf> [Accessed 5 May 2011].

National Strategy for Sustainable Development of tourism in Republic of Bulgaria, Bulgarian State Tourism Agency. [Online] Available at <http://www.tourism.government.bg/bg/tourism_politic.php?menuid=51&id=58> [Accessed 5 May 2011].

National Sustainable Development Strategy Romania, 2013–2020–2030, 2008. Government of Romania and UNDP. [Online] Available at <http://www.un.org/esa/dsd/dsd_aofw_ni/ni_pdfs/NationalReports/romania/Romania.pdf> [Accessed 5 May 2011].

National Waste Management Programme 2003–2007. Government of Bulgaria. [Online] Available at <http://www.upc.edu/sostenible2015/menu–5/seminaris/Seminari_STD_09/docs/nwmp_2003–2007en_fin.pdf> [Accessed 5 May 2011].

Nature Protection Act of Croatia, 2003. Croatian Parliament, provisional translation by Ministry of European Integrations. [Online] Available at <http://www.hah.hr/pdf/Nature_Protection_Act.pdf> [Accessed 11 August 2011].

Nilsson, M. and Eckerberg, K., 2007. *Environmental policy integration in practice*. London: Earthscan.

Novinite, 2010. *Barosso Devastatingly Critical of Bulgaria's Failure to Absorb EU Funds*. [Online] Available at <http://www.novinite.com/view_news.php?id=123510> [Accessed 11 August 2011].

Novinite, 2010. *EC Urges Bulgaria to Reform Water Infrastructure*. [Online] Available at <http://www.novinite.com/view_news.php?id=123235> [Accessed 11 August 2011].

Novinite, 2011. *EU Funds Minister 'Meets Promises' as Bulgaria Reaches 10% Absorption*. [Online] Available at <http://www.novinite.com/view_news.php?id=123803> [Accessed 11 August 2011].

Operational Programme Environment 2007–2013, 2007. Sofia: Republic of Bulgaria. [Online] Available at <http://ope.moew.government.bg/uf/other/OPE_FINAL_EN.doc> [Accessed 4 May 2011].

Operational Programme of Environmental and Transport Infrastructure Development for the Period 2007–2013, 2007. Unofficial Translation. Ljubljana, Slovenia. [Online] Available at <http://www.svlr.gov.si/fileadmin/svlsrp.gov.si/pageuploads/KOHEZIJA/KOHEZIJA_-_angleska_stran/OP_ENVIRN_ENG.pdf> [Accessed 4 May 2011].

Operational Programme for Strengthening Regional Development Potentials for the period 2007–2013, 2007 Ljubljana: Slovenian Government Office for Local Self-government and Regional Policy. [Online] Available at <http://www.svlr.gov.si/fileadmin/svlsrp.gov.si/pageuploads/KOHEZIJA/Programski_dokumenti/OP_Strength_regional_dev_potentials_FINAL.pdf> [Accessed 4 May 2011].

Operativni program zmanjševanja emisij toplogrednih plinov do leta 2012 (OP TGP–1), 2009. Ljubljana: Republic of Slovenia. [Online] Available at <http://www.mop.gov.si/fileadmin/mop.gov.si/pageuploads/zakonodaja/okolje/varstvo_okolja/operativni_programi/op_toplogredni_plini2012_1.pdf> [Accessed 4 May 2011].

Organization for Economic Co-operation and Development. *Conclusion and Recommendation: Bulgaria*. [Online] Available at <http://www.oecd.org/dataoecd/7/51/2452640.pdf> [Accessed 4 May 2011].

Ozdilek, H., 2006. An analogy on assessment of urban air pollution in turkey over the turn of the millennium (1992–2001), *Environmental Monitoring and Assessment* 122:1–3 pp.203–219.

Paradiž, B. and Kranjc, A., 2002. *Slovenia's First National Communication under the UN Framework Convention on Climate Change*. Ljubljana, Slovenia: Slovenian Ministry of Environment, Spatial Planning and Energy. [Online] Available at <http://unfccc.int/resource/docs/natc/sloencl.pdf> [Accessed 4 August 2011].

Peeva, V., Doukov, D., Stoykov, A., Chobanova, B. and Stoykova, T., n.d. in : Petkova, E. and Varaday, G., (eds), *Good Practices in Policies and Measures for Climate Change Mitigation A Central and Eastern European Perspective*. Szentendre, Hungary: The Regional Environmental Center for Central and Eastern Europe (REC). [Online] Available at <http://archive.rec.org/Climate/Publications/goodpractices/> [Accessed 4 May 2011].

Petresin, E. and Fridl, S., 2003. Slovenian Water Management and EU – Challenge and Opportunity. *European Water Management*. [Online] Available at <http://www.ewaonline.de/journal/2003_05.pdf> [Accessed 4 August 2011].

Pitija, 2010. *Review of EEA and Norway Grants Biodiversity Support*. Ljubljana, Slovenia: [Online] Available at <http://www.eeagrants.org/asset/1703/1/1703_1.pdf> [Accessed 4 August 2011].

Point Carbon, 2010. *JI/AAU Host Country Ratings*. [Online] Available at <http://int.pointcarbon.com/CDMper_cent20&per_cent20JI/category.php?categoryID=160> [Accessed 4 August 2011].

Protected Areas Law of Bulgaria, 1998. National Assembly of Bulgaria. [Online] Available at <http://eelink.net/~asilwildlife/Bulgaria1.html> [Accessed 4 June 2011].

Pulpanova, L., 2006. Trends in Government Expenditure by Function, 2000–2004. *Statistics in Focus 11/2006*. European Communities. [Online] Available at <http://epp.eurostat.ec.europa.eu/cache/ITY_OFFPUB/KS-NJ–06–011/EN/KS-NJ–06–011-EN.PDF> [Accessed 16 July 2011].

Ray, A. J., 2007. Findings on the Physical Basis of Climate Change and Adaptation, Impacts and Vulnerability. *IPCC Fourth Assessment Report*. [Online] Available at <http://wwa.colorado.edu/admin/publication_files/resource–2523-Alvord_ipcc.pdf> [Accessed 10 August 2011].

Regional Environmental Center and Umweltbundesamt GmbH. *Handbook on the Implementation of EC Environmental Legislation*. [Online] Available at <http://ec.europa.eu/environment/enlarg/handbook/handbook.pdf> [Accessed 4 May 2011].

Regulation (EC) No. 1013/2006 of the European Parliament and of the Council of 14 June 2006 on shipments of waste. [Online] Available at <http://trade.ec.europa.eu/doclib/docs/2006/october/tradoc_130521.pdf> [Accessed 4 May 2011].

Regulation (EC) No. 443/2009 of the European Parliament and of the Council of 23 April 2009 setting emission performance standards for new passenger cars as part of the Community's integrated approach to reduce CO_2 emissions from light-duty vehicles. [Online] Available at <http://eur-lex.europa.eu/LexUriServ/LexUriServ.do?uri=OJ:L:2009:140:0001:0015:EN:PDF> [Accessed 4 May 2011].

Republic of Bulgaria, 1996. *The First National Communication on Climate Change*. Sofia: UNFCCC. [Online] Available at <http://unfccc.int/resource/docs/natc/bulnc1.pdf> [Accessed 4 August 2011].

Republic of Bulgaria, 1998. *The Second National Communication on Climate Change*. Sofia: UNFCCC. [Online] Available at <http://unfccc.int/resource/docs/natc/bulnc2.pdf> [Accessed 4 August 2011].

Republic of Bulgaria, 2002. *The Third National Communication on Climate Change*. Sofia: UNFCCC. [Online] Available at <http://unfccc.int/resource/docs/natc/bulnc3.pdf> [Accessed 4 August 2011].

Republic of Bulgaria, 2006. *The Fourth National Communication on Climate Change*. Sofia: UNFCCC. [Online] Available at <http://unfccc.int/resource/docs/natc/bgrnc4.pdf> [Accessed 4 August 2011].

Republic of Bulgaria, 2010. *The Fifth National Communication on Climate Change*. Sofia: UNFCCC. [Online] Available at <http://unfccc.int/resource/docs/natc/bgr_nc5.pdf> [Accessed 4 August 2011].

Resolution on the National Environmental Action Programme 2005–2012, 2005. National Assembly of the Republic of Slovenia. [Online] Available at <http://www.ecolex.org/server2.php/libcat/docs/LI/MON–083604.pdf> [Accessed 4 May 2011].

Romanian Ministry of Environment and Water Management, 2005. *Romania's Third National Communication on Climate Change under the United Nations Framework*. [Online] Available at <http://unfccc.int/resource/docs/natc/romnc3.pdf> [Accessed 4 May 2011].

Romanian Ministry of Environment and Water Management, 2006. *Report on Demonstrable Progress in Implementing the Kyoto Protocol: Romania*. Bucharest: [Online] Available at <http://www.mmediu.ro/protectia_mediului/schimbari_climatice/1_Documentatie/Romania_Report_Demonstrable_Progress2005.pdf> [Accessed 4 May 2011].

Romanian Ministry of Environment and Sustainable Development, 2007. *National EPER Report 2005 of Romania Emission Data of Individual Facilities*. Bucharest: Submission under Article 1 sub 2 and 3 of the EPER Decision. [Online] Available at <http://www.eper.ec.europa.eu/eper/Documents/RO_EPER_Data_Romania_2005_final_6may2007.pdf> [Accessed 4 May 2011].

Saith, A, 2006. From Universal Values to Millennium Development Goals: Lost in Translation. *Development and Change*, 37: 1167–99.

Sectoral Operational Programme: Environment 2007–2013, 2007. Romanian Ministry of Environment and Sustainable Development. [Online] Available at <http://www.google.com/url?sa=t&rct=j&q=sectoral%20operational%20programme%3A%20environment%2Bromania&source=web&cd=1&ved=0CB0QFjAA&url=http%3A%2F%2Fwww.posmediu.ro%2FShowDocument.aspx%3Fpath%3DNFw1XDQucGRm&ei=OFOpTvHjDur–4QT01pwC&v6u=http%3A%2F%2Fdualstack.ipv6-exp.l.google.com%2Fgen_204%3Fip%3D161.53.89.213%26ts%3D1319719736591276%26auth%3Doegoczkd2cqpbxauirmg7xnduqhaqrmn%26rndm%3D0.7125397315254319&v6s=2&v6t=943&usg=AFQjCNHQAsm4xNpZzDc8epP2x2c8csFxvA&sig2=9n2KYi62ft0qmEIBbjV2gQ&cad=rja> [Accessed 4 May 2011].

Shirishtov, K. and Stoyanoff, P., 2011. *The International Comparative Legal Guide to Environment and Climate Change Law 2011*. Global Legal Group.

Silva-Jauregu, C., 1999. *Slovenia: Economic Transformation and EU Accession Vol. 1: Summary Report*. Washington DC: World Bank.

Šimleša, D., 2010. *Ekološki otisak, Kako je razvoj zgazio održivnost*. Zagreb: Tiskara Zelina.

Slovenian Environmental Agency, 2009. *Area Under Organic Farming*. [Online] Available at <http://kazalci.arso.gov.si/?data=indicator&ind_id=289&lang_id=94> [Accessed 4 May 2011].

Slovenian Environmental Agency, 2009a. *Damage Caused by Protected Animal Species*. [Online] Available at <http://kazalci.arso.gov.si/?data=indicator&ind_id=218&lang_id=94> [Accessed 4 May 2011].

Slovenian Ministry of Agriculture, Forestry and Food, 2007. *Rural Development Programme of the Republic of Slovenia 2007–2013*. [Online] Available at <http://www.arsktrp.gov.si/fileadmin/arsktrp.gov.si/pageuploads/Aktualno/Aktualno/2010/RDP2007–2013__en.pdf> [Accessed 4 May 2011].

Slovenian Ministry of the Environment and Physical Planning, 1999. *National Environmental Action Programme*. [Online] Available at <http://www.mop.gov.si/fileadmin/mop.gov.si/pageuploads/publikacije/drugo/en/okolje.pdf> [Accessed 4 May 2011].

Slovenian Ministry of the Environment and Spatial Planning, 2003. *Strategic Reference Framework for Cohesion Fund Assistance: Environmental Sector*. [Online] Available at < http://www.rupprecht-consult.de/iczmdownloads/strategic_framework_en.pdf> [Accessed 4 May 2011].

Slovenian Ministry of the Environment and Spatial Planning, 2007. *Natura 2000 Site Management Operational Programme 2007–2013*. [Online] Available at <http://www.natura2000.gov.si/uploads/tx_library/NATURA_ANG_2008.pdf> [Accessed 4 May 2011].

Spassov, Y., Krustev, A. and Nikolovska, V., 2011. Lowest-cost Abatement in Light of the EU ETS and Renewable Feed-in Tariffs in the Electricity Sector in Bulgaria. *Journal of Energy and Natural Resource Law* Vol. 29(2): 281–303. [Online] New York: UN. Available at <http://www.dgkv.com/uf/publications/IBA_Article_Journal%20of%20ENRL.pdf> [Accessed 18 February 2011].

Spurgeon, J. Marchesi, N. Mesic, Z. and Thomas, L., 2009. *Sustainable Financing Review for Croatia Protected Areas*. Environmental Resource Management. [Online] New York: World Bank. Available at <http://www.profor.info/profor/sites/profor.info/files/docs/SustainableFinancingReview-Croatia-Oct2009.pdf> [Accessed 18 March 2011].

Stahl, Jr., R. G., Kapustaka, L. A., Munns, Jr., W. R. and Bruins, R. J. F., 2003. *Valuation of Ecological Resources, Integration of Ecology and Socioeconomics in Environmental Decision Making*. New York: CRC Press.

Stec, S. and Casey- Lefkowitz, S, 2000. *The Aarhus Convention Implementation Guide*. Geneve: United Nations. [Online] Available at <http://www.unece.org/fileadmin/DAM/env/pp/acig.pdf> [Accessed 22 May 2011].

Stoltenberg, J. and Zenawi, M., 2010. *Report of the Secretary-General's High Level Advisory Group on Climate Change Financing*. New York: UN. [Online] Available at <http://www.un.org/wcm/webdav/site/climatechange/shared/Documents/AGF_reports/AGF_Final_Report.pdf> [Accessed 18 February 2011].

Strategy of Waste Management in the Republic of Croatia, 2005. *Official Gazette No. 178/04*. [Online] New York: UN. Available at http://www.fzoeu.hr/hrv/pdf/Waste_Management_Strategy.pdf> [Accessed 6 May 2011].

Šušteršič, J. Rojec, M. and Korenika, K., 2005. *Slovenia's Development Strategy*. Ljubljana, Slovenia: Tiskarna Solos; New York: UN. [Online] Available at <http://www.arrs.gov.si/en/agencija/inc/ssd-new.pdf> [Accessed 10 June 2011].

Tišma, S. and Butković, H., 2008. Main Challenges in Adopting Environmental Acquis. In: Samardžija, V. and Dukes, A., (eds), 2008. *Communciating Integration Impact in Croatia and Ireland*. Zagreb: Institute for International and European Affairs and Institute for International Relations, pp. 175–90.

Tišma, S. and Čermak, H., 2010. Environmental Dimension of the Lisbon Strategy and the EU 2020 Strategy. In: Samardžija, V. and Butković, H., (eds), 2010. *From the Lisbon Strategy to Europe 2020*. Zagreb: Institute for International Relations, pp. 250–70.

Tišma, S. and Maleković, S., 2009. *Environmental Protection and Regional Development – Experiences and Perspectives*. Zagreb: Institute for International Relations.

Tonchevski, A. and Lust, A., 2006. *National Evaluation Report for Bulgaria*. Brussels and London: GHK. [Online] Available at <http://ec.europa.eu/regional_policy/sources/docgener/evaluation/pdf/evalstrat_env/bu_main.pdf> [Accessed 21 May 2011].

Torcu-Tas, E. C., 2009. Implementation of EU Water Policies for Accession in Turkey. *Fifth World Water Forum*. Istanbul, 19 March 2009. [Online] Available at <http://www.rec.org.tr/dyn_files/42/389-rectr-suforumu-yanetkinlik-sunum–05.pdf> [Accessed 18 March 2011].

Turkish Court of Accounts, 2007. *Waste Management in Turkey National Regulations and Evaluation of Implementation Results*. Performance Audit Report. [Online] Available at <http://www.sayistay.gov.tr/english_tca/Performance/TCA_Waste_Management_Report.pdf> [Accessed 18 March 2011].

Turkish Grand National Assembly, 2006. *Ninth Development Plan (2007–2013)*. [Online] Available at <http://ekutup.dpt.gov.tr/plan/ix/9developmentplan.pdf> [Accessed 18 March 2011].

Turkish Ministry of Environment and Forestry, 2004. Used Batteries and Accumulators Control Regulation. *Official Gazette No. 25569*. [Online] Available at <http://www.projegelistirme.com/yonetmelik/eng/Regulation6.doc> [Accessed 18 March 2011].

Turkish Ministry of Environment and Forestry, 2006. *EU Environmental Approximation Strategy 2007–2023*. [Online] Available at <http://www.delta-eko.org/_docs/f6e6cf8efd_uces_eng.pdf> [Accessed 18 March 2011].

Turkish Ministry of Environment and Forestry, 2007. *Environment Operational Programme.* Ankara: [Online] Available at <http://www.ipa.gov.tr/Files/EOP.pdf> [Accessed 18 March 2011].

Turkish Ministry of Environment and Forestry, 2007a. *The National Biological Diversity Strategy and Action Plan.* [Online] Available at <http://www.cbd.int/doc/world/tr/tr-nbsap-v2-en.pdf> [Accessed 18 March 2011].

Turkish Ministry of Environment and Forestry, 2010. *National Climate Change Strategy 2010–2020.* [Online] Available at <http://www.iklim.cob.gov.tr/iklim/Files/Stratejiler/National%20Strategy.pdf> [Accessed 18 March 2011].

TurkStat, 2011. *Turkish Statistical Institute.* [Online] Available at <http://www.turkstat.gov.tr/Start.do > [Accessed 18 March 2011].

UNDP and GEF, n.d. *Conservation and Sustainable Use of Biodiversity in the Dalmatian Coast through Greening: Coastal Development – COAST.* UNDP Project Document. [Online] Available at [Online] Available at <http://www.thegef.org/gef/sites/thegef.org/files/repository/Croatia_Conservation_Sust_Use_BD_Dalmatian_Coast.pdf> [Accessed 28 May 2011].

UNDP Romania, 2008. *Small Grants Programmes.* [Online] Available at <http://www.nug.bg/lang/2/index> [Accessed 28 May 2011].

UNDP Turkey, 2006. *Capacity Building for Climate Change Management in Turkey Project.* [Online] Available at <http://www.undp.org.tr/Gozlem2.aspx?WebSayfaNo=1892> [Accessed 28 May 2011].

UNDP Turkey, 2006a. *Developing Turkey's National Climate Change Action Plan Project.* [Online] Available at <http://www.undp.org.tr/Gozlem2.aspx?WebSayfaNo=2057> [Accessed 28 May 2011].

UNDP Turkey, 2011. *Global Environment Facility – Small Grants Programme (GEF-SGP).* [Online] Available at <http://www.undp.org.tr/Gozlem2.aspx?WebSayfaNo=33> [Accessed 28 May 2011].

UNEP, 2011. *Towards a Green Economy: Pathways to Sustainable Development and Poverty Eradication – A Synthesis for Policy Makers.* [Online] Available at <http://www.unep.org/greeneconomy/Portals/88/documents/ger/GER_synthesis_en.pdf> [Accessed 28 May 2011].

UNFCCC, 2007. *Report of the individual review of the Greenhouse Gas Inventory of Turkey Submitted in 2007.* [Online] Available at <http://unfccc.int/resource/docs/2007/arr/tur.pdf> [Accessed 18 September 2011].

UNFCCC, 2007a. *Report of the Review of the Initial Report of Slovenia.* [Online] Available at <http://unfccc.int/resource/docs/2007/irr/svn.pdf> [Accessed 18 September 2011].

UNFCCC, 2008. *Investment and Financial Flows to Address Climate Change: an update.* [Online] Available at <http://unfccc.int/resource/docs/2008/tp/07.pdf> [Accessed 18 September 2011].

UNFCCC, 2008a. *Report of the Review of the Initial Report of Bulgaria.* [Online] Available at <http://unfccc.int/resource/docs/2008/irr/bgr.pdf> [Accessed 18 September 2011].

UNFCCC, 2008b. *Report of the Review of the Initial Report of Romania.* [Online] Available at <http://unfccc.int/resource/docs/2008/irr/rou.pdf> [Accessed 18 September 2011].

UNFCCC, 2009. *Report of the Individual Review of the Greenhouse Gas Inventories of Turkey Submitted in 2007 and 2008.* [Online] Available at <http://unfccc.int/resource/docs/2009/arr/tur.pdf> [Accessed 18 September 2011].

UNFCCC, 2009a. *Report of the Review of the Initial Report of Croatia.* [Online] Available at <http://unfccc.int/resource/docs/2009/irr/hrv.pdf> [Accessed 18 September 2011].

UNFCCC, 2009b. *Questions of Implementations – Croatia.* [Online] Available at <http://unfccc.int/kyoto_protocol/compliance/enforcement_branch/items/5456.php> [Accessed 18 September 2011].

UNFCCC, 2010. Appeal by Croatia against a final decision of the enforcement branch of the Compliance Committee, *Sixth session of Conference of the Parties Serving as the Meeting of the Parties to the Kyoto Protocol.* 29 Nov.–Dec. 2010. [Online] Available at <http://unfccc.int/resource/docs/2010/cmp6/eng/02.pdf> [Accessed 18 September 2011].

UNFCCC, 2010a. *National Greenhouse Gas Inventory Data for the Period 1990–2008.* [Online] Available at <http://unfccc.int/resource/docs/2010/sbi/eng/18.pdf> [Accessed 18 September 2011].

UNFCCC, 2011. *Report of the Individual Review of the Annual Submission of Turkey Submitted in 2010.* [Online] Available at <http://unfccc.int/resource/docs/2011/arr/tur.pdf> [Accessed 18 September 2011].

Vukadin, B. and Polanec, V., 2009. *Waste Management.* Environmental Agency of the Republic of Slovenia. [Online] Available at <http://kazalci.arso.gov.si/?data=indicator&ind_id=403&lang_id=94> [Accessed 25 May 2011].

Water Management Strategy, 2008. Government of Republic of Croatia. [Online] Available at <http://narodne-novine.nn.hr/clanci/sluzbeni/2008_08_91_2900.html> [Accessed 25 May 2011].

Worboys, G. L., Francis, W. L. and Lockwood, M. (eds), 2010. *Connectivity Conservation Management, A Global Guide (with particular reference to mountain connectivity conservation).* London and Washington DC: Earthscan.

World Bank, 2006. *Turkey Public Expenditure Review.* Report No. 36764-TR. [Online] Available at <http://siteresources.worldbank.org/INTTURKEY/Resources/361616–1173282369589/tr_per_cr.pdf> [Accessed 24 June 2011].

World Bank, 2011. *Open Data.* [Online] Available at <http://data.worldbank.org/> [Accessed 15 March 2011].

World Databank, 2011. *World Development Indicators (WDI) and Global Development Finance (GDF).* [Online] Available at <http://databank.worldbank.org/ddp/home.do> [Accessed 15 March 2011].

Winter, G., 1988. *Business and the Environment.* Hamburg: McGraw-Hill Book Company.

Yapanoglu, P., 2009. *Sector Report: Environment: Turkey.* Ankara: UK Trade & Investment. [Online] Available at <http://www.google.com/url?sa=t&rct=j&q=yapanoglu%2C%202009%2B100%20billion%20euros&source=web&cd=1&ved=0CBkQFjAA&url=http%3A%2F%2Fwww.ukti.gov.uk%2Fdownload%2F110268_101314%2FEnvironment%2520Sector%2520in%2520Turkey%2520-%2520Dec%252009.html&ei=u4WmToCCL5SL4gS4–7Ee&usg=AFQjCNHxmwZSk71H1yR7oalVcRYMNvH8Rg&cad=rja> [Accessed 10 May 2011].

Yapanoglu, P., 2010. *Sector Report: Water Sector – Turkey.* Ankara: UK Trade & Investment. [Online] Available at <http://www.google.com/url?sa=t&rct=j&q=sector%20report%3A%20water%20sector%3A%20turkey&source=web&cd=1&ved=0CB0QFjAA&url=http%3A%2F%2Fwww.ukti.gov.uk%2Fdownload%2F112444_101940%2FWater%2520Sector%2520in%2520Turkey.html&ei=0lepTqvPEqXh4QSq2onrDw&usg=AFQjCNGle0s–04H5iAoHv75G5nUBak3lMQ&sig2=9j-dyifHiFT_uuoMcscGaQ&cad=rja> [Accessed 10 May 2011].

Yavuz, E. and Altintas, B., 2009. Kyoto Ushers in New Era for Turkey. *Today's Zaman 07 February 2009.* [Online] Available at <http://www.todayszaman.com/newsDetail_getNewsById.action?load=detay&link=166219> [Accessed 10 September 2011].

Zachau, U., 2009. *New Economic Realities and the Water Sector.* Istanbul: Strategic, Technical, Economic Research Center. [Online] Available at <http://siteresources.worldbank.org/TURKEYEXTN/Resources/361711–1260521694635/6640655–1263801597244/20090617_New_Economic_Realities_and_the_Water_Sector.pdf> [Accessed 10 June 2011].

Zakon o podnebnih spremembah 3. Osnutek, 2011. Republika Slovenija. [Online] Available at <http://www.svps.gov.si/fileadmin/svps.gov.si/pageuploads/3._osnutek/ZPS_140210_vse.pdf> [Accessed 9 August 2011].

Index

For Product Safety Concerns and Information please contact our EU representative GPSR@taylorandfrancis.com
Taylor & Francis Verlag GmbH, Kaufingerstraße 24, 80331 München, Germany

www.ingramcontent.com/pod-product-compliance
Lightning Source LLC
Chambersburg PA
CBHW050450051126
54379CB00003B/86
9780415586092